REASON *in* LAW

EIGHTH EDITION

LEIF H. CARTER
and
THOMAS F. BURKE

WITH A FOREWORD BY
SANFORD LEVINSON

THE UNIVERSITY OF CHICAGO PRESS
CHICAGO AND LONDON

The University of Chicago Press, Chicago 60637
The University of Chicago Press, Ltd., London
© 2010 by Lief H. Carter and Thomas F. Burke
All rights reserved. Published 2015.
Printed in the United States of America

24 23 22 21 20 19 18 17 16 15   1 2 3 4 5

ISBN-13: 978-0-226-34049-4 (paper)

This book was previously published by: Pearson Education, Inc. Any
questions concerning permissions should be directed to Permissions
Department, The University of Chicago Press, Chicago, IL.

♾ This paper meets the requirements of ANSI/NISO Z39.48-1992
(Permanence of Paper).

REASON *in* LAW

Contents

6 Law and Politics   134

Appendix A: Introduction to Legal Procedure and Terminology   159

Appendix B: The Rule of Law and the Presidency of George W. Bush   165

Foreword

I am pleased to write a few words about what is truly an outstanding book, *Reason in Law*. Although I am not a rigorous Darwinian, it nonetheless is worth noting that the very fact that you hold in your hand the eighth edition is a testament to its ability to survive—indeed, to flourish—in a very competitive world. Most books suffer the sad fate immortalized in David Hume's lament (which turned out to be false) that his books "fell stillborn from the press." It is no small matter for a book to establish itself as a classic, which *Reason in Law* is, and to live unto the next generation.

Central to any explanation for its survival is that both Lief Carter and his more recent collaborator, Thomas Burke, have a capacity to write with admirable clarity about complex issues in legal analysis. As a professor of law, I can vouch for the fact that they introduce central topics in an extraordinarily reader-friendly way. Whether one is interested in classic common-law reasoning, statutory interpretation, or my own specialty, constitutional interpretation, there is much to savor in this slim book.

The authors clearly admire law as a means of dispute resolution that serves to preserve social peace and order. But, of course, commands issued by an all-powerful Hobbesian sovereign could serve this role. As suggested by the American author Ring Lardner, " 'Shut up,' he explained" is an ever-present possibility when responding to someone dissatisfied with the way he or she is being treated. Every parent has taken refuge in such a posture, and every child no doubt has felt frustrated by the perceived failure to be taken seriously. Carter and Burke know that "shut up" is indeed inadequate. Winners may be delighted simply to be told, "you can do what you'd like," but losers want to know *why* they are not being allowed. Receiving an adequate answer is essential to believing that one is being treated with the proper concern and respect that political philosophers John Rawls and Ronald Dworkin have identified as the essence of a defensible political order.

Reason in Law is based on the assumption that *someone* actually reads judicial decisions, and that the quality of reasoning will assuage the feelings even of those who disagree with the outcomes. *Who* reads judicial opinions is, of course, an interesting question in itself. Carter and Burke appear to agree with political scientists like Gerald Rosenberg that members of the general public rarely read judicial decisions; *their* responses are far more likely to depend on the bottom-line result—and how that result is portrayed in the popular press—than in the chain of legal reasoning supporting it. For better and, undoubtedly, for worse, one can be confident that very few Americans actually read the various judicial decisions on the Terri Schiavo case that are carefully delineated in [the seventh edition's] Appendix B.[1]

What one can be certain of, though, is that the lawyers involved in specific cases will surely read the opinions, and that it is particularly important that the losers in such cases feel

---

[1] Appendix B of this edition features an analysis of "The Bush Administration and the Rule of Law." If you are interested in reading about the Terry Schiavo case to which Prof. Levinson refers, you may read the seventh edition Appendix B, which is available at: http://www.pearsonhighered.com/carter8e.

some measure of satisfaction after reading the court's explanation of why they lost. The central question posed by Carter and Burke is whether this dream is utopian. Do we have sufficient faith in our legal system—and in those who inhabit judicial office—to take the necessarily disinterested stance it requires even when we are deeply committed to the losing side? This is an *empirical* question. One can easily imagine communities where such faith in law and legal officials exists. But, of course, it is as easy to imagine communities that are rent by a variety of cleavages, in which one trusts neither the law nor those who purport to "interpret" it. This phenomenon could certainly be observed by supporters of Ms. Schiavo's parents. (It is completely question-begging to describe them as supporters of Ms. Schiavo herself.) And one should note, incidentally, that one need not mistrust law per se in order to mistrust those who claim to speak in its name.

A special problem with regard to the role of "Reason in Law" is presented, as Carter and Burke clearly acknowledge, by the reliance on previously decided cases. The paradox of precedent is that what might be termed "pure precedent-based argument" is strongest precisely when the precedent is least persuasive or "reasonable." If one agrees with a precedent, then one isn't really "following precedent"; one is doing what one's own reason suggests is the right thing to do. A "strong" precedentialist will follow the prior decision even when it appears unreasonable or simply wrong. Whether this constitutes reason in law is, of course, an important question! "The deference that is due to the determination of former judgments," wrote Jeremy Bentham, "is due not to their wisdom, but to their authority." And one should certainly take note of one of the most famous passages in Oliver Wendell Holmes' "The Path of the Law," perhaps the most important speech on law in American history. Speaking to the students and faculty of Boston University Law School in 1897, Holmes thundered, "It is revolting to have no better reason for a rule of law than that so it was laid down in the time of Henry IV. It is still more revolting if the grounds upon which it was laid down have vanished long since, and the rule simply persists from blind imitation of the past." One suspects that Carter and Burke would agree. They are scarcely uncritical devotees of what might be termed almost mindless stare decisis, such as that exhibited by the Supreme Court in the baseball cases that Carter and Burke draw on in their own discussion. At the very least, it should be clear that legal opinions call for critical analysis, and not for thoughtless acceptance.

Critical analysis is encouraged by one very strong feature of the American legal system that is illustrated throughout this book: American judges, to a degree unusual among the world's legal systems, are institutionally encouraged to write dissenting opinions. This is no small matter. The European Court, for example, issues only one opinion, in the name of "the Court," as was the case in Germany prior to 1971 and is the case today in other countries, such as Greece or Ireland. The presumed reason is that the possibility of a dissent, which can sometimes be quite harshly written and accuse the majority of exhibiting "unreason in law," works to undercut the faith of the citizenry—and especially the losers—that they have been treated with the dignity they wish. There is more than one dissent in the pages of the *United States Reports,* for example, that basically accuses the majority of being closer to Ring Lardner's character than to what is required of what we might label a "Carter–Burke model judge." Readers might ask themselves if the critical stance that is so much a feature of this book would be possible if Carter and Burke offered only unanimous opinions or suppressed the fact that there were vigorous— and often utterly convincing—dissents.

There is one last point worth mentioning. If I have a disagreement with the authors, it is in the extent to which "law" is identified as the workproduct of judges. In the American constitutional system, it is not only judges who are invited to become constitutional interpreters. Presidents and members of Congress must wrestle with their own oaths of office, which require fidelity to the Constitution—and not simply to "the Constitution as interpreted by the majority of the Supreme Court." This casts into sharp relief the importance of President Andrew Jackson's statement in his famous 1832 veto of a bill renewing the charter of the Bank of the United States, whose constitutionality had been affirmed in John Marshall's classic opinion in *McCulloch v. Maryland* (1819). Jackson disagreed: "The authority of the Supreme Court must not, therefore, be permitted to control the Congress or the Executive when acting in their legislative capacities, but *to have only such influence as the force of their reasoning may deserve*" (emphasis added). And in a "republican" political order like the United States, which emphasizes the importance of participation by all citizens in civic governance, individuals themselves must develop confidence in their own capacity to critically analyze public officials' assertions about constitutional meaning. Very few readers of this book will become judges, but almost all will become citizens. Its fundamental importance is therefore not vocational job training, but rather enabling each and every one of you to become a more effective citizen by deciding what standards of reasoning a court (or any other constitutional interpreter) must meet and what follows if one is not persuaded.

Sanford Levinson
W. St. John Garwood and W. St. John
 Garwood Centennial Chair in Law
University of Texas Law School
Professor, Department of Government,
University of Texas at Austin

Preface to the Eighth Edition

This eighth edition of *Reason in Law* marks the 30th birthday of its debut. Although the book has had eight incarnations, its major themes have not significantly changed. We can't fully understand a human creation—a game of baseball, a symphony, a Rembrandt painting, anything that people make and do—unless we understand how the creators "play with" the formal and abstract rules and structures of their game so as to produce something concrete and new. And once we understand this creative process, we can judge for ourselves whether someone else—a player, a composer, or an artist—has created well or badly. The same is true of judges and the goodness of the legal decisions they make. Just as baseball aficionados can learn to judge a manager's decision without playing the game themselves, and film buffs can tell better movies from worse ones without sitting in the director's chair, non-lawyers can learn the abstract materials of the legal game so that they—you!—can evaluate the quality of judicial decisions in the United States.

We believe that the political history of the United States over these past thirty years—and particularly the past eight years—has made it increasingly clear that to make smart political judgments, citizens must be able to differentiate good and bad law-doing. Without citizens who actively and critically evaluate legal reasoning, we are in danger of descending to a police state, in which those with the raw power of guns and muscle make up the law as they go along, just as a bully in a playground changes the rules of the game to allow him to win. The Bush administration's troublesome handling of law, especially its cavalier treatment of the rules governing the American struggle with terrorism, together with the Obama administration's attempt to reformulate those rules, makes the need to become critical judges of legal reasoning all the more crucial. Much of what is new in this edition, particularly Appendix B, asks you to analyze the persuasiveness of the Bush administration's legal reasoning so as to make political judgments about its wisdom. To promote that goal, this edition for the first time includes Weblinks to appendices of the previous two editions, first the sixth edition's analysis of the issues in the much-criticized case of *Bush v. Gore*, and then the seventh edition's examination of the legal and political debates about whether to maintain an apparently brain-dead woman, Terri Schiavo, on life support.[2]

There is another, subtler, theme embedded here, one that this edition does not directly address. The Bush administration's careless disregard for the practices and habits of mind that nourish the rule of law may have flowed from its broader failures of political judgment, and indeed of careful reasoning of any kind. Commentators across the political spectrum frequently complained that key deciders in the Bush administration did not engage in careful thinking about the purposes they hoped to achieve. Too often they engaged in wishful or magical thinking about real-world constraints on their actions. Too often they did not connect the hard facts

---

[2] These appendices are available at: http://www.pearsonhighered.com/carter8e.

on the ground with their own social values. Good legal reasoning is, we think, merely a subset of good political reasoning, which in turn is a subset of wise reasoning in all of life. And so we hope that the ways of thinking presented here will give you, the reader, both an introduction to legal reasoning and some guidance in how to reason wisely and well, both in your civic and public roles and in your private and personal life.

We wish to thank our editor Eric Stano at Longman, and the many far-flung contractors who these days put academic books together.

As always, Tom Burke thanks the administrators of the political science department, Cyndy Northgraves and Lynda Jeha, as well as the dedicated and delightful students of Wellesley College. Most of all, Tom thanks his long-suffering but always even-tempered and witty coauthor, from whom he has learned so much about law over the past two decades, extending back to his own years as an undergraduate. Lief Carter, belatedly, thanks Martin Shapiro of the University of California, Berkeley, for his wisdom over many years. He benefits from the effective administration of his department at Colorado College by Jenn Sides. And he specially thanks his wife, Marilyn Vickers, for her wise counsel on all manner of things and her steadfast affection. It's mutual!

Lief H. Carter
Thomas F. Burke

About the Authors

Lief Carter grew up in the Seattle area in the age of "innocent" rock 'n roll (the 1950s). He earned his AB from Harvard College (1962) and his law degree from Harvard Law School (1965). The Vietnam War ended his career as a legal practitioner just as it started. He served in the Peace Corps (Bolivia) as an alternative form of service in 1966–1967 and then returned to graduate school at the University of California-Berkeley, where he earned his Ph.D. in political science (1972). His dissertation received the Corwin Award of the American Political Science Association. He taught at the University of Georgia from 1973 until 1995 and then served for a decade as the McHugh Family Distinguished Professor at The Colorado College. In addition to *Reason in Law*, he has published books on criminal prosecution, administrative law, and theories of constitutional interpretation. He comprehensively explores the similarities between the requirements of good competitive games—and particularly the requirement that the umpires and referees be impartial—and the requirements of good law doing in his recent publication, "Law and Politics as Play," which appears in the *Chicago-Kent Law Review*, volume 3 (2008). Lief lives in Manitou Springs, Colorado.

Tom Burke is proud to have been born and raised in the city of Minneapolis, Minnesota, and to have received his undergraduate degree from the University of Minnesota. Nonetheless, he is also glad to have left his native state for the warm California sun. He received his Ph.D. from the University of California-Berkeley in 1996. At Berkeley, Tom studied with many of the professors who two decades earlier had taught Lief Carter, and, like Lief, he received the Corwin Award of the American Political Science Association for his dissertation. In 1996 he began teaching at Wellesley College, just outside of Boston, Massachusetts, where he is the Jane Bishop '51 Associate Professor of Political Science. He has written articles on campaign finance, the European Union, the Americans with Disabilities Act, how organizations respond to legal mandates, empirical rights scholarship, the Bush administration's approach to legal politics, and the place of rights in American politics. Among his recent articles is "Political Regimes and the Future of the First Amendment," *Studies in Law, Politics and Society* 44 (2008): 107–139. Tom lives in Cambridge, Massachusetts.

I was much troubled in spirit, in my first years upon the bench, to find how trackless was the ocean on which I had embarked. I sought for certainty. I was oppressed and disheartened when I found that the quest for it was futile. I was trying to reach land, the solid land of fixed and settled rules, the paradise of a justice that would declare itself by tokens plainer and more commanding than its pale and glimmering reflections in my own vacillating mind and conscience. . . . As the years have gone by, and as I have reflected more and more upon the nature of the judicial process, I have become reconciled to the uncertainty, because I have grown to see it as inevitable. I have grown to see that the process in its highest reaches is not discovery, but creation; and that the doubts and misgivings, the hopes and fears, are part of the travail of mind, the pangs of death and the pangs of birth, in which principles that have served their day expire, and new principles are born.

What is it that I do when I decide a case? To what sources of information do I appeal for guidance? In what proportions do I permit them to contribute to the result? In what proportions ought they to contribute? If a precedent is applicable, when do I refuse to follow it? If no precedent is applicable, how do I reach the rule that will make a precedent for the future? If I am seeking logical consistency, the symmetry of the legal structure, how far shall I seek it? At what point shall the quest be halted by some discrepant custom, by some consideration of the social welfare, by my own or the common standards of justice and morals? Into that strange compound which is brewed daily in the caldron of the courts, all these ingredients enter in varying proportions. I am not concerned to inquire whether judges ought to be allowed to brew such a compound at all. I take judge-made law as one of the existing realities of life. There, before us, is the brew. Not a judge on the bench but had a hand in the making.

—JUDGE BENJAMIN N. CARDOZO,
THE NATURE OF THE JUDICIAL PROCESS (1921)

CHAPTER 1

What Legal Reasoning Is, and Why It Matters

I have grown to see that the [legal] process in its highest reaches is not discovery, but creation.

—BENJAMIN N. CARDOZO

They ain't nuthin' until I calls 'em.

—ATTRIBUTED TO UMPIRE BILL KLEM

AN OVERVIEW OF LAW AND POLITICS

While driving home from work the evening of March 10, 2004, the acting attorney general of the United States, James Comey, received a disturbing call. It came from an aide to Comey's boss, John Ashcroft. Ashcroft had suffered an acute illness that required his gall bladder to be removed, so Comey was acting as attorney general while Ashcroft recovered. The aide told Comey that Andrew Card, President George W. Bush's chief of staff, along with White House Counsel Alberto Gonzales, was driving to Ashcroft's room at George Washington University Hospital, just five and a half blocks up Pennsylvania Avenue from the White House.

Comey realized immediately that they were not visiting to pay their respects. Gonzales and Card needed to get the attorney general's office to recertify the legality of the Bush administration's secret surveillance program, created without authorization by Congress after 9/11. Under this program, government officials, assisted by private telecommunications companies, and without judicially approved search warrants, eavesdropped on calls and e-mails between the United States and foreign countries. Every 45 days, the Justice Department was required to certify that the program was operating legally. Comey and several others in the department were, however, refusing to sign off on the program because they were concerned that it violated federal law. The Federal Intelligence Surveillance Act (FISA) required that a special FISA court give prior approval for surveillance of U.S. citizens, and several U.S. Supreme Court cases, beginning in 1804, held that the president had no constitutional power to disobey a direct statutory command from Congress.[1] Prior to his sudden and potentially fatal illness, Ashcroft had, with Comey, concluded that the program as written violated FISA and hence went beyond the constitutional powers of the executive. As the 45-day deadline loomed, Comey, temporarily acting in Ashcroft's capacity, refused to reauthorize the program. Now the president's men, Card and Gonzales, seemed to be taking advantage of Ashcroft's illness to try to obtain the certification anyway.

On receiving the call, James Comey telephoned FBI director Robert Mueller and alerted him to the situation, then ordered his driver to turn around, switch on the car's sirens, and head for the hospital. When he reached Ashcroft's room, Comey found Ashcroft nearly delirious from his illness and from heavy medication. Yet a few minutes later when Card and Gonzales presented Ashcroft with the reauthorization form to sign, Ashcroft revived. Jack Goldsmith, the head of the Office of Legal Counsel in the Department of Justice, had also rushed to the hospital and described to the PBS program *Frontline* what he saw:

> He had tubes going in and out of him. He looked ashen, and I actually thought he looked near death. . . . Attorney General Ashcroft . . . kind of lifted himself up and gave about a two or three minute speech, or talk . . . in which he basically, I can't get into the details, but he showed enormous, unbelievable clarity about what the issues were and what was going on, and he explained why he would also not approve the program, and he read them a bit of the riot act, and then . . . at the end of all this he said, 'And in any event, I'm not the Attorney General now, Jim Comey is.' . . . And with that extraordinary performance—and it was . . . one of the most amazing things I've ever seen in my life . . . he just receded into the bed, and I really worried at that moment that he was going to expire, and it looked like he had given it the last of his energy.

Card and Gonzales left without acknowledging Comey's presence. Comey, Goldsmith, and FBI director Mueller then prepared letters of resignation and threatened to submit them if the Bush administration continued the surveillance program without modifying it to make it lawful. Eventually, the Bush administration did so.[2]

A dramatic story. But what, you might ask, does it have to do with a book on legal reasoning? We, the authors, believe that legal reasoning at its core is about *the trustworthiness of the reasons people in power give to justify their actions.* Those who rule must explain their decisions in ways that serve the community, not merely personal or partisan interests. The rule of law requires a commitment to this process of justification. When

---

[1] See *Little v. Barreme,* 6 U.S. 170 (1804) and *Youngstown Sheet & Tube v. Sawyer* 343 U.S. 579 (1952). Appendix B of this book, beginning on p. 165, analyzes President Bush's claim that congressional limits on executive power to combat terrorism are unconstitutional. The letter abbreviations following the names of cases identify the series of books that contains the judicial opinion deciding the case; in this instance "U.S." stands for "U.S. Reports." The first number indicates the volume in the series that contains the opinion, and the second number is the starting page of the opinion. If you want to follow up on one of the cases cited in this book, you can usually "Google" them by name and citation; almost all of them are available online.

[2] *Frontline,* "Cheney's Law" WGBH, October 16, 2007; and and Dan Eggen and Paul Kane, "Gonzales Hospital Episode Detailed: Ailing Ashcroft Pressured on Spy Program, Former Deputy Says," *The Washington Post,* May 16, 2007, p. A1. Our account of the hospital story is drawn from the *Frontline* documentary, the *Post* article, Assistant Attorney General James Comey's testimony before Congress, and two books that put the story in a broader context: Eric Lichtblau, *Bush's Law: The Remaking of American Justice* (New York: Pantheon, 2008) and Charlie Savage, *Takeover: The Return of the Imperial Presidency and the Subversion of American Democracy* (New York: Little Brown, 2007). For an argument that the surveillance program was within the president's powers and not restricted by federal laws on wiretapping, see John Yoo, *War by Other Means: An Insider's Account of the War on Terror* (New York: Atlantic, 2006), pp. 99–127.

Comey and Ashcroft found they could not justify the surveillance program as consistent with FISA and the Constitution, they chose fidelity to the legal process over loyalty to the Bush administration. Conversely, when Card and Gonzales, the president's advisors, faced the same struggle, they chose not to modify the surveillance program or to find a trustworthy legal basis for it, but to try to take advantage of a sick man. When justification proved difficult, they went outside the rule of law to get what they wanted.

This is why the story, when it was revealed more than three years later—and after President Bush was reelected in the fall of 2004—disturbed so many. When those in power no longer respect the need to justify their decisions to others, the rule of law breaks down, and those on either side of social and political divides lose trust in the goodness and integrity of their communities. Legal reasoning matters because it is how legal officers, and particularly judges, justify their decisions, and so fortify social trust. Legal reasoning may seem a dry and technical "prelaw" topic, but the hospital story demonstrates why it is so important. Legal reasoning serves simultaneously as the velvet glove covering the fist of governmental power and as the sincerest expression of our ideals of justice and of community.[3] Understand legal reasoning and you understand the rule of law itself.

In Chapter Six and in Appendix B we explore the intersections between legal reasoning and politics more fully, but here are three specific signposts to get you oriented.

The Law Is All Around Us

Opponents of the United States' war in Iraq argued strenuously that without the approval of the United Nations, the war violated international law. Because no "World Court" had the power to resolve the matter and enforce its judgment, that legal issue remained just another political shouting match. Law becomes "the rule of law" only when courts have the power to resolve legal claims or when people, knowing that powerful courts can step in to settle matters for them, "bargain in the shadow of the law."[4]

The political system of the United States, unlike the international system, incorporates a powerful and independent judiciary. Our nation thereby claims to honor the rule of law. Alexis de Tocqueville wrote long ago that "there is hardly a political question in the United States that does not sooner or later turn into a judicial one."[5] The daily flow of news regularly reaffirms Tocqueville's observation. Here are just a few recent examples:

■ In 2008, the U.S. Supreme Court ruled that Kentucky's method of executing inmates by injecting them with a combination of three drugs did not violate the Constitution's ban on "cruel and unusual punishment." Critics argued that if one of the drugs, meant to render inmates unconscious, was not administered properly, it would make the excruciating pain caused by the injection of the other drugs undetectable. Chief Justice

---

[3] *Community* can mean very different things depending on the context in which people use this (or any) word. We can speak of a community of Internet users or of hip-hop fans. For our purposes here, *community* means the physical space that courts rule. California courts, for example, speak on matters of California law to the community of everyone in California, including prisoners, infants, and illegal aliens, because the California courts have power over them. The Supreme Court speaks to the community of all people in the United States.

[4] See Robert H. Mnookin and Lewis Korhauser, "Bargaining in the Shadow of the Law: The Case of Divorce," 88 *Yale Law Journal* 950 (1979).

[5] Alexis de Tocqueville, *Democracy in America*, J.M. Mayer, tr. (New York: Harper and Row, 1969), p. 270.

Roberts concluded, however, that Kentucky's procedure included adequate safeguards and so did not create a "substantial risk of serious harm."[6]

■ In 2006, the Arkansas Supreme Court unanimously struck down a state agency's rule barring gays and lesbians from serving as foster parents, concluding that the rule was based on the moral views of some members of the community rather than the needs of foster children. The Court found no evidence that homosexual foster parents were harmful to the well-being of foster children and ruled that the state's Child Welfare Agency Review Board had improperly tried to regulate public morality, a goal that was beyond its legal powers. (In response, Arkansas voters in 2008 enacted a law barring unmarried couples from providing foster care to children.)[7]

■ During its 2007–2008 term, the U.S. Supreme Court decided such controversial issues as whether the Second Amendment protects an individual's right to own a gun, whether states that require voters to show photo identification violate the Equal Protection Clause of the Fourteenth Amendment, and what rights those held in the Guantanamo military base as "enemy combatants" have to contest their detention.[8]

The Rule of Law Keeps the Peace

Many people, no doubt, react to such politically charged cases by comparing the legal result against their own moral convictions. Liberals opposed to the death penalty criticized the Supreme Court's decision on lethal injections; death penalty advocates supported the ruling. But if you stop and think about it, judging a legal result simply in terms of one's own sense of right and wrong won't do. The whole point of the rule of law is to set standards of governance that transcend individual moral feelings. If all we have are our moral feelings, we are no better than religious and political fundamentalists who insist that *their* moral scheme justifies destroying other incompatible moral systems. The claim of moral right-eousness and superiority has driven many of our species' worst atrocities, such as the Holocaust, the genocide of American Indians, and the killing of millions of "enemies of the state" in communist regimes.

The rule of law substitutes legal reasoning for moral righteousness. In the sample of cases above, the legal reasoning question is not whether we "like" the result but whether the judge has given reasons we find trustworthy. If this distinction seems too abstract, think of an organized sport or game, one with umpires or referees. You may root passion-ately for one side, but when a referee's call goes against your team, you don't automati-cally condemn it. You ask if you trust it, whether the facts on the field fit the call. It is indeed extraordinary that sports and games, contests among emotionally charged people whose self-respect and wealth may be on the line, remain for the most part civil and peaceful.[9]

---

[6] *Baze v. Rees* 553 U.S. _____ (2008).

[7] *Department of Human Services v. Howard*, 367 Ark. 55 (Arkansas Supreme Court, June 29, 2006). The Court's opinion is available online: http://courts.state.ar.us/opinions/2006a/20060629/05-814.pdf. On the ballot measure, see Robbie Brown, "Antipathy Toward Obama Seen as Helping Arkansas Limit Adoption," *The New York Times*, November 8, 2008.

[8] The cases are *Heller v. D.C.*, 554 U.S. _____ (2008); *Crawford v. Marion County Election Board*, 553 U.S. _____ (2008); and *Boumediene v. Bush*, 553 U.S. _____ (2008).

[9] Lief Carter explains in detail the peace-keeping tendencies of "good games" in "Law and Politics as Play," 83 *Chicago-Kent Law Review* 1333 (2008).

The Critical Importance of Judicial Impartiality

Reflect a bit further on your experience of sports referees and you will soon realize that a critical call against the home team does not normally turn a peaceful home crowd into a rebellious mass of frothing maniacs (who would throw beverage bottles at the refs if glass containers were still allowed in the stands). Only blatantly erroneous calls and, worse, a *pattern* of wrong calls that suggests a bias against the home team cause fan rage. The impartiality of legal judges is as necessary for political peace as the impartiality of referees and umpires is to keeping peace in the stands.

Indeed, we find that in most human societies, trusted third parties routinely resolve disputes. Alec Stone Sweet and Martin Shapiro (who originated the concept formally known as "triadic dispute resolution") described the phenomenon this way:

> If a conflict arises between two persons and they cannot resolve it themselves, then in all cultures and societies it is logical for those two persons to call upon a third to assist in its resolution. That assistance falls along a spectrum that stretches from the mediator to the arbitrator to the judge. . . . The triad contains a basic tension. To the extent that the triadic figure appears to intervene in favor of one of the two disputants and against the other, the perception of the situation *will shift from the fairest to the most unfair of configurations: two against one.* Therefore the principal characteristics of all triadic conflict resolvers will be determined by the need to avoid the perception of two against one, for only then can they rely on their basic social logic.[10]

How can judges, the triadic conflict resolvers we are concerned with, overcome the "two against one" perception? In most nontrivial appeals cases, judges write opinions explaining and thereby justifying the results they reach.[11] This makes appellate judges different from baseball umpires, who make most of their calls automatically. It is the job of appeals judges to write opinions that justify their decisions on impartial grounds, grounds that don't seem to take partisan sides. (The concept of "impartiality" will be explored more fully in the concluding chapter.)

Because law gains its authority through impartiality, people often assume that law isn't "political." We, however, view law and legal reasoning as a special kind of politics. *Politics,* in our definition, refers to all the things people do in communities in order to minimize threats to their well-being. People sometimes cooperate with each other to resist perceived threats, but sometimes they fight. Political behavior sometimes tries to conserve what is and sometimes tries to change what is. Hence, like other forms of politics, law can either preserve communities or change them. By the end of this book, you will have encountered many examples of legal actions that resulted in both change and preservation.

If referees and umpires do triadic dispute resolution badly, public belief in the integrity of a game can suffer. If *judges* do triadic dispute resolution badly, the problem can undermine the entire community. When people believe that judges cynically manipulate legal language to reach partisan and self-interested political ends, faith in fairness and equity ebbs, motives for social cooperation falter, and communal life becomes more nasty and brutish. The sense of injustice can cause explosive social damage. When, for example, a suburban Los Angeles jury acquitted the white police officers who beat Rodney King, a black man, minority communities throughout the United States were outraged by what they saw as a racially biased

---

[10] Martin Shapiro and Alec Stone Sweet, *On Law, Politics, and Judicialization* (Oxford: Oxford University Press, 2002), p. 211 *(emphasis added).*

[11] For an introduction to the legal procedures and terms by which cases reach the appellate level, see Appendix A, beginning at p. 159.

verdict. Major riots erupted in Los Angeles and several other cities. Distrust in the impartiality of judges creates disrespect for legal institutions and ultimately the rule of law.

The problem of judicial impartiality seems particularly acute in the United States today because of growing controversy over the selection of judges. Other books examine judicial selection in more detail.[12] We must, however, report that the systems of judicial selection in the United States are not designed to recruit judges on the basis of their ability to reason well and rule impartially. Nor does the United States systematically teach future judges about the basic social logic that avoids "two against one." Indeed, compared with the systems of judicial selection in Europe (or most organized sports leagues!), American approaches seem almost designed to make this problem worse. Many state judges are elected, and campaigns for judicial office can be polarizing and partisan.[13] Other judges are appointed by politicians—for life in the case of federal judges—for partisan reasons.

No one would trust a home plate umpire who calls pitches before they leave the pitcher's hand. Should the public trust those who become judges only because they have already taken sides on legal issues? Remember that this book has ruled out the simplest method of judging judges: We can't simply respect the ones who decide as we like and scorn those who don't. Instead we must decide whether judges have used their power legitimately. We may believe that an umpire blew the call on a particular pitch, or that a referee missed calling an obvious foul under the basket, and still believe that overall they are judging the game fairly, even when a particular "bad call" hurts our team. Similarly, we must trust that judges decide impartially across the full spectrum of cases they decide, even when we think a particular decision rules against what we think is right. At bottom, then, this book explores a classic political question: By what standards can we say that someone we disagree with nevertheless acts and argues with integrity? By what standards can we say that Comey and Ashcroft justified the decisions they made in that hospital room, while Card and Gonzales did not? Our answer is that judges can convince others of their integrity when they use "good legal reasoning." The rest of this book is an account of what "good legal reasoning" means.

A DEFINITION OF LAW

Law is a language, not simply a collection of rules. What distinguishes law from other ways of making sense of life? Lawyers and judges attempt to prevent and solve other people's problems, but so do physicians, priests, professors, and plumbers. The term *problem solving* therefore includes too much. Lawyers and judges work with certain kinds of problems that can lead to conflicts, even physical fights, among people. Contrary to the impression from television that law is all about courtroom battles, most lawyers generally practice "preventive law." They help people discover ways to reduce their taxes or write valid wills and contracts. They study complex insurance policies and bank loan agreements. Such efforts reduce the

---

[12] See, for example, Keith J. Bybee, ed., *Bench Press: The Collision of Courts, Politics and the Media* (Palo Alto, CA: Stanford University Press, 2007); Michael Dorf, *No Litmus Test: Law Versus Politics in the Twenty-first Century* (New York: Rowman and Littlefield, 2006); Nancy Scherer, *Scoring Points* (Palo Alto, CA: Stanford University Press, 2005); Sheldon Goldman, *Picking Federal Judges* (New Haven: Yale University Press, 1999); and David Yalof, *Pursuit of Justices: Presidential Politics and the Selection of Supreme Court Nominees* (Chicago: University of Chicago Press, 1999).

[13] Matthew J. Streb, ed., *Running for Judge: The Rising Political, Financial and Legal Stakes of Judicial Elections* (New York: New York University Press, 2007); and James Sample, Lauren Jones and Rachel Weiss, *The New Politics of Judicial Elections 2006* (Washington, D.C.: Justice at Stake Campaign, 2007), available at http://www.justiceatstake.org/files/NewPoliticsofJudicialElections2006.pdf.

probability of conflict. Most lawyers usually play a planning role. They help people create their own "private laws" governing their personal affairs and no more.

Yet some conflicts start anyway, perhaps because a lawyer did the planning and preventing poorly, or because the client did not follow a lawyer's good advice. Sometimes lawyers cannot find in rules of law a safe plan with which to prevent a conflict. Many conflicts, such as the auto collision, the dispute with a neighbor over a property line, or the angry firing of an employee, begin without lawyers. Then people may call them in after the fact, not for an ounce of prevention but for the pounding of a cure.

If a battle erupts spontaneously, lawyers may find a solution in the rules of law, though once people get angry with each other, they may refuse the solution lawyers offer. If the lawyers don't find a solution or negotiate a compromise, then either one side gives up or the opponents go to court; they call in the judges to resolve their dispute.

You may now think you have a solid definition of law: Law is the process of preventing or resolving conflicts between people. Lawyers and judges do this; professors, plumbers, and physicians, at least routinely, do not. But parents prevent or resolve conflicts among their children daily. And parents, perhaps exasperated from coping with family fights, may turn to a family counselor to deal with their own conflicts. Many ministers no doubt define one of their goals as reducing conflict. Lawyers, then, aren't the only people who try to resolve conflicts.

Law, like the priesthood and professional counseling, encounters an immense variety of problems. Law requires the ability to see specifics and to avoid premature generalizing and jumping to conclusions. So do good counseling, good "ministration," and good parenting. But what distinguishes the conflict solving of lawyers and judges from the conflict solving of parents, counselors, or ministers? Consider these three cases. What makes them distinctively *legal* problems?

- A young man, entranced by the thought of flying, steals a Cessna from an airstrip in Rhode Island and manages to survive a landing in a Connecticut corn patch. He is prosecuted under the National Motor Vehicle Theft Act, which prohibits transportation "in interstate or foreign commerce [of] a motor vehicle, knowing the same to have been stolen . . ." The statute defines *motor vehicle* to "include an automobile, automobile truck, automobile wagon, motorcycle, or any other self-propelled vehicle not designed for running on rails." Does the pilot's brief flight amount to transportation of the plane "in interstate . . . commerce?" Is an airplane a "vehicle" within the meaning of the act?[14]

- "Equal" and "Splenda" are competing artificial sweeteners. Equal, often called "aspartame," was once the dominant sugar substitute, but since its manufacturers introduced Splenda in 1999, Splenda has gained more than 60 percent of the market. The makers of Equal, however, claim that Splenda's advertising slogan—"made from sugar, so it tastes like sugar"—is misleading. Equal's makers claim that the slogan makes consumers think that Splenda is not an artificial sweetener. Splenda's makers reply that the laboratory process that produces Splenda in fact starts with pure cane sugar, while that which produces Equal does not. Does Splenda's slogan mislead? Is it unfair to the makers of Equal?[15]

---

[14] *McBoyle v. United States*, 283 U.S. 25 (1931). Appendix A discusses *McBoyle* further.

[15] Lynnley Browning, "Makers of Artificial Sweeteners Go to Court," *The New York Times*, April 6, 2007, p. C5.

■ Cockfighting is illegal in virtually all U.S. states, but the operators of "toughsportslive. com" use the Internet to broadcast live cockfights from Puerto Rico, where cockfighting is legal. A 1999 federal law makes it a crime to profit from depictions of animal cruelty, but there is an exception for works of "serious religious, political, scientific, educational, journalistic, historical, or artistic value." The attorney for the website company argues that cockfighting is as integral to Puerto Rican culture as bullfighting is to Spanish culture. Does this cultural argument protect the operators of "toughsportslive.com" from criminal conviction? If not, does prosecuting them violate their First Amendment free speech or free press rights?[16]

These are legal problems, not counseling or parental problems, because we define their nature and limits—though not necessarily their solution—in terms of rules that the state, the government, has made. Criminal statutes passed by legislatures define, among many concepts, how the government may deal with thieves and purveyors of animal cruelty. Federal law gives businesses the right to sue competitors for false advertising. The First Amendment prohibits public officials from abridging freedom of speech. The process of resolving human conflicts through law begins when people decide to take advantage of the fact that the government has made rules to prevent or resolve such conflicts. When people convert a problem into a legal conflict by taking it to court, the court's resolution of the problem has the force of the government behind it. Even in a noncriminal case, if the loser or losers don't pay up, the judge may order jail terms.

The law, then, is a language that lawyers and judges use when they try to prevent or resolve problems—human conflicts—using official rules made by the state as their starting point. To study reason in this process is to study how lawyers and judges justify the choices they inevitably make among various legal solutions. For example, legal reasoning studies how they justify saying an airplane is or is not a "vehicle" in the context of the National Motor Vehicle Theft Act. Throughout this book, we shall study the legal process by asking the central questions lawyers and judges ask themselves as they do their work: What does the law mean as applied to the problem before me? What different and sometimes contradictory solutions to the problem does the law permit in this case?

Now stop and compare this definition of law and legal reasoning with your own intuitive conception of law, with the definition of the legal process you may have developed from television, movies, and other daily experiences. Do the two overlap? Probably not very much. The average layperson usually thinks of law as trials, and criminal trials at that. But trials, by our definition, are one of the less legal, or "law-filled," parts of the legal process because much of the conflict-settling work of lawyers and judges involves deciding not what law means but what happened. Those who followed the trial of R. Kelly, the singer accused of appearing in a sex video with an underage minor, did not need to be expert in the intricacies of child pornography law. Trials are not so much legal reasoning as they are a microscopic kind of historical research. The R. Kelly trial revolved around very simple questions of fact: Was the singer actually in the video, or had it been digitally altered to look that way? Was the female in the video an underage minor?[17] We are confident enough that such historical problems do not require legal reasoning that we often turn the job of solving them over to groups of amateur historians, better known as juries.

---

[16] Adam Liptak, "First Amendment Claim in Cockfight Suit," *The New York Times*, July 11, 2007, p. A13.

[17] The jury acquitted apparently because jurors thought the prosecution had not proven that it was Kelly and an underage girl who appeared on the tape. Stacy St. Clair, "R. Kelly Verdict: Not Guilty," *The Chicago Tribune*, June 13, 2008.

Rules do tell juries what facts to seek. Child pornography laws told jurors in the Kelly case to look for evidence that the woman in the video was underage. If Kelly's lawyers had claimed the insanity defense, the jurors would have looked for evidence about Kelly's sanity as defined by the law in Illinois, the state in which the trial took place.

Facts and the law, then, are intertwined. Yet the heart of the reasoning part of law, and the subject of this book, does not involve figuring out the facts about what happened to the parties in the case. Instead, legal reasoning concerns what to make of the facts once we "know" them. In the airplane theft case, for example, the historical problem was whether the defendant flew someone else's plane to another state without permission. The legal reasoning problem was whether the statute's definition of a "vehicle" included airplanes.

The illustrative case at the end of this chapter sets out the distinction between trial and appellate decisions. In that case, a trial court had decided that a certain Mr. Prochnow was the father of his wife's baby. The facts—which included a suspicious liaison between the wife and another man, the physical separation of the husband and wife except for one encounter eight months before the birth of a full-term baby, and the incompatibility of the husband's blood type with that of the child—seemed to point conclusively in the other direction. Nevertheless, certain official rules of law, as interpreted by the appellate court, seemed to prevent the trial judge from holding that the husband was not the child's natural father. This case also provides our first full-length example of a court trying (and in our judgment failing) to do legal reasoning well.

A DEFINITION OF LEGAL REASONING

The story about the Bush advisors who tried to get their way by taking advantage of a sick man worries us because it showed that the Bush administration could not justify, even to its own appointees, the legality of the surveillance program they were operating. It is a fundamental political expectation in the United States that those in power justify the way in which they use that power. We expect, both in private and in public life, that people whose decisions directly affect our lives will show how their decisions serve common rather than purely selfish ends. We expect teachers articulate to grading standards. We expect elected politicians to respond to the needs of voters. In all such cases, we reject the authoritarian notion that power justifies itself, that those with money or political office can do whatever they please.

Holding public officials responsible for justifying their power may seem obvious to us, but this practice is actually a fairly recent development in Western political philosophy. The alternatives—governing through greater physical strength and brute force, or governing through tradition and authoritarian right (as did kings when they proclaimed "divine right" to rule)—may have seemed acceptable when people believed that God willed everything. However, religious theories of government, still prevalent in many parts of the world, tend to produce so much warfare and bloodshed that liberal philosophers from John Locke forward have tried to substitute reason and justification for the force of armies and for the unchallengeable authority of kings, tyrants, and other "supreme leaders."[18]

The rule of law transforms the way power is exercised. Yet we must never forget that law itself is a form of power. Indeed, though law may seem civilized, even erudite, it is also violent, as the essays of Robert Cover remind us. "Legal interpretation," he wrote, "takes place in a field of pain and death." Law often justifies violence that has occurred or that is

---

[18] Lief Carter develops this theme further in his first chapter of *An Introduction to Constitutional Interpretation: Cases in Law and Religion* (White Plains, N.Y.: Longman, 1991).

about to occur.[19] Judicial outcomes in lawsuits can literally kill and bankrupt people. Courts govern, and government, at its core, is the collective use of authority backed by threats of violence. Whether appellate judges meet or fail to meet our fundamental expectation about the use of judicial power depends on the quality of their legal reasoning. We hold legislators, governors, presidents, and many other politicians to account by forcing them to run for election, but we hold appellate judges accountable primarily by examining the honesty and quality of their opinions.[20]

LEGAL REASONING DOES NOT DISCOVER THE "ONE RIGHT ANSWER"

Our culture reinforces some misunderstandings of legal reasoning. Perhaps because, starting in the Renaissance, a stream of discoveries about the physical world has continuously bombarded Western civilization, we too often assume that legal reasoning is good when it discovers the law's "right answer," the correct legal solution to a problem. The idea that we live under a government of laws, not men, seems based on the assumption that correct legal results exist, like undiscovered planets or subatomic particles, quite independent of man's knowledge.

Of course if law (and science) actually worked that way, a book on legal reasoning would be absurd. To see whether a judge settled a contract dispute correctly, we would simply study the law of contract. In all cases, trained lawyers and legal scholars would, like priests in olden days, have access to correct answers that laypeople—most readers of this book—could not hope to match. A layperson would either defer to the conclusion of the expert or rebel.

Appellate judges do justify their power through the quality of the opinions they write. The quality of their opinions, however, depends on something other than proving that they found the one correct legal answer. After all, when the law is clear enough that people on opposite sides of a case can agree on what law commands, they usually don't spend the many thousands of dollars that contesting a case in an appellate court requires. Legal reasoning, in other words, describes what judges do to justify their decision when they *cannot* demonstrate or prove that they have reached the "right answer." As Benjamin Cardozo pointed out the better part of a century ago (see the opening epigraph, p. xiv), appellate judges usually *create* law. The uncertainties and imperfections in law force judges to choose what the law *ought* to mean, not merely report on what it does mean.

THE FOUR ELEMENTS OF LEGAL REASONING

To persuade us that the law ought to mean what the judge has decided, the well-reasoned judicial opinion will harmonize the following four basic building blocks present in every case:

1. The *case facts* established in the trial and preserved in the record of the evidence produced at the trial
2. The facts, events, and other conditions that we observe in the world, quite apart from the case at hand, which we call *social background facts*

---

[19] Robert Cover, "Violence and the Word," in *Narrative, Violence and the Law: The Essays of Robert Cover,* Martha Minow, Michael Ryan, and Austin Sarat, eds. (Ann Arbor: University of Michigan, 1995), p. 203.

[20] All federal judges who are appointed under Article III of the Constitution, the judicial article, serve for life. Impeachment and removal from office are rare.

3. What the *rules of law,* that is, the official legal texts created by the state, say about cases like this

4. Widely shared moral *values* and social principles.

These four building blocks are the foundation of all legal reasoning. Sometimes judges hide them, but these four elements drive all well-reasoned judicial decisions. And thus we arrive at our definition of legal reasoning:

Legal reasoning describes how a legal opinion combines the four elements: the facts established at trial, the rules that bear on the case, social background facts, and widely shared values. When a judge reasons well, the opinion harmonizes or "fits together" these four elements.

This definition, no doubt, seems abstract and fuzzy at first. We hope that by the time you finish this book, you will understand this definition and see that it is not simply an academic theory of law. These four building blocks are so essential to legal reasoning that you should practice learning how to identify and distinguish them in concrete cases. Here are illustrations of how each of the four elements works in the legal reasoning in specific cases.

Case Facts

Of the four building blocks, case facts are perhaps the easiest to understand. These are facts about the dispute between the parties in the case as developed in a trial. In a jury trial, the judge usually charges the jury that it must find certain things to be true in order to find for the plaintiff, or to find a defendant guilty; a jury verdict of guilt or liability necessarily finds such facts to be true. In a trial where a judge sits without a jury, the judge will usually read into the court record her findings of fact. In either situation, the only way an appellate court can overturn a trial court's factual conclusions is to hold that they have no substantial basis in the evidence and are therefore "clearly erroneous,"[21] a rare event.

A case fact was central in the Supreme Court's decision that suspected "enemy combatants" imprisoned at Guantanamo Bay had constitutional habeas corpus rights to challenge their detention. The Court found that though the Guantanamo facility was based in Cuba, the terms under which the United States leased the land gave it, in practice, "complete jurisdiction and control" over the area. This was a crucial finding of fact, because it led the Court to conclude that the U.S. government had "functional sovereignty" over the area, so that those imprisoned there had habeas corpus rights under the Constitution. Under the Court's interpretation of the Constitution, if the area was not completely controlled by the United States, as in for example a war zone, the detainees would not have had habeas corpus rights.[22]

Social Background Facts

Social background facts are conclusions about the world independent of the specific case facts that the parties are disputing. Social background facts often play a dramatic role in the harmonizing process. Sometimes the parties will contest them. For example, in medical malpractice suits, the parties often argue over what the "standard and commonly accepted" treatment of a given medical condition would be. That is a crucial point, because medical providers who do not follow the "standard and commonly accepted" practice can be deemed negligent, so the two sides will often call expert witnesses who debate what is standard and commonly accepted.

---

[21] See Rule 52A, Federal Rules of Civil Procedure.

[22] *Boumediene v. Bush* 553 U.S. _____ (2008), and see Appendix B.

More often, however, the social background facts in a case are fairly obvious and uncontested. For example, in *Prochnow v. Prochnow*, the child support case presented at the end of this chapter, both sides acknowledged that babies do not arise spontaneously in the womb but must be created by a sperm inseminating an ovum. Even when the social background facts in a case are not clear, judges and juries nonetheless often rely on hunches about them, something Judge Learned Hand does openly in a case you will read in Chapter 2, *United States v. Repouille*.

In a 2007 ruling striking down the Environmental Protection Administration's (EPA) refusal to develop rules regulating greenhouse gas emissions, Justice John Paul Stevens' opinion rested on several social background facts about global warming. He concluded that "the harms of global climate change are serious and well recognized," including a rise in sea levels and "severe and irreversible changes to natural ecosystems." The EPA, Justice Stevens noted, did not dispute the causal connection between greenhouse gas emissions and global warming.[23] In her opinion in a 2003 case upholding the constitutionality of an affirmative action program at the University of Michigan law school, Justice Sandra Day O'Connor supported her decision with several social background facts—facts not about Michigan specifically but about affirmative action programs more generally. She cited studies that suggest "student body diversity promotes better learning outcomes," and she quoted from a "friend of the court" brief submitted by a number of senior military officials, who claimed that for the military to fulfill its mission, it must maintain racial diversity in the academies in which officers are trained. These were contested social background facts—some opponents of affirmative action took issue with them—but they were important premises in O'Connor's opinion.[24]

Rules of Law

Judges must take account of all the rules of law that are relevant to a case. Rules of law come from statutes or constitutions, but they can also come from precedents—previously decided cases. The justices in the majority in *Carhart v. Gonzales*, a 2007 case upholding a federal law criminalizing "partial birth abortion," had to take account of a very similar precedent decided just seven years before, *Stenberg v. Carhart*. In *Stenberg*, the Court struck down a Nebraska law banning some late-term abortion procedures in part because the law did not contain an exception for cases in which those procedures were necessary to protect the health of the mother. (The law did have an exception for when an abortion was necessary to *save the life* of the mother.) Justice Kennedy's opinion in *Carhart v. Gonzales*, however, concluded that where medical authorities differed on the necessity of using partial-birth abortion to protect the mother's health, legislatures need not include the exception.[25]

Widely Shared Values

To be convincing, judges must also take account of social values. This is not an invitation for judges to recite their own values nor to pick the values they deem most worthy. Instead, judges must try to persuade communities they have considered widely shared values that ordinary members of the community can see embedded in the dispute.

Two widely shared values, freedom and privacy, were cited in *A.Z. v. B.Z.* In this dispute, a woman who wanted to implant frozen embryos in her womb was opposed by her ex-husband,

---

[23] *Massachusetts v. EPA*, 549 U.S. 497 (2007).

[24] *Grutter v. Bollinger* 536 U.S. 306, at 331–332 (2003).

[25] *Stenberg v. Carhart* 530 U.S. 914 (2000); *Carhart v. Gonzales* 550 U.S. 124 (2007).

who did not want any more children with her. The frozen embryos were left over from fertility treatments the couple had taken while married. The ex-husband had signed seven consent forms saying that if the couple separated, the wife would retain the choice of whether to implant them. The ex-wife argued strongly for the moral importance of keeping one's formal contractual promises. Nonetheless, the Supreme Judicial Court of Massachusetts ruled in the husband's favor, concluding that "respect for liberty and privacy requires that individuals be accorded the freedom to decide whether to enter into a family relationship." Thus, the Court refused to enforce the consent forms.[26]

You can imagine how all four building blocks of legal reasoning play some role in each of these cases: *Rules of law* about when contracts can be disregarded also shaped the ruling in the frozen embryos case. The *widely shared value* of preserving the environment was central in the global warming case. And it is a *social background fact* that fathers usually feel responsible for their offspring, a factor in the *Prochnow* case. All cases have each of the four building blocks in them, though sometimes the opinion in the case fails to identify them clearly or even attempts to hide them.

Several immensely important corollaries follow from our definition of legal reasoning. First, two judges may reach different results in the same case, yet each may reason equally well or badly. Like two excellent debaters, two opposing opinions may still persuade us that each judge has fit together the four elements into a vision of justice that we trust.

Second, legal reasoning is ultimately political. Laypeople who read judicial opinions can and should react to them and decide whether the opinion actually persuades them. No single opinion will persuade everyone. Reactions for and against judicial decisions about such volatile issues as abortion, global warming, and gay rights inevitably shape the development of law in the future.

Third, legal reasoning does *not* refer to the specific calculations that go on in a judge's head. In 1929, U.S. District Judge Joseph Hutcheson confessed that the actual decision-making process revolved around the judicial "hunch."[27] Professor Warren Lehman in 1986 agreed: "What we call the capacity for judgment . . . is an intellectualized account of the capacity for decision making and action, whose nature is not known to us."[28] Legal reasoning justifies the decision but does not explain how the judge arrived at it. In theory, a devilishly partisan judge could decide cases solely to advance her political agenda yet write masterful opinions that appear fair and impartial. A truly apathetic judge could flip a coin to make a decision, then write a brilliant opinion that convincingly justified it. We will never know with certainty why judges decide as they do, and it would be foolish to assume that a judge's opinion is some kind of record of the decision process.

Psychologically speaking, however, a judge's internal mental process and the quality of her public justification for the result presumably interact. The discipline of writing thoughtful

---

[26] A.Z. v. B.Z., 431 MA. 150; 725 N.E.2d 105 (2000).

[27] Joseph C. Hutcheson, Jr., "The Judgment Intuitive: The Function of the 'Hunch' in Judicial Decision," 14 *Cornell Law Quarterly* 274 (1929). Hutcheson defined *hunch* as "a strong intuitive impression that something is about to happen."

[28] Warren Lehman, *How We Make Decisions* (Madison: Institute for Legal Studies of the University of Wisconsin Law School, 1986), p. 12. The current research describing how the brain integrates its right and left hemispheres to solve, by "insight," complex problems is particularly well summarized by Jonah Lehrer, "The Eureka Hunt," *The New Yorker,* July 28, 2008, pp. 40–45. "The answer will arrive when you least expect it," Lehrer writes (p. 44). See also the reflections of a respected judge in Richard Posner, *How Judges Think* (Cambridge, MA: Harvard University Press, 2008), and Carter, "Law and Politics as Play," 1342–1348.

opinions, can, through a mental feedback loop, make the judge's decision making more thoughtful and well-considered. Psychologists have found that when people learn to think in new ways, they can literally reshape their brains and thus improve the way they make decisions.[29] It is no stretch to believe that judges who write well-reasoned opinions are also likely to make good decisions. Still, there is always a gap between the decision and the reasoning that explains it. A judge's opinion is a public justification of the choice she has made, not a moving brain scan of a mind at work.

Finally, the process by which judges seek to fit the four elements of legal reasoning together inevitably requires them to simplify and distort each element to some degree. Therefore, most opinions will fail to meet the requirements of formal logic. (The Supreme Court's rulings about establishment of religion—which allow churches and church schools many tax advantages yet prohibit the government from providing certain forms of financial aid to church schools—are notoriously incoherent by purely logical standards.) So, too, opinions will simplify the moral and empirical issues in them. Simplification and alteration are facts of life. We always must reshape raw materials if we want to fit them together smoothly.

Thus we return to the point made previously: Law does not provide a technique for generating "right answers." This book's analysis assumes that nothing, including science and technology, can ever be correct in an absolute demonstrable sense. For the same reasons, pitches in baseball become balls and strikes, for all practical purposes, because the umpire calls them that way—even when we may see the pitch differently. Just so with judges and lawyers, who agree to follow certain procedures and to use a common vocabulary of legal reasoning but do not automatically agree on legal outcomes—or even on which techniques of legal reasoning to use and when to use them.

SOURCES OF OFFICIAL LEGAL TEXTS

The range of legal problems and conflicts is practically infinite, but lawyers and judges will, one way or another, resolve the issues by referring to and reasoning about official legal texts created by the state ("rules of law," or just "legal rules" for short). Despite the endless variety of legal problems, lawyers and judges usually resort to four categories of official texts: *statutes, common law, constitutional law,* and *administrative regulations.*

The easiest category to understand is what we often call "laws"—the *statutes* passed by legislatures. Laypeople tend to think of statutes as the rules defining types of behavior that society wishes to condemn: crimes. However, legislatures enact statutes governing (and sometimes creating!) many problems without enacting criminal statutes—civil rights, income tax rates, and social security benefit levels, for example. For our purposes, statutory law, the subject of Chapter 4, also includes the local ordinances passed by the elected bodies of cities and counties.

But there is a problem here. Legislatures do not enact statutes to cover everything. And when lawyers and judges face a problem without a statute, they normally turn to that older set of legal texts called *common law,* the subject of Chapter 3.

Judges make law in a way completely different from legislators. Instead of meeting together to draft, argue about, and vote on proposals to change the law, judges decide cases—and in doing, create legal rules. Common-law rules emerged through a process introduced in England before the discovery of the New World. The process began because the king of England chose to assert national authority by sending judges throughout the country to decide cases in the name

---

[29] Susan C. Vaughn argues that successful psychotherapy creates this structural transformation. See Vaughn, *The Talking Cure: The Science Behind Psychotherapy* (New York: Henry Holt, 1998).

of the Crown. The king did not write rules to govern all judges' decisions. It was because the judges acted in the name of the central government, a shaky government by our standards, that their decisions became law common to the king's entire domain. Many common-law rules originated in local custom or in the minds of the judges themselves.

Chapter 5 explores the third category of official legal texts, *constitutional law.* The Constitution of the United States and the 50 state constitutions set out the structure and powers of government. They also place legal limits on the way those who govern can use their power. While statutes, and common law, where statutory law is silent, can govern anybody, constitutions govern the government.[30] The U.S. Constitution even governs presidents, although most constitutional cases involve an alleged conflict between the national or state constitutions and a decision made and enforced by lesser public administrators, who claim to act under statutory authority.

Administrative regulations—of the Internal Revenue Service, or the San Francisco Zoning Board, or any of the thousands of national, state, and local administrative agencies—make up the fourth category of legal texts. Executives and nonelected administrators can make rules only when a constitution or a statute gives them the authority to do so. Problems in administrative law can fascinate and perplex as much as any. Because this book's length and your time both have limits, we shall examine reasoning about administrative regulations only indirectly. Do not, however, let this deliberate neglect mislead you into thinking the subject is unimportant. Administrative regulations are shaping law and our lives more and more.[31] The scope of this book, however, is mainly confined to historically more developed official legal texts: *statutes, common law,* and *constitutional law.*

THE CHOICES THAT LEGAL REASONING CONFRONTS

While official legal texts are the starting point for legal reasoning, they are rarely the endpoint. If judges could resolve disputes simply by reciting the words of a legal text, disputes would not come to court in the first place. Anybody can read. People can usually find ways to dispute what words mean: The Bush administration engaged in a long-running dispute over the meaning of the word "torture," as used in international treaties and federal law, at one point defining it so narrowly as to include only techniques that inflict pain that one would feel from "organ failure, impairment of bodily function or even death."[32] For better or worse, it takes judicial reasoning and judgment to say what legal texts actually mean in the context of specific cases. In most cases, judges must reconcile the potential inconsistencies and contradictions among widespread values, the actual words of legal rules and

---

[30] If I, as a private citizen, don't like a speech of yours and forcibly remove you from your podium, I will probably violate a principle of common or statutory law. I will also violate the value favoring free exchange of ideas. But I will not violate the First Amendment of the U.S. Constitution. If, however, I did this while employed by a government agency, such as the FBI, my action could be a constitutional violation.

[31] See Lief Carter and Christine Harrington, *Administrative Law and Politics,* 4th ed. (Washington, D.C.: CQ Press, 2009). The U.S. Congress generally enacts a few hundred statutes per year, but the federal bureaucracy issues 3,000 to 5,000 rules per year.

[32] John Yoo, Deputy Assistant Attorney General, Memorandum to White House Counsel Alberto Gonzales regarding Standards of Conduct for Interrogation Under 18 U.S.C. 2340–2340A, August 1, 2002. This memo, as well as other documents from the Bush administration regarding torture, is reprinted in Karen J. Greenberg, ed., *The Torture Debate in America* (New York: Cambridge University Press, 2006), p. 317.

prior judicial opinions, and their own views of the case facts and the social background facts in the cases before them. Judges must make difficult choices such as the following:

■ Does the case before me call for continued adherence to the historical meaning of legal words? Must I do what the framers of statutory or constitutional language intended their language to accomplish? Isn't it impossible to know what other people in the past intended? When do social, political, and technological changes permit or require a different or revised interpretation of legal concepts?

■ Should I always follow the literal meaning of words? In what circumstances can I ignore the literal meaning of words altogether?

■ Does this case obligate me to follow a judicial precedent the wisdom of which I doubt? When am I free to ignore a relevant precedent? Just what makes a precedent relevant in the first place?

Throughout the following chapters, we shall see that choices such as these—the choice of change or stability and of literal or flexible interpretation of words and precedents, for example—have no "right answer." Judges inevitably have discretion to decide.

Judges also must make choices when a case pits widely shared moral values against each other. Thus the Constitution contains language protecting the freedom of the press. It also contains language ensuring the fairness of criminal trials. But an unrestrained press can do much to prejudice the members of the jury who follow the news, and hence impair the fairness of a trial.

In this instance, perhaps judges can do justice by reaching a fair compromise between values. A more difficult problem arises not when two values collide but when two ideas of justice itself collide. One such collision pits *general* justice against *particular* justice. Is it just for bus drivers and train engineers always to pull away from the station exactly on time, even if it means that a soldier on leave and racing down the platform to get home for Christmas will miss his ride? Is it not true in the long run, to paraphrase Professor Zechariah Chafee, that fewer people will miss buses and trains if they all know that buses and trains always leave on the dot, that more people will miss if they assume that they can dally and still find the vehicle at the station? While it is often possible to engineer compromises among competing values, it is often impossible to compromise between different visions of justice itself. Unless they are corrupt or lazy, judges will *strive* to do justice, but whether they succeed often remains debatable.

Because legal decisions require choices from among competing values, judges and others who analyze legal problems cannot be "objective." The problem of general versus particular justice is a good illustration. A value, a preference, or a moral "feeling" is not a concept we can prove to be right or wrong. Those who adopt values that conflict with yours will call you biased, and you may feel the same way about them. In the final chapter, we will examine more fully the nature of bias and impartiality in law. If "biases" and "values" are identical psychological feelings or beliefs about right and wrong, then legal reasoning cannot eliminate them, but we will see that judges can act impartially nevertheless. The impartial judge will persuasively harmonize, or coherently fit together, the four elements described in this chapter. We trust that with the next four chapters under your belt, you will follow easily the more complete development of this idea in the final chapter.

Impartiality, however, does not eliminate the tragic element in law. In Martha Nussbaum's *The Fragility of Goodness*, we learn that tragic situations exist whenever circumstances pull people in two inconsistent but equally good directions at once. Imagine yourself having to decide the frozen embryo case mentioned earlier, and you will feel its inherently tragic nature. Immanuel Kant believed, as Nussbaum puts it, "that objective practical rules be in every situation consistent, forming a harmonious system like a system of true beliefs. . . ."

Nussbaum (and most contemporary moral philosophers), however, rejects Kant's claim that an internally consistent structure of rules can eliminate the need to make tragic choices in life. Think of all the tragic consequences that even the routine award of child custody in a contested divorce case can have on the parent denied custody, and perhaps on the child. Impartiality requires judges to persuade us that they have reached the better result. But if a judge denies the tragic choices in a case by pretending it has an easy answer, she will not persuade us to trust her exercise of power over us. We will know better because we know, from Greek mythology and from our own experience, that we often cannot do right without doing wrong. Legal reasoning matters because, done well, it helps communities survive and transcend life's tragic side. As Nussbaum writes, "If we were such that we could in a crisis dissociate ourselves from one commitment because it clashed with another, we would be less good."[33]

ILLUSTRATIVE CASE

Each chapter ends with an illustrative case that gives you a chance to apply what you have learned to an example of legal reasoning. After presenting the Prochnow case, we pose questions that will help you identify the four legal reasoning elements in its majority and dissenting opinions.

Prochnow v. Prochnow

Supreme Court of Wisconsin 274

Wisconsin 491 (1957)

A husband appeals from that part of a decree of divorce which adjudged him to be the father of his wife's child and ordered him to pay support money. The actual paternity is the only fact which is in dispute.

Joyce, plaintiff, and Robert, defendant, were married September 2, 1950, and have no children other than the one whose paternity is now in question. In February 1953, Robert began his military service. When he came home on furloughs, which he took frequently in 1953, he found his wife notably lacking in appreciation of his presence. Although he was home on furlough for eight days in October and ten in December, after August 1953, the parties had no sexual intercourse except for one time, to be mentioned later. In Robert's absence, Joyce had dates with a man known as Andy, with whom she danced in a tavern and went to a movie, behaving in a manner which the one witness who testified on the subject thought unduly affectionate. This witness also testified that Joyce told her that Robert was dull but that she and Andy had fun. She also said that a few days before Friday, March 12, 1954, Joyce told her she had to see her husband, who was then stationed in Texas, but must be back to her work in Milwaukee by Monday.

On March 12, 1954, Joyce flew to San Antonio and met Robert there. They spent the night of the 13th in a hotel where they had sex relations. The next day, before returning to Milwaukee, she told him that she did not love him and was going to divorce him. Her complaint, alleging cruel and inhuman treatment as her cause of

---

[33] Martha Nussbaum, *The Fragility of Goodness: Luck and Ethics in Greek Tragedy and Philosophy* (New York: Cambridge University Press, 1986), pp. 31 and 50.

action, was served on him April 8, 1954. On September 16, 1954, she amended the complaint to include an allegation that she was pregnant by Robert and demanded support money.

The child was born November 21, 1954. Robert's letters to Joyce are in evidence in which he refers to the child as his own. He returned to civilian life February 13, 1955, and on February 18, 1955, answered the amended complaint, among other things denying that he is the father of the child born to Joyce; and he counterclaimed for divorce alleging cruel and inhuman conduct on the part of the wife.

Before trial, two blood grouping tests were made of Mr. and Mrs. Prochnow and of the child. The first was not made by court order but was ratified by the courts and accepted in evidence as though so made. This test was conducted in Milwaukee on March 21, 1955. The second was had in Waukesha September 29, 1955, under court order. The experts by whom or under whose supervision the tests were conducted testified that each test eliminated Robert as a possible parent of the child. An obstetrician, called by Robert, testified that it was possible for the parties' conduct on March 13, 1954, to produce the full-term child which Mrs. Prochnow bore the next November 21st. Mrs. Prochnow testified that between December 1953 and May 1954, both inclusive, she had no sexual intercourse with any man but her husband . . .

Brown, Justice.

The trial judge found the fact to be that Robert is the father of Joyce's child. The question is not whether, on this evidence, we would have so found: we must determine whether that finding constituted reversible error.

Section 328.39 (1) (a), Stats., commands:

> Whenever it is established in an action or proceeding that a child was born to a woman while she was the lawful wife of a specified man, any party asserting the illegitimacy of the child in such action or proceeding shall have the burden of proving beyond all reasonable doubt that the husband was not the father of the child. . . .

Ignoring for the moment the evidence of the blood tests and the effect claimed for them, the record shows intercourse between married people at a time appropriate to the conception of this baby. The husband's letters after the child's birth acknowledge it is his own. The wife denies intercourse with any other man during the entire period when she could have conceived this child. Unless we accept the illegitimacy of the baby as a fact while still to be proved, there is no evidence that then, or ever, did she have intercourse with anyone else. The wife's conduct with Andy on the few occasions when the witness saw them together can justly be called indiscreet for a married woman whose husband is absent, but falls far short of indicating adultery. Indeed, appellant did not assert that Andy is the real father but left that to the imagination of the court whose imagination, as it turned out, was not sufficiently lively to draw the inference. Cynics, *among whom on this occasion we must reluctantly number ourselves* [emphasis supplied], might reasonably conclude that Joyce, finding herself pregnant in February or early March, made a hasty excursion to her husband's bed and an equally abrupt withdrawal when her mission was accomplished. The subsequent birth of a full-term child a month sooner than it would usually be expected if caused by this copulation does nothing to dispel uncharitable doubts. But we must acknowledge that a trial judge, less inclined to suspect the worst, might with reason recall that at least as early as the preceding August, Joyce had lost her taste for her husband's embraces. Divorce offered her freedom from them, but magnanimously she might determine to try once more to save the marriage: hence her trip to Texas. But when the night spent in Robert's arms proved no more agreeable than such nights used to be she made up her mind that they could live together no more, frankly told him so and took her departure. The medical testimony concerning the early arrival of the infant does no more than to recognize eight months of gestation as unusual. It admits the possibility that Robert begat the child that night in that San Antonio hotel. Thus, the mother swears the child is Robert's and she knew, in the Biblical sense, no other man. Robert, perforce, acknowledges that it may be his. Everything else depends on such reasonable inferences as one chooses to draw from the other admitted facts and circumstances. And such inferences are for the trier of the fact. Particularly, in view of Sec. 328.39 (1) (a), Stats., supra, we cannot agree with appellant that even with the blood tests left out of consideration, the record here proves beyond a reasonable doubt that Joyce's husband was not the father of her child.

Accordingly we turn to the tests. The expert witnesses agree that the tests excluded Mr. Prochnow from all possibility of this fatherhood. Appellant argues that this testimony is conclusive; that with the tests in evidence Joyce's testimony that she had no union except with her husband is insufficient to support a finding that her husband is the father. . . . But the Wisconsin statute authorizing blood tests in paternity cases pointedly refrains from directing courts to accept them as final even when they exclude the man sought to be held as father. In its material parts it reads:

> Sec. 325.23 *Blood tests in civil actions.* Whenever it shall be relevant in a civil action to determine the parentage or identity of any child, . . . the court . . . may direct any party to the action and the person involved in the controversy to submit to one or more blood tests, to be made by duly qualified physicians. Whenever such test is ordered and made the results thereof shall be receivable in evidence, but only in cases where definite exclusion is established. . . .

This statute does no more than to admit the test and its results in evidence—there to be given weight and credibility in competition with other evidence as the trier of the fact considers it deserves. No doubt in this enactment the legislature recognized that whatever infallibility is accorded to science, scientists and laboratory technicians by whom the tests must be conducted, interpreted, and reported retain the human fallibilities of other witnesses. It had been contended before this that a report on the analysis of blood is a physical fact which controls a finding of fact in opposition to lay testimony on the subject, and the contention was rejected. . . . When the trial judge admitted the Prochnow tests in evidence and weighed them against the testimony of Mrs. Prochnow he went as far in giving effect to them as our statute required him to do. Our opinions say too often that trial courts and juries are the judges of the credibility of witnesses and the weight to be given testimony which conflicts with the testimony of others for us to say that in this case the trial court does not have that function. . . .

The conclusion seems inescapable that the trial court's finding must stand when the blood-test statute does not make the result of the test conclusive but only directs its receipt in evidence there to be weighed, as other evidence is, by the court or jury. We hold, then, that the credibility of witnesses and the weight of all the evidence in this action was for the trial court, and error cannot be predicated upon the court's acceptance of Joyce's testimony as more convincing than that of the expert witnesses.

Judgment affirmed.

Wingert, Justice (dissenting). With all respect for the views of the majority, Mr. Chief Justice Fairchild, Mr. Justice Currie, and the writer must dissent.

In our opinion the appellant, Robert Prochnow, sustained the burden placed upon him by Sec. 328.39 (1) (a), Stats., of proving beyond all reasonable doubt that he was not the father of the child born to the plaintiff.

To meet the burden, appellant produced two classes of evidence, (1) testimony of facts and circumstances, other than blood tests, which create grave doubt that appellant is the father, and (2) the evidence of blood tests and their significance, hereinafter discussed. In our opinion the blood test evidence should have been treated as conclusive in the circumstances of this case.

Among the numerous scientific achievements of recent decades is the development of a method by which it can be definitely established in many cases, with complete accuracy, that one of two persons cannot possibly be the parent of the other. The nature and significance of this discovery are summarized by the National Conference of Commissioners on Uniform State Laws, a highly responsible body, in the prefatory note to the Uniform Act on Blood Tests to Determine Paternity, as follows:

> In paternity proceedings, divorce actions and other types of cases in which the legitimacy of a child is in issue, the modern developments of science have made it possible to determine with certainty in a large number of cases that one charged with being the father of a child could not be. Scientific methods may determine that one is not the father of the child by the analysis of blood samples taken from the mother, the child, and the alleged father in many cases, but it cannot be shown that a man is the father of the child. If the negative fact is established it is evident that there is a great miscarriage of justice to permit juries to hold on the basis of oral testimony, passion, or sympathy, that the person charged is the father and is responsible for the support of the child and other incidents of paternity. . . . There is no need for a dispute among the experts, and true experts will not disagree. Every test will show the same results. . . .
>
> [T]his is one of the few cases in which judgment of court may be absolutely right by use of science. In this kind of a situation it seems intolerable for a court to permit an opposite result to be reached when the judgment may scientifically be one of complete accuracy. For a court to permit the establishment of paternity in cases where it is scientifically impossible to arrive at that result would seem to be a great travesty on justice. (Uniform Laws Annotated, 9 Miscellaneous Acts, 1955 Pocket Part, p. 13.)

In the present case the evidence showed without dispute that the pertinent type of tests were made of the blood of the husband, the wife, and the child on two separate occasions by different qualified pathologists, at separate laboratories, and that such tests yielded identical results, as follows:

	3/17/55	9/29/55
	Blood types	
Robert Prochnow (Husband)	AB	AB
Joyce Prochnow (Wife)	O	O
David Prochnow (Child)	O	O

There is no evidence whatever that the persons who made these tests were not fully qualified experts in the field of blood testing, nor that the tests were not made properly, nor that the results were not correctly reported to the court. . . .

Two qualified experts in the field also testified that it is a physical impossibility for a man with type AB blood to be the father of a child with type O blood, and that therefore appellant is not and could not be that father of the child David. Both testified that there are no exceptions to the rule. One stated "There is no difference of opinion regarding these factors amongst the authorities doing this particular work. None whatsoever." The evidence thus summarized was not discredited in any way and stands undisputed in the record. Indeed, there was no attempt to discredit it except by the wife's own self-serving statement that she had not had sexual relations with any other man during the period when the child might have been conceived. . . .

QUESTIONS ABOUT THE CASE

1. This case requires the court to interpret several statutes. Which are they? The case also involves a procedural rule that differentiates the work of appellate courts from that of trial courts. What is that rule?

2. What factual assertions about this dispute did the trial court accept as proved? What factual assertions did it reject?

3. What social background facts are at issue here? What choice did the appellate court have to make about social background facts in order to decide this case?[34]

4. Did not the majority's decision to reject the conclusive proof of the blood tests rest on some value choices? Does the court articulate these choices? If not, what might they have been? Does this decision necessarily depend on a fundamentalist religious conviction that God can always alter nature if He wishes? Or might the court have believed that, in the interest of giving David any father at all, it was best to assign paternity to Robert despite science?[35]

5. Why was the law ambiguous in this case?

6. Do you find that the majority or the dissenting opinion does a better job of legal reasoning? Why?

7. How does this opinion change the law? That is, if the dissent had prevailed in this case, how would the reading of the rules of law at issue in this case change?

---

[34] *Hint:* Don't discount the social background fact that medical practitioners make mistakes. In 1995, a Harvard School of Public Health research team studying two well-regarded Boston hospitals found 334 errors in drug delivery to patients over a 6-month period. ("Hundreds of Drug Errors Are Found at Two Hospitals," *The New York Times,* July 6, 1995, p. A8.) Doesn't the possibility of error help explain why the statute uses the phrase "receivable in evidence"?

[35] A twenty-first century Massachusetts case may offer a clue to the *Prochnow* court's thinking. The Massachusetts Supreme Judicial Court rejected a man's motion to be released from paying child support to his seven-year-old daughter after DNA tests revealed that the man was not in fact the father of the child. The court reasoned that "Cheryl's" interest in having the "legal rights and financial benefits of a parental relationship" outweighed the man's interests, particularly because he had delayed for several years in contesting a paternity agreement. (*In Re Cheryl,* 434 MA 23; 746 N.E.2d 488, 2001.) Most state courts, faced with a wave of DNA-based lawsuits, have ruled similarly, fearing the consequences of leaving children "fatherless." (Kathleen Burge, "SJC Says Fatherhood Goes Past DNA Test," *Boston Globe,* April 25, 2001, p. A1.)

CHAPTER 2

Change and Stability in Legal Reasoning

*The mystery of life is not a problem to be solved, but
a reality to be experienced.*

—AART VAN DER LEEUW

The first chapter began to narrow this book's scope of inquiry. We do not put ourselves in the shoes of legislators, nor do we examine how elections or lobbying or presidential leadership produce new law. But while this book does not explore many important political issues, it inevitably steers us into thinking about politics, for three reasons.

First, studying legal reasoning shows us that "the law" does not substitute for politics—it is politics. Unless the parties agree that "the law" automatically resolves a case (and when this happens, they usually don't go to court in the first place), the judge will make and defend a choice. That is, the judge will use his or her political power to change people's lives—to send them to jail or the death chamber, to bankrupt them, to humiliate them or vindicate them. Legal reasoning, as explained in the first chapter, becomes the language we use for analyzing whether the judge has used this political power fairly and persuasively.

Second, once we learn from studying legal reasoning that the most impartial and fair judges inevitably make political choices when they decide cases, we learn that we must take other questions about legal politics very seriously. Whom we elect as president, for example, will affect the selection of people who sit on the federal courts, and that, in turn, will inevitably affect who wins and who loses in the judicial system. At a hearing on his nomination to the Supreme Court, Clarence Thomas once asserted that he would "strip down like a runner" and leave a life's worth of beliefs and political attitudes behind him when he ascended to the bench. If Thomas was simply promising that he would not allow his attitudes to *predetermine* his decisions, his statement was unremarkable. If instead Thomas's pledge was to become an attitudeless judge, his promise was not simply unrealistic but nonsensical.[1]

---

[1] David Broder, "A Justice with No Agenda," *Washington Post,* September 15, 1991, p. C7. Martha Minow makes Justice Thomas's comments the starting point of her analysis in her article "Stripped Down Like a Runner or Enriched by Experience," in G. Larry Mays and Peter R. Gregware, eds, *Courts and Justice: A Reader* (Prospect Heights, IL.: Waveland Press, 1995), pp. 366–382.

A long line of political science research demonstrates that the worldviews and experiences of judges affect the decisions they make.[2] Professors David Schkade and Cass Sunstein reported strikingly different outcomes in the U.S. Court of Appeals depending on whether the judges were appointed by a Republican or Democratic president.[3] Judges of the U.S. Court of Appeals are assigned randomly to hear cases in clusters of three-judge panels. Women who sued for sex discrimination won 75 percent of the time when a panel of three Democratic-appointed judges decided their case—but only 31 percent when three Republican-appointed judges presided. Research findings such as these, we emphasize, do *not* reflect some monstrous failure by judges to achieve objective, and hence "correct," legal judgments. There is, remember, no single "right answer" to legal questions, so it is absurd to condemn a judge for making an "incorrect" or "biased" decision merely because he or she disagrees with another judge about a case.[4]

That said, judges can be evaluated based on how well they explain their decisions. If a judicial opinion uses the elements of legal reasoning nonsensically, then those who read the opinion may infer, rightly or wrongly, that in the judge's decision, reason in law took a backseat, and other factors, including partisan views, or worries about political pressures, predominated. Judges don't find right answers to legal questions, but in their opinions they do create "good" and "bad" answers, and bad answers have consequences. Judges who use good legal reasoning bolster a community's confidence in the legal system by demonstrating they have thought carefully about the factors that are relevant to a decision. That—not "attitudelessness"—should be our standard for judging judges. Invariably, then, judges bring their attitudes with them when they ascend to the bench, and controversy over judicial appointments such as Thomas's is to be expected.

Third, as our emphasis on good reasoning suggests, the legal process, for all its political characteristics, is still a distinctive kind of politics. The practices, customs, and norms that go with being a U.S. congressperson or senator inevitably shape how that kind of politician thinks. Judges, because they have been trained in the law and are constantly exposed to legal arguments, think differently about politics than do legislators. Moreover, the audience for legal opinions expects a different set of justifications for political action than does the audience for legislative decisions. It is, for example, perfectly acceptable for senators to explain that they made a particular decision because it benefited their home state or some interest group they support (and, alas, that most likely supported them through a major donation to their campaign); a judge who explained his vote in this way would be considered corrupt or incompetent.

Law, like any language practice, limits what becomes thinkable within that framework. What counts as good evidence, or an appropriate case to hear, or a recognizable social background fact, or legitimate social value all depends on the tradition of legal practices that

---

[2] Empirical studies of judicial decision making support the approach we take here. See for example Thomas G. Hansford and James F. Spriggs, *The Politics of Precedent on the U.S. Supreme Court* (Princeton, N.J.: Princeton University Press, 2006); Jeffrey A. Segal and Harold J. Spaeth, *The Supreme Court and the Attitudinal Model Revisited* (New York: Cambridge University Press, 2002); *Majority Rule or Minority Will: Adherence to Precedent on the U.S. Supreme Court* (New York: Cambridge University Press, 1999); and Saul Brenner and Harold Spaeth, *Stare Indecisis* (Cambridge: Cambridge University Press, 1995).

[3] David Schkade and Cass R. Sunstein, "Judging by Where You Sit," *The New York Times,* June 11, 2003, p. A29. See Cass Sunstein, Davide Schkade, Lisa M. Ellman, and Andres Sawicki, *Are Judges Political? An Empirical Analysis of the Federal Judiciary* (Washington, D.C., The Brookings Institution, 2006).

[4] For a wide-ranging treatment of why language and logic do not yield objectively "correct" interpretations of the world, see Stanley Fish's essays collected in *There's No Such Thing as Free Speech* (New York: Oxford University Press, 1994).

make such things thinkable in the first place. So, as you grapple with legal reasoning issues throughout this book, please keep in the back of your mind that you are simultaneously studying the political language by which the law creates and perpetuates its power.[5]

The first section of this chapter explores why legal language does not generate "correct" answers to contested legal questions. The second section asserts that this uncertainty and ambiguity, on balance, benefit us more than they harm us. The third section examines the other side of the uncertainty coin, the general philosophical conditions in which judges should choose legal clarity and stability at the expense of other values. This chapter's concluding section reviews some general and inevitable characteristics of law that make it forever changing, never perfected.

SOURCES OF UNPREDICTABILITY IN LAW
The Disorderly Conduct of Words

Cases often go to courts (and particularly to appellate courts) because the law does not determine the outcome. Both sides believe they have a chance to win. The legal process is in these cases *unpredictable*. Legal rules are made with words, and we can begin to understand why law is unpredictable by examining the ambiguity of words, the "disorderly conduct of words," as Professor Chafee put it.[6] Sometimes our language fails to give us precise definitions. There is, for example, no way to define the concept of *table* so as to exclude some items we call "benches," and the reverse.[7] As fans of the "planet" Pluto learned to their dismay in 2006, there exists no single correct definition of a planet.[8] More often, words that seem clear enough in the abstract may nevertheless have different meanings to each of us, because we have all had different experiences with the objects or events in the world that the words have come to represent.

To illustrate, consider the U.S. Equal Employment Opportunity Commission's basic description of illegal sexual harassment:

> Unwelcome sexual advances, requests for sexual favors, and other verbal or physical conduct of a sexual nature constitutes sexual harassment when submission to or rejection of this conduct explicitly or implicitly affects an individual's employment, unreasonably interferes with an individual's work performance or creates an intimidating, hostile or offensive work environment.

---

[5] Stanley Fish's essay, "The Law Wishes to Have a Formal Existence," in *There's No Such Thing as Free Speech*, pp. 141–179, describes this phenomenon particularly well. We're grateful to Michael McCann for showing us why specifying this point is so essential to this book's larger argument. For a thorough description of how law helps constitute the hopes and expectations of laypersons outside the judicial system, see McCann's *Rights at Work* (Chicago: University of Chicago Press, 1994).

[6] Zechariah Chafee, "The Disorderly Conduct of Words," 41 *Columbia Law Review* 381 (1941). Seemingly objective photographs, videos and digital imagery are no less ambiguous as spoken or written words when used as evidence in law, see Jessica Silbey, "Judges As Film Critics: New Approaches to Filmic Evidence," 37 *Michigan Journal of Law Reform* 493 (2004).

[7] If you don't believe it, try creating this definitional distinction—paying attention to coffee tables and tool benches. Further suppose a state enacts a statute exempting from its sales tax all "food and foodstuffs." What is *food*? Is chewing gum food? Is coffee? Is beer? Who, for that matter, should count as a "terrorist?" See Martin Kaste, "Oregon Environmental Activists Sentenced," *Morning Edition*, (National Public Radio, May 24, 2007).

[8] In 2006 the International Astronomical Union demoted Pluto to the status of "dwarf planet," though controversy over the definition of "planet" continues. Dennis Overbye, "Vote Makes It Official: Pluto Isn't What It Used to Be," *The New York Times*, August 25, 2006. "The Society for the Preservation of the Pluto as a Planet" continues to fight the decision, see www.plutoisaplanet.org.

How would you define the words "sex" and "sexual"? What does the phrase "implicitly affects an individual's employment" mean? What would a "reasonable" interference with work performance look like? What is "offensive"?[9]

Or consider another context in which "sex" leads to complications. Many states now have laws barring "same-sex marriage." Would such a law bar the marriage between a man and a person who was born male but who has become transgendered, and so has lived his life as a female? What factors should weigh in such a determination? Hormone levels? Surgical alteration of the genitalia? Words, in this case the word "sex," or "bride" and "groom," do not by themselves resolve these questions, as a case that actually arose in Virginia demonstrated.[10]

Words are slippery because their meaning always depends on their context. John Train has developed lists of what he calls "antilogies," words that can have opposite meanings in different contexts.[11] Thus the infinitive *to dust* can refer to removing dust or to laying down dust, as in crop dusting. *To continue* can mean to proceed or to delay a proceeding. *To sanction* both authorizes and condemns. *To buckle* can mean to fasten together or fall apart.

The disorderly conduct of words affects legal reasoning most immediately when a judge faces the task of interpreting a statute for the first time and no judicial precedent helps the judge to find its meaning. Therefore, we shall refine the problem of disorderly words in Chapter 4, which examines judicial choices in statutory interpretation "in the first instance."

For now it suffices to say that, while words can have important practical consequences, and judges must pay close attention to their meaning, words never "speak for themselves." Consider three examples:

■ The U.S. Constitution requires a president to be a "natural born Citizen" of the United States. Senator John McCain, the unsuccessful Republican candidate for the presidency in 2008, was born in 1936 to citizen parents on a military base in the Panama Canal Zone. The Canal Zone was a legally recognized U.S. territory, but Congress conferred U.S. citizenship on people born in the Canal Zone only a year after he was born. The "natural born" provision bars Americans who were born outside the United States and subsequently became citizens from the presidency. Is McCain a "natural born Citizen"?[12]

■ In *Massachusetts v. EPA*, a case we described briefly in Chapter 1, the Supreme Court wrestled with, among other issues, whether carbon dioxide is an "air pollutant" and thus subject to regulation under the Clean Air Act. It is a social background fact that the emission of carbon dioxide is causing global warming, yet we breathe this gas every day, and the plants that sustain us would not exist without it. So, is carbon dioxide an "air pollutant"?[13]

---

[9] See http://www.eeoc.gov/facts/fs-sex.html. These are not trivial questions. Cases have been documented in which older or unpopular workers were fired based on extremely loose interpretations of these words. See Vicki Schultz, "The Sanitized Workplace," 112 *Yale Law Journal* 2061 (2003).

[10] Michelle Washington, "One Small Hitch in the Wedding," *The Virginian-Pilot*, May 23, 2008, p. B1.

[11] See "Antilogies," *Harvard Magazine*, November–December 1985, p. 18, and "More Antilogies," *Harvard Magazine*, March–April 1986, p. 17.

[12] Adam Liptak, "McCain's Eligibility is Disputed by Professor," *The New York Times*, July 11, 2008, p. A11.

[13] The Supreme Court ruled that carbon dioxide is an "air pollutant," under the Clean Air Act, though Justice Scalia dissented on this point, arguing that the Environmental Protection Agency reasonably concluded that CO_2 was not covered by the statute. *Massachusetts v. EPA*, 549 U.S. 497 (2007).

■ Everyone has experienced the emotion of hatred at times, and so we assume that we know what would count as a "hate crime." Of course, hatred motivates many crimes that are not classified hate crimes—wives, for example, sometimes murder abusive husbands because of hatred. Thus a hate crime is typically defined by a categorical hatred of the class of people, like racial minorities or homosexuals, to which the victim belongs. But what about a 2007 case in which practiced muggers used the Internet to lure gay men to known trysting spots only to rob them? They were charged with a hate crime, but they swore that they bore no hatred of gay men; they simply found them to be particularly easy marks. Does targeting a particular group, by itself, make a crime a "hate crime"?[14]

The Unpredictability of Precedents

We have argued that precedents help narrow the range of legal choices judges face when they justify a decision. Indeed, precedents do just that, but they never provide complete certainty. Reasoning by example also perpetuates a degree of unpredictability in law. To see why, we proceed through six analytical stages.

Stage One: Reasoning by Example in General

Reasoning by example, in its simplest form, means accepting one choice and rejecting another because the past provides an example that the accepted choice somehow "worked." Robert, for example, wants to climb a tree but wonders if its branches will hold. He chooses to attempt the climb because his older sister has just climbed the tree without mishap. Robert reasons by example. His reasoning hardly guarantees success: His older sister may still be skinnier and lighter than he. Robert may regret a choice based on a bad example, but he still reasons that way. If he falls and survives, he will possess a much better example from which to reason in the future.

The most important characteristic of reasoning by example in any area of life is that no rules tell the decider *how* to decide which facts are similar and which are different. Let us therefore see how this indeterminacy occurs in legal reasoning.

Stage Two: Examples in Law

In law, decisions in prior cases provide examples for legal reasoning. For starters, a precedent contains the analysis and the conclusion reached in an earlier case in which the facts and the legal question(s) resemble the current conflict a judge has to resolve. Even when a statute or a constitutional rule is involved, a judge will look at what other judges have said about the meaning of that rule when they applied it to similar facts and answered similar legal questions. A judge hearing the case of the airplane thief would not simply read the National Motor Vehicle Theft Act, just as the Supreme Court justices who considered the constitutionality of the District of Columbia's handgun ban didn't simply stare at the words "right to bear arms" in the Second Amendment. Both would primarily look at previous cases in which judges had interpreted these rules.

To understand more fully how precedents create examples, we must return to the distinction between law and history. How does a judge know whether facts of a prior case really do resemble those in the case now before the court?

---

[14] Clyde Haberman, "An Easy Target, But Does That Mean Hatred?" *The New York Times*, June 26, 2007, p. B1.

Trials themselves do *not* normally produce precedents. As we have seen, trials seek primarily to find the immediate facts of the dispute, to discover who is lying, whose memory has failed, and who can reliably speak to the truth of the matter. When a jury hears the case, the judge acts as an umpire, making sure the lawyers present the evidence properly to the jury so that it decides the "right" question. Often judges do the jury's job as well. The law does not allow jury trials in some disputes, and even where it does, sometimes both parties prefer to use a judge. The parties may feel the issues are too complex for laypeople or that a "bench trial" will take less time and cost less money.

Whether or not a jury participates in a trial, it is up to the trial judge to decide the issues of law that the lawyers raise. The conscientious trial judge will explain to the parties orally for the record why and how she resolves the key legal issues in their case. In some instances, she will give them a written opinion explaining her legal choices, and this may be published. But since at trial the judge pays most attention to the historical part of the case, deciding what happened, she usually keeps her explanations at the relatively informal oral level. As a result, other judges will not find these opinions reported anywhere; they cannot discover them even if they try. Hence few trial judges create precedents even though they resolve legal issues.

Thus, the masses of legal precedents that fill the shelves of law libraries mostly emerge from the appellate process. You should not, however, lose sight of the fact that lawyers use many of the same legal reasoning techniques when formulating their arguments and advising their clients, usually so that the client can safely stay out of court altogether.

Stage Three: The Three-Step Process of Reasoning by Example

Legal reasoning often involves reasoning from the examples of precedents. Powerful legal traditions impel judges to solve problems by using solutions to similar problems reached by judges in the past. Thus a judge seeks to resolve conflicts by discovering a statement about the law in a prior case—the example—and then applying this statement or conclusion to the current case. Lawyers who seek to anticipate problems and prevent conflicts follow much the same procedure. Professor Levi calls this a three-step process in which the judge sees a factual similarity between the current case and one or more prior cases, announces the rule of law on which the earlier case or cases rested, and applies the rule to the current case.[15]

Stage Four: How Reasoning by Example Perpetuates Unpredictability in Law

To understand this stage, we must return to the first step in the three-step description of reasoning by example, when the judge decides which precedent governs. The judge must *choose* the facts in the current case that resemble or differ from the facts in the case, or line of cases, in which prior judicial decisions first announced the rule. The judge no doubt accepts the obligation, made powerful by legal tradition, to "follow precedent," but the judge is under no obligation to follow any particular precedent. He completes step one *by deciding for himself* which of the many precedents are similar to the facts of the case before him and *by deciding for himself* what they mean.

No judicial opinion in a prior case can require that a judge sift the facts of the present case one way or another. She is always free to do this herself. A judge writing an opinion can

---

[15] Edward Levi, *An Introduction to Legal Reasoning* (Chicago: University of Chicago Press, 1949), p. 2. Please do not confuse the six analytical stages we use in this chapter with the three-step reasoning process inherent in the legal system itself.

influence a future user of the precedent she creates by refusing to report or consider some potentially important facts revealed in the trial transcript. But once she reports them, judges in later similar cases can use the facts in their own way. They can call a fact critical that a prior judge reported but deemed insignificant; they can make a legal molehill out of what a prior judge called a mountain. Thus the present judge, the precedent user, retains the freedom to choose the example from which the legal conclusion follows.

We call judicial freedom to choose the governing precedent by selectively sifting the facts of prior cases and weighing their relative significance *fact freedom*. This is a major source of uncertainty in law, because it is impossible to predict with total accuracy how judges will use their fact freedom. Thus we cannot say that "the law" applies known or given rules to diverse factual situations' because we don't know the applicable rules until after the judge uses fact freedom to choose the precedent.

Stage Five: An Illustration of Fact Freedom in Action

Consider the following example from the rather notorious history of the Mann Act. The Mann Act, passed by Congress in 1910, provides in part that "Any person who shall knowingly transport or cause to be transported . . . in interstate or foreign commerce . . . any woman or girl for the purpose of prostitution or debauchery, or for any other immoral purpose . . . shall be deemed guilty of a felony." Think about these words for a minute. Do they say that if I take my wife to Tennessee for the purpose of drinking illegal moonshine whiskey with her, I have violated the Mann Act? What if I take her to Tennessee to rob a bank? Certainly robbing a bank is an "immoral purpose." Is it "interstate commerce"? But we are jumping prematurely to Chapter 4's discussion of statutes and Chapter 5's analysis of constitutional law. For the moment, you should see that the U.S. Congress has chosen some rather ambiguous words, and then turn your attention to the main problem: deciding how best to read the facts from one Mann Act case, *Caminetti v. United States*, to come to a decision about the criminal prosecution of the Mortensens.

Mr. and Mrs. Mortensen, owners and operators of a house of prostitution in Grand Island, Nebraska, went with two employees on a well-earned vacation to Yellowstone and Salt Lake City. The girls did lay off their occupation completely for the duration of the trip, and they paid for much of the vacation themselves. Upon their return, they resumed their calling. More than a year later, federal agents arrested the Mortensens and, on the basis of the vacation trip, charged them with violation of the Mann Act. The jury convicted the Mortensens, but their lawyer appealed to an appellate court judge.

Unpredictability in law arises when the judge cannot automatically say that a given precedent is or isn't factually similar. To simplify matters here, let us now assume that only one precedent exists, the decision of the U.S. Supreme Court in *Caminetti v. United States*, announced in 1917.[16] Assume that in *Caminetti*, two married men took two young women (aged 19 and 20) who were not their wives from Sacramento, California, to a cabin near Reno, Nevada, where they had sexual relations. The girls went voluntarily; they were neither prostitutes nor known to be "fast." By traveling to Reno, the men may have hoped to avoid prosecution by California state officials. On these facts, the Supreme Court in *Caminetti* upheld the conviction under the Mann Act.

---

[16] *Caminetti v. United States*, 242 U.S. 470 (1917).

Does *Caminetti* seal the Mortensens' fate? Does this precedent require the courts to find Mr. and Mrs. Mortensen guilty under the Mann Act? To answer these questions, the judge must decide whether this case is factually similar to *Mortensen*. Is it?

In one sense, of course it is. In each case, the defendants transported women across state lines, after which sex out of wedlock occurred. In another sense, it isn't. Without going to Reno, the girlfriends might not have slept with the defendants. But if the Mortensens had not sponsored the vacation, the women would have continued their work. The Mortensens' transportation *reduced* the frequency of prostitution; the two boyfriends, by bringing their girlfriends on a trip, may or may not have increased the amount of "illicit sex." Should this difference matter? The judge is free to select one interpretation of the facts in order to answer this question. Either decision will create a new legal precedent. It is precisely this freedom to decide either way that increases unpredictability in law.

Stage Six: Reasoning by Example Facilitates Legal Change

Why does judicial fact freedom make law change constantly? Legal rules change every time they are applied because no two cases ever have exactly the same facts. Although judges treat cases as if they were legally the same whenever they apply the rule of one case to another, deciding the new case in terms of the rule adds to the list of cases a new and unique factual situation. To rule in the Mortensens' favor, as the Supreme Court did in 1944, gave judges new ways of looking at the Mann Act.[17] With those facts, judges after 1944 could, if they wished, read the Mann Act more narrowly than they did in *Caminetti*. *Mortensen* thus potentially changed the meaning of the Mann Act, thereby changing the law.

But as the situation turned out, the change did not endure. In 1946, the Court upheld the conviction under the Mann Act of certain Mormons, members of a branch known as Fundamentalists, who took "secondary" wives across state lines. No prostitution at all was involved here, but the evidence did suggest that some of the women did not travel voluntarily. Fact freedom worked its way again.[18] The Court extended *Caminetti* and by implication isolated *Mortensen*. The content of the Mann Act, then, has changed with each new decision and each new set of facts.

Is law always as confusing and unclear as these examples make it seem? In one sense, certainly not. To the practicing lawyer, most legal questions the client asks possess clear and predictable answers. But in such cases—and here we return to the definition of legal conflicts in Chapter 1—the problems probably do not get to court at all. Uncertainty helps convert a human problem into a legal conflict. We focus on uncertainty in law because that is where reason in law takes over.

In another sense, however, law never entirely frees itself from uncertainty. Lawyers always cope with uncertainties about what happened, uncertainties that arise in the historical part of law. If they go to trial on the facts, even if they think the law is clear, the introduction of new evidence or the unexpected testimony of a witness may raise new and uncertain legal issues the lawyers didn't consider before the trial. Lawyers know they can never fully predict the outcome of a client's case, even though much of the law is clear to them most of the time.

---

[17] *Mortensen v. United States*, 322 U.S. 369 (1944).
[18] *Cleveland v. United States*, 329 U.S. 14 (1946).

IS UNPREDICTABILITY IN LAW DESIRABLE?

Is it desirable that legal rules do not always produce clear and unambiguous answers to legal conflicts? Should the legal system strive to reach the point where legal rules solve problems in the way, for example, that the formula for finding square roots of numbers provides automatic answers to all square root problems?

Despite the human animal's natural discomfort in the presence of uncertainty, some unpredictability in law is desirable. Indeed, if a rule had to provide an automatic and completely predictable outcome before courts could resolve conflicts, society would become intolerably repressive, if not altogether impossible. There are two reasons why.[19]

First, since no two cases ever raise entirely identical facts, society must have some way of convincing litigants that treating different cases *as if they were the same* is fair. But if the legal system resolved all conflicts automatically, people would have little incentive to *participate* in the process that resolves their disputes. If the loser knew in advance he would surely lose, he would not waste time and money on litigation. He would not have the opportunity to try to persuade the judge that his case, always factually unique, *ought* to be treated by a different rule. Citizens who lose will perceive a system that allows them to "make their best case" as fairer than a system that tells them they lose while they sit helplessly.

Only in unpredictable circumstances will each side have an incentive to present its best case. When the law is ambiguous, each side thinks it might win.[20] This produces an even more important consequence for society as a whole, not just for the losers. The needs of society change over time. The words of common law, precedents, statutes, and constitutions must take on new meanings. Ambiguity encourages litigants to constantly bombard judges with new ideas. The ambiguity inherent in reasoning by example gives the attorney the opportunity to persuade the judge that the law *ought* to say one thing rather than another. Lawyers thus keep pushing judges to make their interpretation of "the law" fit new circumstances and changes in social values.

We do not encourage legislators and judges to celebrate legal uncertainty, much less to maximize it by deliberately crafting vague statutes and ambiguous opinions. Rather, we argue that uncertainty in law is unavoidable. This uncertainty is, however, more a blessing than a curse. The participation that uncertainty in law encourages gives the legal process and society itself a vital capacity to change its formal rules as human needs and values change.

VERTICAL AND HORIZONTAL STARE DECISIS: A STABILIZING AND CLARIFYING ELEMENT IN LAW

This discussion of unpredictability in law should not lead you to believe that law is never clear, or at least "clear enough" to discourage parties from fighting over the meaning of the law in court. Government by law cannot function without some consensus on the meaning of laws. If society is to work, most law must be clear much of the time. We must be able to make wills and contracts, to insure ourselves against disasters, and to plan hundreds of other decisions with the confidence that courts will back our decisions if the people we trust with our freedom and our property fail us.

---

[19] Levi, *An Introduction to Legal Reasoning,* pp. 1–6.

[20] The process also has the desirable effect of encouraging negotiation and compromise. Each side has an incentive to settle because each side knows it could lose.

There is indeed a force pushing toward stability within reasoning by example itself: Once judges determine that a given precedent is factually similar enough to determine the outcome in the case before them, then in normal circumstances they follow the precedent. This is the doctrine of *stare decisis,* meaning, "we let the prior decision stand."

Stare decisis operates in two dimensions. In the first, or *vertical,* dimension, it acts as a marching order in the chain of judicial command. Courts in both the state and federal systems are organized in a hierarchy within their jurisdictions. Thus the supreme court of each state, as well as the U.S. Supreme Court, sits atop an "organization chart" of courts. The rulings of the highest court in any jurisdiction legally control all the courts beneath it. Stare decisis stabilizes law vertically because no court should ignore a higher authoritative decision on a legal point. As long as the U.S. Supreme Court holds that airplanes are not "vehicles" within the National Motor Vehicle Theft Act (NMVTA), all courts beneath it must legally honor that ruling in any future airplane theft case that may arise under the Act.

There is, however, a more interesting *horizontal* dimension to stare decisis. Horizontal stare decisis is the binding force of a precedent *on the court that created it* over time. What should a court do if it makes a decision that, a few years or decades later, judges come to believe made "bad" law, or law that is outdated because of changes in social background facts or social values? Horizontal stare decisis describes the circumstances in which judges should continue to follow and apply their court's own decisions even when they believe that those decisions were misguided or are outdated.

The U.S. Supreme Court's decision in June of 1992 to continue to follow *Roe v. Wade*— and to reaffirm that the Constitution implicitly grants a female a right to choose whether to continue a pregnancy prior to viability—amounted to a debate about this very principle. The *New York Times* quoted on its front page the essence of the Court's horizontal stare decisis reasoning. Justice O'Connor extolled the importance of keeping law clear and stable. "Liberty finds no refuge in a jurisprudence of doubt . . . ," her opinion began. Justice Kennedy wrote of the importance of respecting the interest in relying on the law: "An entire generation has come of age free to assume *Roe's* concept of liberty in defining the capacity of women to act in society, and to make reproductive decisions." And Justice Souter spoke eloquently of preserving the Court's image: "A decision to overturn . . . would address error, if error there was, at the cost of both profound and unnecessary damage to the Court's legitimacy, and to the Nation's commitment to the rule of law."[21]

Eleven years later, the same three justices encountered another prominent—and problematic—precedent, this one involving laws criminalizing sodomy. In *Lawrence v. Texas,* the Court considered the case of two men convicted under Texas's "Homosexual Conduct" law. The men argued that the law violated their liberties under the Due Process Clause of the Fourteenth Amendment—an argument the Supreme Court had rejected in a very similar 1986 case, *Bowers v. Hardwick.* Writing for the majority, which included Justice Souter,[22] Justice Kennedy concluded that "*Bowers* was not correct when it was decided, and it is not

---

[21] *The New York Times,* June 30, 1992, p. A1; and *Planned Parenthood v. Casey,* 505 U.S. 833 (1992). See also *Dickerson v. United States,* where the Supreme Court voted to retain its controversial "*Miranda* rule" requiring advising a criminal of his rights before obtaining any incriminating evidence for use in trial. Chief Justice Rehnquist, who had expressed skepticism about the rule, wrote, "Whether or not we would agree with *Miranda's* reasoning and its resulting rule, were we addressing the issue in the first instance, the principles of stare decisis weigh heavily against overruling it now." 530 U.S. 428 (2000).

[22] Justice O'Connor, who had voted in 1992 to uphold *Roe* despite her misgivings, also voted to strike down the law in *Lawrence* but on separate equal protection grounds.

correct today." And though "The doctrine of *"stare decisis"* is essential to the respect accorded to the judgments of the Court and to the stability of the law," it is not "an inexorable command."[23] Unlike *Roe*, Kennedy argued, no one was relying on *Bowers*, so overruling it would do more good than harm.

Justice Scalia found the distinction unconvincing. He argued that the Court and many other institutions had relied on *Bowers* in criminalizing private sexual behavior. The overruling of *Bowers*, Scalia predicted, would create "a massive disruption in the current social order."[24]

Scalia's dissent raises the central issue in stare decisis: Under what conditions should judges ignore or follow what they consider to be bad case law? Professor Thomas S. Currier has examined the values justifying the principle of horizontal stare decisis. He suggests five values that should lead judges toward continuing to follow otherwise "bad" precedents:

> 1. *Stability*. It is clearly socially desirable that social relations should have a reasonable degree of continuity and cohesion, held together by a framework of reasonably stable institutional arrangements. Continuity and cohesion in the judicial application of rules [are] important to the stability of these institutional arrangements, and society places great value on the stability of some of them. Social institutions in which stability is recognized as particularly important include the operation of government, the family, ownership of land, commercial arrangements, and judicially created relations. . . .
>
> 2. *Protection of Reliance*. [T]he value here is the protection of persons who have ordered their affairs in reliance upon contemporaneously announced law. It is obviously desirable that official declarations of the principles and attitudes upon which official administration of the law will be based should be capable of being taken as determinate and reliable indications of the course that such administration will in fact take in the future. . . . This value might be regarded as a personalized variation on the value of stability; but it is broader in that it is recognized even where no social institution is involved, and stability as such is unimportant.
>
> 3. *Efficiency in the Administration of Justice*. If every case coming before the courts had to be decided as an original proposition, without reference to precedent, the judicial workload would obviously be intolerable. Judges must be able to ease this burden by seeking guidance from what other judges have done in similar cases.
>
> 4. *Equality*. By this is meant the equal treatment of persons similarly situated. It is a fundamental ethical requirement that like cases should receive like treatment, that there should be no discrimination between one litigant and another except by reference to some relevant differentiating factor. This appears to be the same value that requires rationality in judicial decision-making, which in turn necessitates that the law applied by a court be consistently stated from case to case. The same value is recognized in the idea that what should govern judicial decisions are rules, or at least standards. The value of equality, in any event, appears to be at the heart of our received notions of justice.
>
> 5. *The Image of Justice*. This phrase does not mean that any judicial decision ought to be made on the basis of its likely impact upon the court's public relations, in the Madison Avenue sense, but merely that it is important not only that the court provide equal treatment to persons similarly situated, but that, insofar as possible, the court

---

[23] *Lawrence v. Texas*, 539 U.S. 558 at 577 (2003), citing *Payne v. Tennessee*, 501 U.S. 808 (1991) at 828.
[24] *Lawrence v. Texas*, 539 U.S. at 591.

should appear to do so. Adherence to precedent generally tends not only to assure equality in the administration of justice, but also to project to the public the impression that courts do administer justice equally.[25]

The following chapters will describe more precisely the circumstances in which Currier's reasons for horizontal stare decisis should and should not compel a judge to follow rather than depart from a precedent. Here you should simply note that, in part because of stare decisis, most law is clear enough to prevent litigation most of the time. Lawyers can advise us on how to make valid wills and binding contracts, trusting that the arrangements they help us make will be upheld by courts. And if someone steals our car and takes it to another state, federal officials, under the authority of the National Motor Vehicle Theft Act, can try to track down the car and the criminal. Without a system of precedents, it would be harder for us to predict judicial decisions and therefore more difficult for us to plan to avoid legal conflicts.[26]

These forces in law pushing toward predictability and stability should not, however, obscure this chapter's main conclusion. Cases routinely arise where the best possible legal reasoning *cannot* provide a "right answer." New mixes of facts and legal rules pop up literally every day. The basic principle of the rule of law obligates judges to justify the result they reach in each new case in such a way that we trust their impartiality. Only good legal reasoning can build and maintain that trust.

ILLUSTRATIVE CASES

In the federal judicial system, it is common for the intermediate appellate courts to hear cases in panels of three judges with the outcome determined by majority vote. Here are two opinions, both interpreting the Nationality Act of 1940, written by Learned Hand sitting on two separate panels. The first is a precedent for the second. Notice that they were decided just a month apart. You should read the second case to see how Judge Hand uses his fact freedom to distinguish *Repouille* from the first case, *Francioso,* then to see how Judge Frank uses fact freedom a different way, and finally to explore the possibility that both judges in *Repouille* have used their fact freedom foolishly.

---

[25] Thomas S. Currier, "Time and Change in Judge-Made Law: Prospective Overruling," 51 *Virginia Law Review* 201 (1965), pp. 235–238.

[26] Judges who refuse to follow the precedents of their superior courts face the embarrassment of having their decisions reversed by a higher court, but judges face no such sanction when they refuse to follow their own court's precedent, and so scholars have wondered why judges often do so. There are at least two possibilities. First, following precedent makes the job of deciding cases easier. As Benjamin Cardozo put it in *The Nature of the Judicial Process,* the "labor of judges would be increased almost to the breaking point if every past decision could be reopened in every case, and one could not lay one's own course of bricks on the secure foundation of the courses laid by others who had gone before him. (*The Nature of the Judicial Process* (1921) p. 149, quoted in Stevens, dissent, *District of Columbia v. Heller,* 554 U.S. _____ (2008)). Second, judges may follow precedent because they have a sense of institutional loyalty and respect for colleagues on the court who created it. These two factors, further, may reinforce each other. For a thorough analysis of the role of precedents in law, see Michael Gerhardt, *The Power of Precedent* (New York: Oxford University Press, 2008). For analyses of why precedent does not seem to be so powerful for justices on the Supreme Court, see the books cited in footnote 2 of this chapter, p. 23.

United States v. Francioso
164 F.2d 163 (Nov. 5, 1947)

L. Hand, Circuit Judge.

This is an appeal from an order admitting the appellee, Francioso, to citizenship. At the hearing the "naturalization examiner" objected to his admission upon the ground that he had married his niece and had been living incestuously with her during the five years before he filed his petition. Upon the following facts the judge held that Francioso had been "a person of good moral character" and naturalized him. Francioso was born in Italy in 1905, immigrated into the United States in 1923, and declared his intention of becoming a citizen in 1924. His wife was born in Italy in 1906, immigrated in 1911, and has remained here since then. They were married in Connecticut on February 13, 1925, and have four children, born in 1926, 1927, 1930, and 1933. Francioso was the uncle of his wife, and knew when he married her that the marriage was unlawful in Connecticut and that the magistrate would have not married them, had they not suppressed their relationship. They have always lived together in apparent concord, and at some time which the record leaves indefinite, a priest of the Catholic Church—of which both spouses are communicants—"solemnized" the marriage with the consent of his bishop.

In United States ex rel. *Iorio v. Day,* in speaking of crimes involving "moral turpitude" we held that the standard was, not what we personally might set, but "the commonly accepted mores": i.e., the generally accepted moral conventions current at the time, so far as we could ascertain them. The majority opinion in the United States ex rel. *Berlandi v. Reimer* perhaps looked a little askance at that decision; but it did not overrule it, and we think that the same test applies to the statutory standard of "good moral character" in the naturalization statute. Would the moral feelings, now prevalent generally in this country, be outraged because Francioso continued to live with his wife and four children between 1938 and 1943? Anything he had done before that time does not count; for the statute does not search further back into the past.

In 1938 Francioso's children were five, eight, eleven and twelve years old, and his wife was 31; he was morally and legally responsible for their nurture and at least morally responsible for hers. Cato himself would not have demanded that he should turn all five adrift. True, he might have left the home and supported them out of his earnings; but to do so would deprive his children of the protection, guidance and solace of a father. We can think of no course open to him which would not have been regarded as more immoral than that which he followed, unless it be that he should live at home, but as a celibate. There may be purists who would insist that this alone was consistent with "good moral conduct"; but we do not believe that the conscience of the ordinary man demands that degree of ascesis; and we have for warrant the fact that the Church—least of all complaisant with sexual lapses—saw fit to sanction the continuance of this union. Indeed, such a marriage would have been lawful in New York until 1893, as it was at common law. To be sure its legality does not determine its morality; but it helps to do so, for the fact that disapproval of such marriages was so long in taking the form of law, shows that it is condemned in no such sense as marriages forbidden by "God's law." It stands between those and the marriage of first cousins which is ordinarily, though not universally, regarded as permissible.

It is especially relevant, we think, that the relationship of these spouses did not involve those factors which particularly make such marriages abhorrent. It was not as though they had earlier had those close and continuous family contacts which are usual between uncle and niece. Francioso had lived in Italy until he was eighteen years of age; his wife immigrated when she was a child of four; they could have had no acquaintance until he came here in August, 1923, only eighteen months before they married. It is to the highest degree improbable that in that short time there should have arisen between them the familial intimacy common between uncle and niece, which is properly thought to be inimical to marriage. . . .

Order affirmed.

Repouille v. United States
165 F.2d 152 (Dec. 5, 1947)

L. Hand, Circuit Judge.

The District Attorney, on behalf of the Immigration and Naturalization Service, has appealed from an order, naturalizing the appellee, Repouille. The ground of the objection in the district court and here is that he did not show himself to have been a person of "good moral character" for the five years which preceded the filing of his petition. The facts are as follows. The petition was filed on September 22, 1944, and on October 12, 1939, he had deliberately put to death his son, a boy of thirteen, by means of chloroform. His reason for this tragic deed was that the child had "suffered from birth from a brain injury which destined him to be an idiot and a physical monstrosity malformed in all four limbs. The child was blind, mute, and deformed. He had to be fed; the movements of his bladder and bowels were involuntary, and his entire life was spent in a small crib." Repouille had four other children at the time towards whom he has always been a dutiful and responsible parent; it may be assumed that his act was to help him in their nurture, which was being compromised by the burden imposed upon him in the care of the fifth. The family was altogether dependent upon his industry for its support. He was indicted for manslaughter in the first degree; but the jury brought in a verdict of manslaughter in the second degree with a recommendation of the "utmost clemency"; and the judge sentenced him to not less than five years nor more than ten, execution to be stayed, and the defendant to be placed on probation, from which he was discharged in December 1945. Concededly, except for this act he conducted himself as a person of "good moral character" during the five years before he filed his petition. Indeed, if he had waited before filing his petition from September 22, to October 14, 1944, he would have had a clear record for the necessary period, and would have been admitted without question.

Very recently we had to pass upon the phrase "good moral character" in the Nationality Act; and we said that it set as a test, not those standards which we might ourselves approve, but whether "the moral feelings, now prevalent generally in this country" would "be outraged" by the conduct in question: that is, whether it conformed to "the generally accepted moral conventions current at the time."[a] In the

---

[a] *United States v. Francioso,* 164 F.2d 163 (2d Cir., 1947). [Footnote in original.]

absence of some national inquisition, like a Gallup poll, that is indeed a difficult test to apply; often questions will arise to which the answer is not ascertainable, and where the petitioner must fail only because he has the affirmative. Indeed, in the case at bar itself the answer is not wholly certain; for we all know that there are great numbers of people of the most unimpeachable virtue, who think it morally justifiable to put an end to a life so inexorably destined to be a burden on others, and—so far as any possible interest of its own is concerned—condemned to a brutish existence, lower indeed than all but the lowest forms of sentient life. Nor is it inevitably an answer to say that it must be immoral to do this, until the law provides security against the abuses which would inevitably follow, unless the practice were regulated. Many people—probably most people—do not make it a final ethical test of conduct that it shall not violate law; few of us exact of ourselves or of others the unflinching obedience of a Socrates. There being no lawful means of accomplishing an end, which they believe to be righteous in itself, there have always been conscientious persons who feel no scruple in acting in defiance of a law which is repugnant to their personal convictions, and who even regard as martyrs those who suffer by doing so. In our own history it is only necessary to recall the Abolitionists. It is reasonably clear that the jury which tried Repouille did not feel any moral repulsion at his crime. Although it was inescapably murder in the first degree, not only did they bring in a verdict that was flatly in the face of the facts and utterly absurd—for manslaughter in the second degree presupposes that the killing has not been deliberate—but they coupled even that with a recommendation which showed that in the substance they wished to exculpate the offender. Moreover, it is also plain, from the sentence which he imposed, that the judge could not have seriously disagreed with their recommendation.

One might be tempted to seize upon all this as a reliable measure of current morals; and no doubt it should have its place in the scale; but we should hesitate to accept it as decisive, when, for example, we compare it with the fate of a similar offender in Massachusetts, who, although he was not executed, was imprisoned for life. Left at large as we are, without means of verifying our conclusion, and without authority to substitute our individual beliefs, the outcome must needs be tentative; and not much is gained by discussion. We can say no more than that, quite independently of what may be the current moral feeling as to legally administered euthanasia, we feel reasonably secure in holding that only a minority of virtuous persons would deem the practise morally justifiable, while it remains in private hands, even when the provocation is as overwhelming as it was in this instance.

However, we wish to make it plain that a new petition would not be open to this objection; and that the pitiable event, now long passed, will not prevent Repouille from taking his place among us as a citizen. The assertion in his brief that he did not "intend" the petition to be filed until 1945, unhappily is irrelevant; the statute makes crucial the actual date of filing.

Order reversed; petition dismissed without prejudice to the filing of a second petition.

Frank, Circuit Judge (dissenting).
This decision may be of small practical import to this petitioner for citizenship, since perhaps, on filing a new petition, he will promptly become a citizen. But the

method used by my colleagues in disposing of this case may, as a precedent, have a very serious significance for many another future petitioner whose "good moral character" may be questioned (for any one of a variety of reasons which may be unrelated to a "mercy killing") in circumstances where the necessity of filing a new petition may cause a long and injurious delay. Accordingly, I think it desirable to dissent.

The district judge found that Repouille was a person of "good moral character." Presumably, in so finding, the judge attempted to employ that statutory standard in accordance with our decisions, i.e., as measured by conduct in conformity with "the generally accepted moral conventions at the time." My colleagues, although their sources of information concerning the pertinent mores are not shown to be superior to those of the district judge, reject his finding. And they do so, too, while conceding that their own conclusion is uncertain, and (as they put it) "tentative." I incline to think that the correct statutory test (the test Congress intended) is the attitude of our ethical leaders. That attitude would not be too difficult to learn; indeed, my colleagues indicate that they think such leaders would agree with the district judge. But the precedents in this circuit constrain us to be guided by contemporary public opinion about which, cloistered as judges are, we have but vague notions. (One recalls Gibbon's remark that usually a person who talks of "the opinion of the world at large" is really referring to "the few people with whom I happened to converse.")

Seeking to apply a standard of this type, courts usually do not rely on evidence but utilize what is often called the doctrine of "judicial notice," which, in matters of this sort, properly permits informal inquiries by the judges. However, for such a purpose (as in the discharge of many other judicial duties), the courts are inadequately staffed, so that sometimes "judicial notice" actually means judicial ignorance.

But the courts are not helpless; such judicial impotence has its limits. Especially when an issue importantly affecting a man's life is involved, it seems to me that we need not, and ought not, resort to our mere unchecked surmises, remaining wholly (to quote my colleagues' words) "without means of verifying our conclusions." Because court judgments are the most solemn kind of governmental acts—backed up as they are, if necessary, by the armed force of the government—they should, I think, have a more solid foundation. I see no good reason why a man's rights should be jeopardized by judges' needless lack of knowledge.

I think, therefore, that, in any case such as this, where we lack the means of determining present-day public reactions, we should remand to the district judge with these directions: The judge should give the petitioner and the government the opportunity to bring to the judge's attention reliable information on the subject, which he may supplement in any appropriate way. All the data so obtained should be put of record. On the basis thereof, the judge should reconsider his decision and arrive at a conclusion. Then, if there is another appeal, we can avoid sheer guessing, which alone is now available to us, and can reach something like an informed judgment.[b]

---

[b] Of course, we cannot thus expect to attain certainty, for certainty on such a subject as public opinion is unattainable. [Footnote in original.]

QUESTIONS ABOUT THE CASES

1. What legal questions does Judge Hand ask about Mr. Francioso's behavior? How does he answer them?

2. What facts about the *Repouille* case make *Francioso* factually similar enough to serve as a precedent?

3. The problem in both cases is how a court should determine whether an applicant for naturalization has the required good moral character. In *Francioso,* Judge Hand uses a method that permits him to conclude that Mr. Francioso should become a citizen. How does he do so?

4. Does Judge Hand use the same method in *Repouille*? If so, what facts distinguish the two cases so that, even though Mr. Francioso won, Mr. Repouille lost?

5. What method would Judge Frank use? How, if at all, does it differ from Hand's method? Which of these two do you prefer? Why?

Common Law

The life of the law has not been logic; it has been experience. The felt necessities of the time, the prevalent moral and political theories, intuitions of public policy, avowed or unconscious, even the prejudices which judges share with their fellow-men, have had a good deal more to do than the syllogism in determining the rules by which men should be governed.

—OLIVER WENDELL HOLMES, JR.

Common law at first may seem a bizarre creature. You have already seen judges interpreting *statutory* law in cases like *Prochnow* and *McBoyle*, the National Motor Vehicle Theft Act case. And you are probably somewhat familiar with *constitutional* law, which empowers judges to set aside statutes or other actions of the government that conflict with the Constitution. We will examine each of these more familiar forms of law in Chapters 4 and 5. In common-law cases, however, judges do not decide what the official rules written in statutes or constitutions mean. They refer instead only to cases other judges decided in the past and the doctrines that have emerged from them. But, you might ask, if judges in common-law cases reason solely from earlier precedents, what were *those* precedents based on? The surprising answer is that they too were based on precedents, in fact chains of precedents that stretch back into the practice of law in England well before Columbus's arrival in America.[1]

ORIGINS OF COMMON LAW

The story of the common law begins with William the Conqueror, who got his name by assembling thousands of troops, crossing the English Channel, and conquering England in battle. In order to watch over the administration of his new possession, William sent his personal advisors around the country administering ad hoc justice in the king's name—settling

---

[1] Plucknett's "concise" history of the common law is over 700 pages long. Theodore F.T. Plucknett, *A Concise History of the Common Law,* 5th ed. (Boston: Little, Brown, 1956). For real conciseness, try Frederick G. Kempin, *Historical Introduction to Anglo-American Law in a Nutshell,* 2nd ed. (St. Paul: West, 1973). To contrast common-law systems with the deductive or "code-based" systems of law on the European and South American continents, see John Henry Merryman and Rogelio Perez-Perdomo, *The Civil Law Tradition: An Introduction to the Legal Systems of Europe and Latin America,* 3rd ed. (Stanford: Stanford University Press, 2007).

land disputes, collecting the king's rents, and keeping the peace. Additionally, William appointed a "Great Council" to handle more serious transgressions, what we would today call *crimes*.

Nonetheless, local courts, not the king's judges, still did much of the adjudicating during William's reign. It was not until a century later that Henry II began the actual takeover of the lower local courts. Initially the king required litigants to get permission to bring a case in local court for any dispute involving title to his land. A litigant would have to obtain from London a *writ of right* and then produce it in the local court. Shortly thereafter, the king's council began to bypass the local courts altogether on matters of land title. Certain council members heard these cases at first, but as they became more and more specialized and experienced, they split off from the council to form the king's Court of Common Pleas.

Similarly, the council members assigned to criminal matters developed into the Court of the King's Bench. The Court of the Exchequer, which handled rent and tax collections, evolved in similar fashion.

Thus the king began supplanting local courts with his own. But whose law would the king's judges apply? In most of Europe, the kings' judges simply adopted the old Roman codes. In England, however—partly because it was easy and partly because it possessed considerable local political appeal—the king's judges adopted the practice of the pre–Conquest local courts. This practice of the lower courts consisted of adopting the local customs of the place and time and applying to daily events what people felt was fair. We might call this *the custom of following custom*.

The custom of following custom, however, created difficulties. In a sparsely populated region—a primitive area by today's standards of commerce and transportation—customs about crimes, land use, debts, and so forth varied considerably from shire to shire, village to village, and manor to manor. But the king's judges could hardly decide each case on the basis of whatever local custom or belief happened to evolve among those living where the dispute arose. To judge that way would amount to judging on shifting and inconsistent grounds. Judging would not occur in the name of the king but in the name of the location where the dispute arose. Following local custom would undercut the king's long-range political objective to have complete control over his lands.

Thus, in an attempt to rule consistently in the king's name, the royal courts slowly adopted some customs and rejected others. Because justice in England rested on the custom of customs, the customs that the royal courts adopted and attempted to apply uniformly became the customs *common* to all the king's realm. Indeed, though the judges no doubt felt that what they decided was right because it had its roots in some customs, it would be wiser to say they created not common custom but common law—law common throughout England.

Though the law in England became "common," it remained complex. Procedure—the correct way to handle a lawsuit—rapidly became rigid, and lawyers who could not master it and who could not remember all the strict technicalities lost their cases. They needed to write the technicalities down to remember them. Out of necessity, some judges and other observers of the English common law began the tradition, very much expanded today, of writing down, in what came to be called "commentaries," the essential facts and conclusions of court decisions. These collected records naturally became a convenient guide for helping judges decide future similar legal cases.

These early common-law judges, did not, however, create the practices of reasoning by example and stare decisis as we now know them. Indeed, until the American Revolution, men actively rejected the notion that judges actually made law as they decided cases. Men believed rather in natural law, if not God's law, at least nature's own. To them, the proper judicial decision rested on "true" law. The decision that rested elsewhere was in a sense unlawful. Prior to and throughout most of the nineteenth century, lawyers and judges thought of common law as a collected body of correct legal doctrine, not the process of growth and change that reasoning by example—to say nothing of the inevitable changes and compromises required in more democratic political systems—makes inevitable. Moreover, the commentaries were

> unofficial, incomplete, and thus unreliable. Only a radical change in viewpoint, the recognition that law comes from politicians and not from God or nature, coupled with accurate court reporting, permitted reasoning by example and stare decisis to flourish.[2]

In calling the common law judge-made law, then, we mean that for a variety of historical reasons, a large body of legal rules and principles exist because judges, without legislative help, have created them in the course of deciding cases. As long as judges continue to apply them, the judges continue to re-create them with each application. The fact that judges for most of this history thought they simply restated divine or natural law matters relatively little to us today. What matters is that the United States has inherited a political system in which, despite legislative supremacy, judges constantly and inevitably make law. How they do so—how they reason, in other words—thus becomes an important question in the study of politics and government. The central question in this book is not *whether* courts should make law but *what* law to make, and *how.*

REASONING BY EXAMPLE IN COMMON LAW

Much of the everyday law around us falls into the category of common law. Although modern statutes have supplanted much of it, particularly in the important area of commercial transactions, even these statutes for the most part preserve basic definitions, principles, and values articulated first in common law. One of the most important common-law categories concerns the law of tort. Tort law wrestles with questions such as these: What defines and limits a person's liability to compensate those whom he injures? What counts as a hurt serious enough to merit compensation? Breaking someone else's leg? Embarrassing someone? When does law impose liability on me if I threaten someone with a blow (assault)? If I strike the blow (battery)? What if I do so in self defense? If I publicly insult another (libel and slander)? What if I can show my insult is factually accurate? If I do careless things that injure other people (negligence)? These may sound like questions of criminal law to you, but they are not, for the law of torts does not expose the lawbreaker to punishment by the state. Instead, tort law gives people the right to sue to collect compensation from those who have injured them. Today tort law is constantly in the news, in lawsuits over the harms caused by prescription drugs, cigarettes, asbestos, even fatty food at fast-food chain restaurants. And as always, tort law is evolving in response to, as Justice Holmes put it in the epigraph for this chapter, the "felt necessities of the time" and the "prevalent moral and political theories" of the day.

---

[2] Kempin, p. 85, suggests that as late as 1825 in the United States and 1865 in England, stare decisis rested on very shaky ground. Anthropologists are quite comfortable with the conclusion that rules of law, in contrast to imperfectly articulated customs and interpersonal understandings, play a relatively insignificant role in many if not most of the world's justice systems. See Stanley Diamond, "The Rule of Law vs. the Order of Custom," 51 *Social Research* 387 (1984). For a particularly concise review of how slowly and fitfully common-law judges came to appreciate that they inevitably make law as they decide each case, see Roger Cotterrell, *The Politics of Jurisprudence* (London: Butterworth and Co., 1989), Chapter 2.

In this section, indeed for the bulk of the chapter, we illustrate common law in action with problems of tort law, mostly of negligence. We do not discuss tort law in its entirety, for it would take a book triple the size of this one to review all the subtleties and uncertainties in this branch of law. We shall instead focus in some detail on an important and perennial question in the law of tort: At what point do the rights and privileges of owning property stop and at what point does our legal obligation not to hurt others who have encroached on our property begin?

We start with some old cases that may seem fairly irrelevant today. In the nineteenth and early twentieth centuries, the legal question often took the following form: To what extent may we hurt other people without incurring a legal liability to compensate those we hurt *because we hurt them on our own land?* By the end of this chapter, you will see that the common-law process has transformed that question about property into this one: Where do the rights and privileges of being private and free stop, and our legal obligation to help others begin? For example, does a therapist have a duty to warn potential targets of a patient who is threatening violence? Or, as in the case at the end of this chapter, do the architects of tall buildings such as the World Trade Center Towers have a duty to design them in ways that protect occupants from catastrophes such as a terrorist attack? No doubt, 50 years from now, the question will have transformed yet again. Common law is a process of continual incremental adjustment, a story that has no final chapter.

Let us begin with a review of some basic rules of common law that seemed to govern in the middle of the nineteenth century. First, the common law of negligence required one to act in a way a reasonable and prudent person would act and to refrain from acting in a way a reasonable and prudent person would refrain from acting. Lawyers would say that a "standard of care" existed. Second, the law defined the classes of persons to whom a "duty" to act carefully was and was not owed. Third, law imposed liability upon those who carelessly violated the "reasonable man" standard. Whether a person in fact acted negligently in a specific case is one of those legal history questions that trial courts, with or without juries, often decide. Fourth, someone to whom a duty is owed must actually suffer an injury as a result of the hurt. Trial courts also usually make this factual decision. Thus the critical legal questions in negligence cases involve the definition of the "reasonable man" standard of care and duty.

Similarly, the law of battery commands us not to strike another deliberately unless a reasonable person would do so, as in self defense. If we strike another unreasonably, then we become liable as long as we owe a duty to the injured person not to strike.

As you may already suspect, the requirement of a duty before liability attaches can make a great difference. One of the common-law principles of the last century quite plainly said that people do not owe a duty to avoid injuring, carelessly or deliberately, people who *trespass* (encroach without express or implied permission) on their property.

We shall examine three common-law cases to illustrate some of the main features of reasoning in common law. These cases provide evidence, or clues, that support the following basic features of the common-law process:

- General principles, including the rules of negligence and battery just described, do not neatly resolve legal problems.

- Precedents do not neatly resolve legal problems, either.

- In reasoning from precedents, judges do make choices and do exercise fact freedom; it is this exercise that best describes how and why they decide as they do.

- Social background facts often influence case outcomes more powerfully than the facts in the litigation itself.

■ The beliefs and values of individual judges do influence law.

■ The precise meaning of common-law rules—here of trespass and of duty—changes as judges decide each new case.

■ Over time, as fundamental values change, the common law shifts in ways that reflect the changes.

■ Judges have shifted their conception of their role from a belief that they are required to apply divine or natural law toward a more pragmatic recognition of the inevitability of judicial lawmaking and its consequences.

■ Judges have also shifted the way they explain their decisions, moving from mechanical jurisprudence to "realism," a style that acknowledges the role of social background facts and changing values (the "felt necessities" and "prevalent moral and political theories" that Justice Holmes described) in their judgments. They have, in short, become more philosophically pragmatic.

Here are the three cases.

The Cherry Tree

It is summer in rural New York. The year is 1865. The heat of midday has passed. Sarah Hoffman, an unmarried woman living with her brother, a country doctor, sets out at her brother's request to pick ripe cherries for dinner.

A cherry tree stands on her brother's land about two feet from the fence separating his land from that of his neighbor, Abner Armstrong. Sarah's previous cullings have left few cherries on Hoffman's side of the fence. Hence, nimbly enough for her age, Sarah climbs the fence and from her perch upon it begins to take cherries from the untouched branches overhanging Abner's yard.

Angered by this intrusion, Abner runs from his house and orders her to stop picking his cherries. She persists. Enraged, he grabs her wrist and strongarms her down from the fence. Ligaments in her wrist tear. She cries from the pain and humiliation. She sues at common law for battery. The trial jury awards her $1,000 damages.

Abner appealed. He claimed that he, not Sarah nor her brother, owned the cherries overhanging his land. Because he owned the cherries, he had every right to protect them, just as he could prevent Sarah from pulling onions in his garden with a long-handled picker from her perch. In other words, Sarah was not a person to whom Abner owed a duty. By her trespassing and her interference with Abner's property, Sarah exposed herself to Abner's legal battery committed in defense of his property.

Abner's lawyer cited many legal sources in support of his argument. He began with the maxim, *cujus est solum, ejus est usque ad coelum et ad inferos*, sometimes translated as "he who has the soil, has it even to the sky and the lowest depths." He then referred the appellate judge to the great English commentator Blackstone, quoting: "Upwards, therefore, no man may erect any building, or the like to overhang another's land." He also cited *Kent's Commentaries, Bouvier's Institutes, Crabbe's Text on Real Property,* and seven cases in support of his position. One of these, an English case titled *Waterman v. Soper,* held "that if A plants a tree upon the extremest limits of his land and the tree growing extends its roots into the land of B next adjoining," then A and B jointly own the tree.[3]

---

[3] *Waterman v. Soper,* 1 Ld Raymond 737 (opinion undated).

Sarah's lawyer responded that, in law, title to the tree depends on who owns title to the land from which the tree grows. Sarah did not trespass; therefore, Abner owed her the duty not to batter her. In support he cited several commentaries, Hilliard's treatise on real property, and four cases. Sarah's lawyer relied especially on a case, *Lyman v. Hale,* decided in Connecticut in 1836.[4] In *Lyman,* the defendant picked and refused to return pears from branches overhanging his yard from a tree the plaintiff had planted four feet from the line. The *Lyman* opinion explicitly rejected the reasoning of the English precedent, *Waterman.* Despite the antiquated language, *Lyman* is a remarkably sensible, unlegalistic opinion. The court held that *Waterman's* "roots" principle is unsound because of the practical difficulties in applying it:

> How, it may be asked, is the principle to be reduced to practice? And here, it should be remembered, that nothing depends on the question whether the branches do or do not overhang the lands of the adjoining proprietor. All is made to depend solely on the enquiry, whether any portion of the roots extend into his land. It is this fact alone, which creates the [joint ownership]. And how is the fact to be ascertained?
>
> Again; if such [joint ownership] exist, it is diffused over the whole tree. Each owns a certain proportion of the whole. In what proportion do the respective parties hold? And how are these proportions to be determined? How is it to be ascertained what part of its nourishment the tree derives from the soil of the adjoining proprietor? If one joint owner appropriates . . . all the products, on what principle is the account to be settled between the parties?
>
> Again; suppose the line between adjoining proprietors to run through a forest or grove. Is a new rule of property to be introduced, in regard to those trees growing so near the line as to extend some portions of their roots across it? How is a man to know whether he is the exclusive owner of trees, growing, indeed, on his own land, but near the line; and whether he can safely cut them, without subjecting himself to an action?
>
> And again; on the principle claimed, a man may be the exclusive owner of a tree, one year, and the next, a [joint owner] with another; and the proportion in which he owns may be varying from year to year, as the tree progresses in its growth.
>
> It is not seen how these consequences are to be obviated, if the principle contended for be once admitted. We think they are such as to furnish the most conclusive objections against the adoption of the principle. We are not prepared to adopt it, unless compelled to do so, by the controuling [sic] force of authority. The cases relied upon for its support, have been examined. We do not think them decisive.[5]

In effect the *Lyman* opinion says property titles must be clear to help us plan our affairs, to help us know whether we can or can't cut down a tree for winter firewood, for example. Given the inescapable social background facts about trees, the roots rule introduces inevitable uncertainty. We must therefore reject it.

The appellate court in New York found *Lyman* most persuasive and followed it. Sarah won.[6]

Abner appealed again, to the state's highest court of appeals. In 1872 (court delays, as Charles Dickens' great novel *Bleak House* teaches, are not a uniquely modern phenomenon), Abner lost again. The attorneys presented the same arguments. Perhaps surprisingly, however, the highest court did not mention *Lyman.* Instead it seemed to say that *Waterman* does

---

[4] *Lyman v. Hale,* 11 CT. Rep. 177 (1836).

[5] *Lyman v. Hale,* 183–184.

[6] *Hoffman v. Armstrong,* 46 Barbour 337 (1866).

correctly state the law, but Abner's lawyer forgot to prove that the cherry tree's roots actually extended across the property line:

> We have not been referred to any case showing that where no part of a tree stood on the land of a party, and it did not receive any nourishment therefrom, that he had any right therein, and it is laid down in Bouvier's Institutes . . . that if the branches of a tree only overshadow the adjoining land and the roots do not enter into it, the tree wholly belongs to the estate where the roots grow.[7]

Therefore Abner lost.

This simple case, occupying only a few pages in the reports of the two New York appellate courts, richly illustrates many features of common law:

1. Note first that none of the judges either in *Hoffman* or in *Lyman* questioned their authority to decide these cases without reference to statutes. The laws, both of assault and battery and of the more fundamental problem of ownership, come from the common-law heritage of cases, commentaries, and treatises. The judges automatically assumed the power to make law governing a very common human conflict—overlapping claims to physical space on this planet. Surely a legislature could legislate on the subject, but judges have no guilt about doing so themselves in the face of legislative silence.

   In this connection, recall that legislatures pass statutes addressing general problems. How likely is it that a legislature would ever pass a statute regulating tree ownership on or near property lines? Is it not better that our government contains a mechanism, the courts, that must create some law on this subject once the problem turns out to be a real one?

2. The general common-law definitions of battery and of property ownership do not resolve this case. Neither do specific precedents. Instead, both sides cite conflicting principles and inconsistent precedents and urge from them contradictory conclusions. The judge must find some justification or reason for choosing, but nothing in either side's argument, at least in this case, compels the judge to choose one way rather than another. Judges possess the freedom to say that either *Lyman* or *Waterman* expresses the right law for resolving this problem.

   Consider specifically the matter of the Connecticut precedent, *Lyman*. Judges possess the freedom to say, as the first appellate court said, "We find the facts of *Lyman* much like those in Abner's conflict with Sarah. We also find *Lyman's* reasoning persuasive; therefore we apply the rule of *Lyman* to this case and rule for Sarah." But judges also possess the freedom to say, as did the second court, "Connecticut precedents do not govern New York. Older common-law precedents and principles from England conflict with Connecticut's law. We choose the older tradition. Abner would win if only he could show that the roots really grew on his property."

   The New York courts in *Hoffman* had other options. The second court could have easily assumed—because of the social background fact that roots underground normally grow about the same distances as do branches above ground—that the roots did cross the line and that their nourishment probably supported the cherries Sarah tried to pick. Or the court could have taken judicial notice of the social background fact that any reasonably sized tree grows roots in all directions more than two feet from its base. But it didn't.

---

[7] *Hoffman v. Armstrong*, 48 N.Y. 201 (1872), 203–204.

Judges must decide which facts in the case before them matter and what they mean. They must simultaneously decide what the facts in often inconsistent precedents mean as well. The two appellate courts reached the same conclusion but by emphasizing different facts. The first court found that roots shouldn't matter. Even though legal authorities sometimes mention them, the court believed the location of roots should have no legal significance. To give root location legal significance suddenly makes our knowledge of what we own more uncertain. Before we can cut down a tree, we must risk illegally trespassing on our neighbor's land and dig a series of holes in his yard looking for roots. And what if the neighbor has flowers growing in a bed near the tree that he doesn't want dug up? The root rule leaves us out on a limb.

3. To understand how these two courts choose differently to reach the same result, examine the difference in their basic approach to the problem. The first appellate court seems eager to assume the responsibility to shape law, to acknowledge relevant background facts, and hence to make laws that promote human cooperation in daily affairs. The second court approaches the problem much more cautiously. It seems to say: "We admit the precedents conflict. Fortunately we do not really need to choose between them. As long as Abner failed to prove the roots grow on his side of the fence, he loses either way. Therefore we choose the path that disturbs common law the least. The lower appellate court explicitly chose to reject *Waterman,* but we don't have to do that, so we won't."

This judicial caution is very common, but it is not particularly wise. Without realizing it, the highest New York court (whose opinion therefore overrides the precedential value of the better opinion of the court below) has made new law. Now we have New York precedent endorsing *Waterman.* Future courts will have to wrestle with the problem of overruling it or blindly follow it and produce all the practical problems against which *Lyman* wisely warned.

The reason these two sets of judges ruled differently, therefore, rests precisely on the fact that they are different people with different values and beliefs about what judges ought to do. Their values help determine the law they create.

4. At a deeper level, the difference reflects much more than a difference in judicial philosophies. These two approaches illustrate two contrasting common-law styles. The final higher court opinion in *Hoffman* views common law as fixed, stable, and true. It wants to avoid upsetting *Bouvier's Institutes* and Blackstone's maxims if it possibly can. The court thinks these are the common law. In contrast, the lower court's *Lyman* approach, while predating *Hoffman* by nearly 40 years, observes the spirit rather than the letter of common law. It views common law as a tradition in which judges seek to adapt law so that it improves our capacity to live together peacefully and to plan our affairs more effectively. It retains the capacity to change with changing conditions. This more modern style comes closer to helping law foster social cooperation—our legal system's most fundamental goal.

5. Finally, the case of the cherry tree illustrates a fundamental difference between common law and statutory interpretation. In statutory interpretation, as we explain in Chapter 4, judges must think carefully about the purposes behind the laws they interpret. Once the court determines a statute's purpose, it has no need to second-guess the wisdom of that purpose.

In common law, however, the judge who reasons from a precedent does not care about what the prior judge thought or about the purpose of the announced rule of law. In common law, the judge is always free to decide on his own what the law ought to say. The prior judge's intent or purpose does not dictate how his opinion will bind as precedent. Put another way, the legislature's classification of what does and does not belong in its legal category, a classification created by the words of the statute, does bind the judge. In common law, the judge deciding the case creates the classification. He sets his own goals.

This goal setting occurred in both the first and second *Hoffman* opinions. The first court wanted to make workable and practical law, not because *Lyman* or any other precedent commanded it to do so but because the court wanted to achieve that goal. The second court ruled as it did not because *Bouvier's Institutes* or *Waterman* commanded it to do so but because that court preferred the goal of changing past formal statements of law as little as possible.[8]

The Pit

Five years after Sarah Hoffman's final victory, New York's highest court faced a related common-law problem. A Mr. Carter, along with several other citizens of the town of Bath, maintained an alley running between their properties: "Exchange Alley," people called it. The public had used the alley for 20 years as a convenient way to travel from one long block to another, but the town never acknowledged Exchange Alley as a public street nor attempted to maintain it. In May 1872, Carter began excavating to erect a building on his land. The construction went slowly, so slowly in fact that on a gloomy night the next November an open pit still remained on Carter's property. That night, a Mr. Beck passed through the alley on his customary way to supper when, rather suddenly, a carriage turned into the alley and rushed toward him. Beck stepped rapidly to his left to avoid the carriage, tripped, and fell headlong into the pit, injuring himself. Although the evidence was never completely clear, since the alley had no marked border, it appeared that the pit began no less than 7 feet away from the outermost possible edge of the "public" alley.

The lawsuit that followed brought much the same kind of issues to the court as had Sarah's problem. Lawyers for Carter cited the common-law rule that landowners have the right to use their property as they please. They have no duty to avoid harming trespassers negligently. The lawyers cited English cases to show that travelers who were hurt falling into pits 5, 20, and 30 feet from a public way could not recover damages because the danger must "adjoin" the public way.

Despite these arguments, the court held for Beck. It had no difficulty whatsoever determining that, even though Carter and others together privately owned Exchange Alley, allowing the public to use the property over time created a duty to the users not to hurt them negligently.[9]

But the pit excavated truly private property. Is a 7-foot distance from a public alley sufficient to exempt the owner from liability to the public, or does the pit legally "adjoin" the alley, thereby creating a duty of care?

---

[8] Judges do not have this discretion in statutory cases. The statutory language of the Mann Act, for example, commands the courts to consider at least the transportation of willing prostitutes a crime, and the courts should not ignore that command.

[9] As an aside, you might try at this point to define *property*. You should observe from this example that, legally speaking, property is not so much what people hold title to as it is what the law says they can and cannot do with a thing, whether they hold title to it or not.

The court ruled that the alley did adjoin. It held Carter negligently responsible for Beck's injuries. It approved the idea that if the hole was "so situated that a person lawfully using the thoroughfare, and, in a reasonable manner, was liable to fall into it, the defendant was liable."[10]

The court did not have to rule this way. It could have defined adjoining pits as holes in the ground that literally touch the outer boundary of the land. Or it could have said that 7 feet was simply too far away to make a landowner liable. But the court offered a better decision. As in *Lyman*, it produced a workable distinction between injuries to deliberate trespassers and to those who reasonably attempt to use either their own space or the public's space. Just as in the *Lyman* and *Hoffman* decisions, the judges in *Beck v. Carter* chose as they did because their values—their beliefs about desirable and undesirable social relations—led them to this conclusion. If they deeply believed in the absolute sanctity of private property, ambiguity in common law would certainly have given them freedom to say, "Landowners must be free to do what they wish with their land. Carter's pit was entirely on his private land 7 feet from the thoroughfare. Therefore Carter owed Beck no duty of care."

The Diving Board

Before you proceed, note how these two principal cases, reduced to their simplest terms, combine to form a seemingly comprehensive statement of law: When the court has no convincing proof that the plaintiff deliberately and intentionally trespassed on the defendant's property, then the defendant owes the plaintiff a duty of care (*Hoffman*). Furthermore, when the plaintiff accidentally does trespass on the defendant's property, but the defendant should have foreseen the injury from such accidental trespass, the defendant is also liable (*Beck*). Thus arises the final question: What result should a court reach when the plaintiff deliberately and unambiguously trespasses on the defendant's property and is injured?

On another summer day in New York—July 8, 1916—Harvey Hynes and two friends had gone swimming at a favorite spot along the Bronx bank of the then relatively unpolluted Harlem River. For five years, they and other swimmers had dived from a makeshift plank nailed to the wooden bulkhead along the river.

The electrified line of the New York Central Railroad ran along the river. The power line was suspended over the track between poles, half of which ran between the track and the river. Legally the railroad owned the strip of riverbank containing track, poles, wires, and bulkhead. Hence, about half of the 16-foot diving board touched or extended over the railroad's land while the rest reached out, at a height of about 3 feet, over the surface of the public river.

As Harvey prepared to dive, one of the railroad's overhead supports for the power line suddenly broke loose from the pole, bringing down with it the writhing electric line that powered the trains. The wires struck Harvey, throwing him from the board. His friends pulled him dead from the waters of the Harlem River.

Harvey's mother sued the railroad for the damages caused by its alleged negligence in maintaining the supports for the wire. Conceding that New York Central's maintenance of the supports failed to meet the "reasonable man" standard of care, the trial court and the

---

[10] *Beck v. Carter,* 68 N.Y. 283 (1876), 293. If you are dubious, measure off 7 feet from your standing place in a very dark room and mark the spot. Then imagine you suddenly must get out of the way of a carriage by moving toward your mark in the dark. If you pass the mark, you've fallen in the pit. In 1996, in a case evaluating the free speech rights of antiabortion protesters at abortion clinics, the Supreme Court debated during oral argument the "meaning" of 15 feet. See Linda Greenhouse, "Court Hears Challenge to Anti-Abortion Curb," *The New York Times,* October 17, 1996, p. A8.

intermediate appellate court nevertheless denied her claim. Harvey was a trespasser, a deliberate trespasser, and property owners have no duty to protect such trespassers from harm.

Before proceeding further, reflect on the cases of the cherry tree and the pit. You are about to see these rather distantly related cases, two cases among thousands that had tried to thrash out the borderline between property and tort, merge as key precedents in the final *Hynes* decision.

The lawyers for the railroad presented many cases in their favor. They cited *Hoffman* to show that while perched on the board—even if he was over the river—Harvey trespassed, because the board was attached to the railroad's land. They also cited cases, *Beck* among them, to establish the point that the trespass was not a temporary and involuntary move from a public space but a sustained series of deliberate trespasses onto the defendant's land.

Three of the justices on New York's highest court agreed. The railroad had no duty of care to this trespasser. But a majority of four, led by Benjamin Cardozo, supported Harvey's mother and reversed.

Cardozo cited relatively few precedents. He did, however, cite *Hoffman* and *Beck*, but not in the way the railroad's lawyers had hoped. The lawyers tried to convince the judges that a mechanical rule commanded a decision for the railroad. Anything, a cherry tree or a diving board, belongs to the railroad if it is affixed to the railroad's land, regardless of what it overhangs. Therefore, Harvey, at the time the wires struck him, trespassed. Since the trespass was deliberate, *Beck* commands a decision for the railroad. Cardozo, however, appealed to the deeper spirit of these cases, a spirit that rejects mechanical rules such as the root rule for determining ownership of cherry trees. The spirit requires enunciating policy—law—that corresponds to a deeper sense of how society ought to regulate rights and responsibilities in this legal, as well as physical, borderland. Cardozo wrote:

> This case is a striking instance of the dangers of "a jurisprudence of conceptions" (Pound, "Mechanical Jurisprudence," 8 *Columbia Law Review,* 605, 608, 610), the extension of a maxim or a definition with relentless disregard of consequences to . . . "a dryly logical extreme." The approximate and relative become the definite and absolute. Landowners are not bound to regulate their conduct in contemplation of the presence of trespassers intruding upon private structures. Landowners *are* bound to regulate their conduct in contemplation of the presence of travelers upon the adjacent public ways. There are times when there is little trouble in marking off the field of exemption and immunity from that of liability and duty. Here structures and ways are so united and commingled, superimposed upon each other, that the fields are brought together. In such circumstances, there is little help in pursuing general maxims to ultimate conclusions. They have been framed *alio intuitu* [in a different way]. They must be reformulated and readapted to meet exceptional conditions. Rules appropriate to spheres which are conceived of as separate and distinct cannot, both, be enforced when the spheres become concentric. There must then be readjustment or collision. In one sense, and that a highly technical and artificial one, the diver at the end of the springboard is an intruder on the adjoining lands. In another sense, and one that realists will accept more readily, he is still on public waters in the exercise of public rights. The law must say whether it will subject him to the rule of the one field or of the other, of this sphere or of that. We think that considerations of analogy, of convenience, of policy, and of justice, exclude him from the field of the defendant's immunity and exemption, and place him in the field of liability and duty. . . . [11]

---

[11] *Hynes v. New York Central R.R.,* 231 N.Y. 229 (1921), 235–236. How should a judge, following *Hynes,* rule in a case identical to *Hoffman* except that Abner picks cherries from the branches overhanging his yard and that, to stop him, Sarah shoots him in the leg with a .22 pistol?

Note again the effect of fact freedom on judicial choices. Although they wrote no dissenting opinion, we can make an intelligent guess that the dissenters in *Hynes* reasoned from *Hoffman* this way: "The fact is that the diving board grew from the railroad's land. If ownership of the cherry tree depends on where it is rooted, then the board belongs to the railroad. Therefore Harvey trespassed." But Cardozo refuses to rest his opinion on the simple analogy between a diving board that hangs over a river and a cherry tree that projects its branches into an adjoining yard. Cardozo in effect responds, "The important fact is that Sarah didn't really trespass. Just as she used what didn't clearly belong to Abner, so these boys diving into the river from a board over the river didn't really interfere with the railroad's property. It's one thing to say that the railroad could have legally evicted trespassers from its land, or taken down the diving board if it had chosen. It's entirely different to say that the railroad can electrocute this boy without paying for its negligence." Cardozo uses his fact freedom to draw on what he considers to be the most important aspect of the precedents. Reason in law does not allow us to say that his choice legally is right and the other legally wrong. After all, with a switch of one vote, *Hynes* would have produced a very different legal precedent. Yet by recognizing that judges have the freedom to choose among different ways of interpreting precedents, we free ourselves to say we favor one choice over another and to justify why we feel that way.

Cardozo's opinion reflects the rise of "realism," an approach to law that rejects the view that legal conflicts can be solved just like mathematical problems, through formal logic. Instead, realism recognizes that, as Justice Holmes says in the epigraph to this chapter, "the life of the law has not been logic, but experience." Experience—changes in social background facts, and changes in social values—is central to Cardozo's justification of his decision. Cardozo's opinion stresses the value of social cooperation over the values of private property and individual autonomy. Cardozo recognizes that Harvey would have been just as dead if he had already dived into the water when the negligently maintained rotten wood gave way and the wire electrocuted him. Accordingly, Cardozo refuses to let the railroad off the liability hook "on a technicality." The more important point, Cardozo argues, is that the railroad had a social responsibility to be careful in its handling of hazardous electrical wires. "We think there was no moment when [Harvey] was beyond the pale of the defendant's duty—the duty of care and vigilance in the storage of destructive forces," Cardozo concluded.[12]

In this respect, the *Hynes* case foreshadowed one of the most dramatic changes in the American legal system, the shift in the twentieth century from a legal philosophy whose principles emphasize property rights and individualism to a system that promotes social caring and cooperation. In tort law, for example, judges have greatly expanded the duty of manufacturers to take care that the goods they make are safe. Lawsuits against manufacturers for injuries caused by unsafe cars, faulty tires, dangerous drugs, toxic chemicals, and even "nondefective" products such as cigarettes and guns would not have been possible without these changes in tort doctrine.[13]

As the example of product liability indicates, realism has deeply influenced judging, so that judges today are more conscious of the importance of social background facts and changes in social values. They are less likely to hide behind a formal statement of law in a treatise, a commentary, or a common-law principle. Judges today are more self-conscious too

---

[12] Ibid., 235.

[13] For a careful analysis of the impact of realism on tort law, see G. Edward White, *Tort Law in America: An Intellectual History* (New York: Oxford University Press, 1980).

about their ability—one might even say their duty—to make good public policy. These changes, have, however, created controversy. As we'll see, judicial policymaking in tort law has become particularly controversial.

KEEPING THE COMMON-LAW TRADITION ALIVE

The preceding section introduces the most typical common-law judicial problem, one in which precedents provide some guidance but do not automatically resolve problems. In the typical situation, the judge faces an array of precedents, some of which may seem inconsistent, some imaginative, and others wedded to past "truths" in common law. None of them automatically controls, so the judge must make a choice. Sometimes the precedent or principle gives the judge no more than a point of departure from which to justify the unexpressed beliefs and values that determine the result.

Sometimes, however, a genuinely new problem arises, one for which precedents prove so remote, so factually different, as to give the judge no meaningful guidance. The judge will see that a decision for either party in the case will create not a new variation on older law but a new and different law—a new and different definition of how people should relate to one another. In other situations, the reverse happens. The judge faces a precedent so factually similar to the one before him that he cannot distinguish or ignore it. If he chooses to reach a new result, he must overrule the precedent.

This section answers questions involving these less typical judicial problems: How should judges proceed when they cannot find common-law cases that seem to apply to the case before them? When should they make common law from whole cloth? Conversely, in what circumstances should courts choose deliberately to reject a case or principle that controls the case before it? How, in other words, does stare decisis operate in common law?

Answers to these questions depend in part on what we think about the proper balance between judicial and legislative lawmaking. What kinds of problems require the kind of fact-gathering and value-balancing techniques available to legislatures but not courts? What types of problems require, for their solution, the creation of complex administrative planning and enforcement apparatus that only legislatures can create, fund, and supervise?

You may have already discerned our general approach to the problem of judicial–legislative balance. Let us make it explicit here. Courts and legislatures have much in common. They both gather evidence in a systematic way, courts through witnesses at trial and through the briefs of the parties on appeal, and legislatures through committee hearings and the many other efforts of lobbyists. Both institutions gather evidence, at least formally, in an open-minded way. Courts hear from at least two sides. Our adversary system requires it. Legislatures also hear competing arguments in committee hearings and through the efforts of competing lobbyists. Furthermore, both courts and legislatures possess lawmaking power. People who look to law to plan their affairs know they should look to both institutions for legal guidance. Finally, politics influences both branches of government. Many state judges win office by election. Politicians appoint federal judges as well as state judges in unelected posts, so political restraints affect both.

In Chapter 5, we will address some important political differences between judges and legislators. Nevertheless, *judges should always presume themselves competent to take the lawmaking initiative when the legislature has not spoken clearly to them.* In other words, because as a general matter courts and legislatures have a similar authority and competence, the burden of proof always rests on the party arguing that the court should remain silent to show that the legislature is better qualified to address social problems.

Making Common Law without Close Precedents

In early March 1928, two seagoing tugboats towing barges of coal set out in good weather from Norfolk, Virginia, bound for New York. About midnight on March 8, under fair skies but with the barometer falling slightly, the tugs passed the Delaware Breakwater, a safe haven for tugs and barges caught in bad weather. The next morning, however, the wind began to freshen. By noon, gale-force winds blew up heavy seas. Early in the afternoon, two barges sprung leaks. Their crews signaled the tugs that they would proceed to anchor the barges and ride out the storm. They did so, but conditions steadily worsened. The Coast Guard heroically rescued the crews of both barges late in the day. The dawn light on March 10 revealed no trace of the barges. By then, both the barges and their cargoes rested on the ocean floor.

The coal owners sued the barge company, alleging both that the company had breached its contract of carriage and that the unseaworthiness of the barges made it liable for the loss of the coal. The barge company in turn sued the tugboat owners for the loss of both the coal and the two barges. The barge owners claimed that the two tugs had not properly handled the cargo. More precisely, they claimed that the tug owners should bear the total loss because they had not provided their tugs with conventional AM radio receivers.

At trial, the barge owners established several critical facts. On March 8, the Arlington weather bureau broadcast a 10:00 A.M. prediction calling for shifting and increasing winds the following day. Another ship in the vicinity of the tugs and barges had received this report on its AM radio. At 10:00 P.M. the same day, the Arlington bureau predicted "increasing east and southeast winds, becoming fresh to strong Friday night and increasing cloudiness followed by rain on Friday." On the basis of the morning report, one tug owner towing cargo in the vicinity had anchored at the Delaware Breakwater. Even the captain of the defendant tug conceded at trial that, had he heard the evening report, he would have done the same.

Place yourself in the position of a judge resolving this case. In your first step, aided by the arguments of the lawyers, you try to discover how much, if any, of this problem the law already makes clear. You soon find that the law of admiralty—a branch of common law for our purposes—imposes an absolute liability on shipowners for the loss of cargoes in their ships if unseaworthiness of the ship caused the loss. Note that this unseaworthiness doctrine does not simply extend the law of negligence to the sea. The shipowner may have no knowledge of the faulty condition. It may have been impossible even for a reasonable and prudent man to prevent the unseaworthy condition—hidden rot in some of a hull's wooden planking, for example. The rule creates a guarantee of seaworthiness.

But is a ship that does not carry a radio in 1928 therefore unseaworthy because it won't receive weather reports? On this point the law gives no help. You find that Congress has passed a statute requiring steamers carrying more than 50 passengers to carry two-way radios so that they can call for help and receive information, but the statute does not include tugs and barges. You find no precedents whatsoever linking seaworthiness with possession of radios or any other new invention. At this point, you have several choices. You might say:

Choice One
Congress in its wisdom chose not to require two-way shortwave radios of tugs and barges. Furthermore, Congress has made no law requiring AM radios. Therefore, Congress has intended that tugs without AM radios are seaworthy and the tug owners are not liable for the loss.

Choice Two
I find no law requiring receiving sets. Since legislatures, not the courts, are the lawmakers in our democratic nation, I have no legal authority to find the tugowners liable. Therefore they are not liable.

You can, we trust, reject both these choices immediately. We have no evidence whatsoever that Congress thought about AM receivers, much less intended or decided to pass a statute declaring that tugs without them are nevertheless seaworthy. We could just as easily conclude that the statute recognizes the general importance of radios in improving navigation safety. Therefore, the statute gives shipowners a positive signal that they should seriously examine whether radios can help them navigate better. If you have any further doubts about the weakness of the first choice, consider the fact that no congressional statute required tugs to carry compasses.

The second choice conflicts with the common-law tradition. Courts do continue to make law as conditions change; over the years, courts have specifically fashioned the principles of admiralty and of seaworthiness within admiralty law. So you might instead say:

Choice Three

I admit that judges retain their general lawmaking power in admiralty. In this case, however, only a legislature can decide whether ships must carry radios. Only through legislative hearings could we learn, for example, how common it was in 1928 for people to own radios. It would hardly be fair to hold the tug owners liable if, in 1928, radios were only novel. Similarly, only legislative hearings can learn whether shipowners themselves carry radios and think it wise or necessary to do so. If they do, then the fact dictates a new policy of seaworthiness, but we can't tell. As in ancient common law, custom may hold the key to justice, but only a legislature today is equipped to find the key.

The third choice may sound like an improvement, but it's not. Its major premise, that courts can't obtain the facts, is false. The actual case, from which this example is derived, shows that the courts were able to make the necessary factual determinations.[14] The brief for the cargo owners documented the phenomenal growth in the sales of radios, over 1,000 percent between 1922 and 1928. It quoted Frederick Lewis Allen's *Only Yesterday* (1931): "At the age of three and a half years, radio broadcasting had attained its majority. Behind those figures of radio sales lies a whole chapter of the life of the Postwar Decade: radio penetrating every third home in the country; giant broadcasting stations with nation-wide hook-ups."[15] The cargo owners also elicited testimony on the witness stand from one tug captain to the effect that, although only one tug line required radios, at least 90 percent of the tugs had them, if only for entertainment.

The lesson here is critically important. As a rule, courts can find background facts as effectively as can legislatures. We applaud the adversary system in courts precisely because we believe it gives lawyers the incentive to present the fullest possible range of facts to support their position. Legislatures may be superior lawmakers where complex problems require a simultaneous set of solutions and the means to coordinate them, but well-established judicial practices allow courts in cases such as this one to establish the background facts that determine whether a given legal choice is wise and fair.

Choice Four

Custom is a time-honored source of common law. In this case, it has been convincingly shown that tugs customarily carry radios. Radio has become a part of our everyday lives. The absence of the radios in this case caused the loss.

---

[14] *The T.J. Hooper,* 60 F.2d 737 (2nd Cir. 1932).

[15] Quoted in Henry M. Hart and Albert M. Sacks, *The Legal Process* (Cambridge: Harvard Law School, 1958), pp. 432–433. Our selection of illustrative cases in this section draws heavily upon the much larger variety of cases that Hart and Sacks provide. Although we use these cases for somewhat different purposes, we cannot improve upon their choice of working materials; here, as elsewhere, we are much indebted to them.

Choice Five
Custom is a time-honored source of common law. In this case, it has been convincingly shown that a majority of tug owners do not customarily require radios. Since we cannot say that the customs of the sea require radios, we cannot conclude that the absence of a radio in this case caused the loss.

Choices four and five are improvements over earlier choices; they are better judicial choices because they do not shrink from judicial responsibility for lawmaking. They succeed where the other choices failed in that they create a clear rule to guide future conduct. But, of course, you should still feel unsatisfied, for custom appears to produce two contradictory results. How should you choose between them? Better to say:

Choice Six
Is it then a final answer that the business had not yet generally adopted receiving sets? There are, no doubt, cases where courts seem to make the general practice of the calling the standard of proper diligence. . . . Indeed, in most cases reasonable prudence is in fact common prudence; but strictly it is never its measure; a whole calling may have unduly lagged in the adoption of new and available devices. It may never set its own tests, however persuasive be its usages. Courts must in the end say what is required; there are precautions so imperative that even their universal disregard will not excuse their omission. . . . We hold the tugs . . . had they been properly equipped . . . would have got the Arlington reports. The injury was a direct consequence of this unseaworthiness.

The language of choice six speaks with a power and persuasiveness the other choices lack because it is Judge Learned Hand's own, taken from his opinion finally disposing of the case.[16] Hand's choice sets a clear standard, one that, anticipating the certain further growth of the radio industry, would occur sooner or later. Note, however, that with the exception of choice four, any other choice could well have created a precedent that would delay considerably any judicial decision requiring tugs to carry radios. These choices say tugs don't need to carry radios. Judicial change would require overruling any of these alternative decisions. In short, the timid and deferential judge potentially creates a common-law precedent with just as much policy impact as does the assertive judge.

Above all, Hand's choice avoids the problem of lawmaking by default. Judges can never know whether or when or how Congress will act on any but dramatic national issues. Courts that wait for better legislative solutions may wait for a solution that never comes. Do you agree that the court's proven capacity to establish the facts about the use of radios—coupled with Hand's sound ethical judgment that tugs ought to carry radios—makes his opinion persuasive?

Eighty years after the case of the radioless tugboat, the Supreme Court considered another dispute arising from a shipping disaster, the wreck of the *Exxon Valdez*, and like Judge Hand, the justices did not hesitate to take the lawmaking initiative in their decision. The *Exxon Valdez* wreck poured 11 billion gallons of crude oil into an otherwise pristine bay on the Alaskan coast, causing an environmental catastrophe that destroyed wildlife in the sea and on the beaches. The captain of the *Exxon Valdez* was found to be legally intoxicated, and not on the bridge during a particularly tricky maneuver that led to the crash. A group of Native Americans, commercial fishers, and landowners affected by the oil spill sued Exxon, claiming that it was responsible for the captain's conduct. A jury returned a verdict of nearly $300 million in compensatory damages and $5 billion in punitive damages, later reduced by an appellate court to $2.5 billion.

---

[16] *The T. J. Hooper,* 740.

Punitive damages are awarded to punish a defendant for particularly egregious conduct and to deter the defendant and others from engaging in that conduct. The jury's verdict—in particular the huge gap between the compensatory and punitive award—raised a perennial problem with the common law of damages: How should punitive damages be calculated, and what counts as an "excessive" award? Because jurors have no knowledge of damages in previous cases, juries can return widely varying punitive awards in similar cases.

The Court could have waited for Congress to weigh in on this issue, but Justice Souter's opinion noted that "courts have accepted primary responsibility for reviewing punitive damages and thus for their evolution, and if, in the absence of legislation, judicially derived standards leave the door open to outlier punitive-damages awards, it is hard to see how the judiciary can wash its hands of a problem it created . . ." Rather than wait for Congress to address the issue, Souter's opinion explored possible rules for punitive damages, canvassing the policies of the 50 states and of other nations, as well as studies on the frequency and variability of punitive damages. Souter announced a new rule for punitive damages in maritime tort cases: Punitive damage awards can be no higher than compensatory damages. He then reduced the Exxon punitive damage award from $2.5 billion to $507.5 million, the total amount of compensation paid by Exxon to the plaintiffs. Souter admitted that many other rules were possible, but defended his Court's decision to create a limit on damages. "History certainly is no support for the notion that judges cannot use numbers," he concluded.[17] Like Judge Hand decades before, Justice Souter was confident of his ability to make law.

Horizontal Stare Decisis in Common Law

We now move to the other end of the spectrum, cases in which the judge confronts close precedents. How should judges respond to precedents that seem to state outdated or "bad" social policy but at the same time seem to completely cover and control the outcomes of cases before them? Lawyers label these precedents "precisely on point" or "on all fours with the case at bar." The existence of these precedents does not, however, contradict the concept that law remains ambiguous. Judges always choose the results. Some judges, faced with a precedent that produces an unwanted conclusion, will choose to ignore it, much to the anger of the losing lawyer. Other judges will overrule the precedent or pointedly refuse to follow it. Choices remain. In these circumstances, a judge's concerns about good social policy must be weighed against the purposes of stare decisis, which, as we have seen, are to promote legal stability, to protect honest reliance, to preserve efficient judicial administration, to maintain similar treatment of persons similarly situated, and to promote public confidence in courts. A judge must give weight to stare decisis only when adherence to a precedent accomplishes at least one of these goals.

Here are two sample cases, one where stare decisis theory was used persuasively and one where the court mindlessly botched the job.

Rightly Adhering to Precedent Because the Need for Stability and Reliance Is Present

The law of tort, especially the law of negligence, creates enticing moral questions because, almost by definition in the case of negligence, courts apply the law only when it has in fact failed to control how people behave. The negligent driver simply does not plan to have or avoid an accident based on his knowledge of negligence law, even if he has some understanding of it. As a result, negligence law does not generally confront a judge with the

---

[17] *Exxon Shipping v. Baker,* 554 U.S. _____ (2008).

problem of upsetting someone's expectations if he changes the law. Negligence law defines when someone owes someone else a remedy for a past wrong, and this focus leads inevitably to the moral question of how we ought to relate to others, be they friends or strangers.

The need for stability in law more often exists with respect to laws that deal with people's business and contractual relations and with their related planning for the use and disposition of their property. Here we may not reach ultimate moral questions so quickly. When plans depend on law, the law's shortcomings may not justify changing it. We therefore temporarily abandon tort law and turn to one very small problem in a very complicated subject—the law of business contracts.

Contracts, among many other things, are agreements among businesspeople that allow them to formalize their buying and selling of each other's goods and services. Plans involving millions or even billions of dollars can rest on such agreements. For example, a construction company specializing in high-rise office buildings may conditionally contract with a supplier of steel to buy steel at a given price in order to know what to bid on a construction project. If the company receives the award, its entire profit margin could disappear if its steel supplier at the last minute insisted on a higher price for the steel. To take a less weighty example, Sasha Baron Cohen, the actor who plays the character "Borat," recently became embroiled in a contract dispute with an etiquette teacher who was shocked to find herself in one of his movies. The etiquette teacher thought she was instructing a Belarusian visitor in American customs for a documentary about the experiences of a foreign journalist traveling through the United States. When she found out that she was appearing instead in a comedy—and one in which, during a particularly memorable scene, "Borat" presented her with a bag of his own feces—she sued Cohen and the other makers of the film for damages, claiming that she had been humiliated. Cohen argued, however, that Martin had signed a contract agreeing not to sue for damages. The makers of *Borat* relied on such contracts to protect themselves, since their film arguably embarrassed nearly everyone who appeared in it.[18]

But what legal rules convert an ordinary agreement—He: "Can you come to dinner at my place at 8:00?" She: "I'd love to! See you then."—into a legally binding contract? In early common law, if a written agreement contained the impression of a promise-making person's seal in wax, then the beneficiary of the promise could hold him to his promise. Men wore signet rings etched with their sign (their seal) with which to impress the wax. An exception, for a time, was the king. He sealed the wax on his agreements with the impression of his front teeth. Gradually, the use of wax, seals, and front teeth declined, to the point where printing the word "Seal" or the letters "L.S." (for the Latin *locus sigilli*) created the contractual tie.

Contract law today does not require a wax seal to make the agreement binding—"Borat" and the etiquette teacher simply signed their contract. But in many jurisdictions in the past, when people sealed their contract (perhaps simply by adding at the end "Seal" or "L.S."), the law made it very difficult for the contracting parties to dispute it. The law has

---

[18] "Borat" won an initial battle with the etiquette teacher when the Alabama Supreme Court upheld a contract provision requiring that any claims against the film's makers be heard in New York state courts. *Ex Parte Sacha Baron Cohen et al. In re: Katherine Martin v. Sacha Baron Cohen et al.* (Supreme Court of Alabama, 2007). Borat is facing a plethora of lawsuits charging him exposing them to embarrassment and humiliation, including one by residents of a remote Romanian village that was portrayed in the movie as Borat's hometown in Kazakhstan. "New York judge questions viability of villagers' 'Borat' lawsuit," *The Associated Press*, December 4, 2006.

rendered it nearly impossible to argue that the contract was made fraudulently or to prove that the promisor already performed the act he promised.

Long after agreements became enforceable in law without a seal, the law preserved some of the special rigidities for those contracts with seals. In one specific example, unlike an unsealed contract, only a person actually named in a sealed contract could be held liable for violating it ("breaching" it, in legal terminology). When, for example, a buyer sought to disguise his interest by having another contract for him, using the agent's name but remaining the interested party, he along with the agent might find himself bound, but only if the contract of sale bears no seal. A sealed purchase contract, however, would bind only the agent named in it, not the interested party.

Businesspeople regularly transact business through agents. Sometimes, and this is particularly true in commercial real estate transactions, a businessperson will fund another to buy or sell property for him. He will fund the agent but insist that the agent assume all the responsibilities of the contract. The legal name for such a backer is "undisclosed principal." This technique of preserving anonymity is not necessarily unfair to the other side. If someone buys up various plots of land in an area in order to build a factory in his own name, the owners approached last may insist on a highly inflated price, knowing that if the buyer fails to get the last lot, all his other purchases will become meaningless.

Beginning in the nineteenth century, by both statute and judicial decision, the legal gap between the protections of sealed and unsealed contracts began to narrow. However, in the 1920s, this New York case arose. In a contract under seal, an agent agreed to buy land without naming an undisclosed principal. The seller agreed, but the agent shortly thereafter withdrew from the agreement. The seller, having learned the name of the principal, sued the principal. He asked the judge to order the principal to pay for the land and accept the deed.

The court in this case, *Crowley v. Lewis,* ruled for the defendant. It noted many New York precedents limiting the significance of a seal on a contract. Nevertheless it concluded:

> We find no authority for the proposition that a contract under seal may be turned into the simple contract of a person not in any way appearing on its face to be a party to or interested in it, . . . and we do not feel at liberty to extend the doctrine applied to simple contracts executed by an agent for an unnamed principal so as to embrace this case. . . .
>
> Neither do we find any authority since 1876 in this court for the proposition. *Briggs v. Partridge*[19] has been cited by us many times with no hint of disapproval. . . . We repeat that we do not feel at liberty to change a rule so well understood and so often enforced. If such a change is to be made it must be by legislative fiat. . . .
>
> . . . Thousands of sealed instruments must have been executed in reliance upon the authority of *Briggs v. Partridge.* Many times the seal must have been used for the express purpose of relieving the undisclosed principal from personal liability. It may not be unwise to preserve the distinction for this special purpose. But whether wise or unwise the distinction now exists.[20]

Any doctrine, stare decisis included, has impact only when it leads to action not likely otherwise. Stare decisis affects judicial choices when, because of judges' commitment to it, they reach decisions they might in general terms think to be poor social policy.

---

[19] *Briggs v. Partridge,* 64 N.Y. 357 (1876).
[20] *Crowley v. Lewis,* 239 N.Y. 264 (1925), 265–267.

In many respects, it is inequitable to allow the undisclosed principal to avoid keeping a promise because of a seal. New York's Justice Crane, who did not participate in the *Crowley* decision, wrote:

> Thus, if an unsealed contract to sell real estate is signed by the agent in his own name, and the fact that he is acting for another and not for himself appears nowhere upon the face of it, the real principal can always sue and be sued upon the instrument. But if it should happen that the printed letters "L.S." appear after the agent's name, all would be different. The principal could neither sue nor be sued. The absurdity of this is apparent upon the face of the statement, and the danger and pitfall of such a doctrine in business transactions is realized when we pause to consider how many printed forms of agreements have the letters "L.S." stamped upon them, or how easy it is to make the scroll.[21]

But another justice who joined the *Crowley* opinion, Benjamin Cardozo, took the opposite view. Although Cardozo admitted that the seal system seemed an anachronism, he concluded that changing the rules about seals would be unfair:

> Men had taken title in the names of "dummies," and through them executed deeds and mortgages with the understanding, shared by the covenantees, that liability on the covenant would be confined to the apparent principal. They had done this honestly and without concealment.

Cardozo also noted that the seal arrangement had some advantages. Like the corporate form, the seal limited liability, facilitating business transactions. Cardozo concluded that "retrospective change would be unjust. The evil, if it was one, was to be eradicated by statute."[22]

Both Crane and Cardozo are in a sense correct. The rule may work to an unfair advantage, and it is the place of courts, not just legislatures, to minimize unfair advantages in law. However, the court rightly left legal change to the legislature because it understood that many businessmen, without acting unfairly, regularly employed that legal technique in planning their affairs. Judicial action would upset existing plans made by fair men, but the legislature would make law for the future. This difference, not a difference in lawmaking authority, gives the *Crowley* decision its wisdom.

The distinction between retrospective and prospective lawmaking is tricky. Every time a court makes new case law, it creates a winner and a loser in a case that happened under the older law. How can this retrospective lawmaking ever be fair and just? Judges can solve the stare decisis dilemma by asking whether it really makes sense to believe that the parties to the conflict planned their lives around the old law. In tort cases, for example, conflicts usually arise because of unplanned events, such as a car crash. In such circumstances, stare decisis dilemmas usually do not arise. But when the conflict involves a contract, breaking with precedent is much more troublesome. The whole point of a contract, after all, is to give those involved a plan on which everyone can rely. Consider from this perspective a dilemma about contracts signed by elders with diminished mental capacity. At common law a contract signed by a minor cannot be enforced, but no such rule ever applied to the elderly. However, tests devised to assess the mental capacities of elders sometimes find that their abilities fall in the same range as youngsters. Should courts stop enforcing contracts made by adults with diminished mental capacities—or would it be wiser to wait for legislatures to address this

---

[21] Frederick E. Crane, "The Magic of the Private Seal," 15 *Columbia Law Review* 24 (1915): 34–35.

[22] Benjamin N. Cardozo, *The Paradoxes of Legal Science* (New York: Columbia University Press, 1928), pp. 70–71.

problem? The process of enacting new legislation, after all, would provide advance warning to seniors and their lawyers.[23]

Wrongly Adhering to Precedent When Stability Is Unnecessary

It would be a mistake to conclude that courts should always follow precedents in business, contract, and property matters but never in the case of negligence. It is not that simple. Tort law can, for example, influence both a person's decision to insure against loss and the rates insurance companies charge for such insurance. Precedents in tort, like precedents in contract, create expectations on which people can rely. In this final illustration, however, let us look at a property problem in which a court, in a thoughtless opinion, followed precedent when the reasons for stare decisis did not support adherence. This case involves the laws of wills and of trusts, areas in which legal stability and reliance—two bedrock justifications for horizontal stare decisis—normally kick in.

The case involved a section of the will of a New Jersey resident. In it the deceased, Rosa E. Green, stated: "I give and bequeath unto my husband, William L. Green, all of the money which I have on deposit at the Paterson Savings and Trust Company, Paterson, New Jersey, however, any money which is in the said account at the time of my said husband's death, the said sum shall be held by my niece, Catherine King Fox, absolutely and forever." William died without removing the money.

Naturally Ms. Fox attempted to withdraw the money from the bank. However, heirs of William claimed that the conditional gift to Ms. Fox was invalid. Lawyers for the heirs cited many New Jersey precedents stating that an unconditional bequest in a will, like the one to William, gave him unconditional ownership. Any conditional gift of the same property would have to be invalid; otherwise, the first gift would not be absolute. William's heirs won. The court said:

> Appellants ask this Court to explicitly and expressly overrule the long established law of this state. This we decline to do. Such action would be fraught with great danger in this type of case where titles to property, held by bequests and devises, are involved. A change of the established law by judicial decision is retrospective. It makes the law at the time of prior decisions as it is declared in the last decision, as to all transactions that can be reached by it. On the other hand a change in the settled law by statute is prospective only.[24]

Think briefly about this result in terms of the reasons for stare decisis. For whom should this law remain stable? Who could plan on the basis of this rule? Certainly not Rosa. She wanted to make a conditional gift to Catherine but failed. William, if he wanted the money, had only to withdraw it. Until the moment of his death (or legal incapacitation), no one but William could make any plans based on what might happen to "Catherine's" money. For William to have relied on New Jersey precedents in this case, we must suppose reasoning such as: "I am going to die. I don't want the money, but I don't want Catherine to obtain the money, either. I could prevent her from receiving it by depositing it in another bank, but,

---

[23] See "Fine Line: Shielding Elders' Money, and Independence," *The New York Times,* December 24, 2007, p. A1. For a discussion of how American courts have increasingly refused to enforce contracts where one party to the contract was clearly at a disadvantage, in knowledge and experience, relative to the other party, see Lief H. Carter, "Politics and the Law of Contracts," in Carter et al., *New Perspectives on American Law* (Durham, NC: Carolina Academic Press, 1997), pp. 295–350.

[24] *Fox v. Snow,* 6 N.J. 12 (1950), 14.

since the clause is invalid, I'll leave it there." Such planning is possible, but is it probable? Is it the sort of planning that the law needs to preserve at the expense of carrying out the wishes of the deceased? Many people do not know rules of law of this kind. Is it not more probable that William also intended the money to go to Catherine? Is it plausible that, once William died leaving the money in the bank, Catherine made plans on the assumption that she did have the money?

Consider the other purposes of stare decisis: Is the image of justice improved by defeating Rosa's wishes? How important is equality of treatment in this kind of situation? How important is it to say that because courts have refused to carry out the wishes of past testators (the creators of wills), they must treat current testators in the same way for equality's sake?

Finally, efficiency in the judicial process does matter. Judges should not have to question the wisdom of every point of law that arises, but that hardly means they can never do so.

One judge disagreed with the majority in *Fox*. Chief Justice Vanderbilt's dissent is one of the finest essays from the bench on stare decisis and more generally on the nobility of the common-law tradition. It provides a fitting summary of this section:

VANDERBILT, C.J. (dissenting)

I am constrained to dissent from the views of the majority of the court, first, because they apply to the case a technical rule of law to defeat the plain intent of the testatrix without serving any public policy whatever in so doing and, secondly—and this seems to me to be even more important—because their opinion involves a view of the judicial process, which, if it had been followed consistently in the past, would have checked irrevocably centuries ago the growth of the common law to meet changing conditions and which, if pursued now, will spell the ultimate ossification and death of the common law by depriving it of one of its most essential attributes—its inherent capacity constantly to renew its vitality and usefulness by adapting itself gradually and piecemeal to meeting the demonstrated needs of the times. . . .

By the words in the third paragraph, "any money which is in said account at the time of my said husband's death, the said sum shall be held by my niece, Catherine King Fox, absolutely and forever," the testatrix beyond any doubt intended that her husband could use up the bank account but that if he did not, the plaintiff should take what was left of it on his death. To hold otherwise is to proceed on the untenable assumption that the quoted words are meaningless and to ignore the elementary principle that the provisions of a will are not to be construed as meaningless except on the failure of every attempt to render them effective. . . . This principle is an integral part of the most fundamental rule of testamentary construction, *i.e.*, the duty of the court is to ascertain what the intent of the testator was and, then, having ascertained it, to give it effect. . . .

The opinion of the majority of the court, like every other decision in this State on the subject, makes no attempt to justify the rule it perpetuates either in reason or on grounds of public policy. Despite the deleterious effects of the rule and the lack of any sound principle to support it, the majority maintains that it should not be overthrown, because it has been the long established law of this State and because over-ruling it "would be fraught with great danger in this type of case where titles to property, held by bequests and devises, are involved" by reason of the retroactive effect of all judicial decisions. This view, if it had been consistently applied in the past, would have prevented any change whatever in property law by judicial decisions. . . . Every change in the law by judicial decision necessarily creates rights in one party to the litigation and imposes corresponding duties on the other party. This is the process by which the law grows and adjusts itself to the changing needs of the times.

The process is necessarily used not only to create new rights and corresponding duties but, where necessary, to strike down old ones. . . . "It is revolting," says Mr. Justice Holmes, "to have no better reason for a rule of law than that so it was laid down in the time of Henry IV. It is still more revolting if the grounds upon which it was laid down have vanished long since, and the rule simply persists from blind imitation of the past," and "To rest upon a formula is a slumber that, prolonged, means death." *Collected Legal Papers* (1920) 187, 306. . . .

To hold, as the majority opinion implies, that the only way to overcome the unfortunate rule of law that plagues us here is by legislation, is to put the common law in a self-imposed strait jacket. Such a theory, if followed consistently, would inevitably lead to the ultimate codification of all of our law for sheer lack of capacity in the courts to adapt the law to the needs of the living present. The doctrine of *stare decisis* neither renders the courts impotent to correct their past errors nor requires them to adhere blindly to rules that have lost their reason for being. The common law would be sapped of its life blood if *stare decisis* were to become a god instead of a guide. The doctrine when properly applied operates only to control change, not to prevent it. As Mr. Justice Cardozo has put it, "Few rules in our time are so well established that they may not be called upon any day to justify their existence as means adapted to an end. If they do not function they are diseased, . . . they must not propagate their kind. Sometimes they are cut out and extirpated altogether. Sometimes they are left with the shadow of continued life, but sterilized, truncated, impotent for harm." *Nature of the Judicial Process* (1921) 98. All lawyers as well as laymen have a perfectly natural longing to think of the law as being as steadfast and immutable as the everlasting hills, but when we face the realities, we must agree with Dean Pound when he says, "Law must be stable, and yet it cannot stand still," *Interpretations of Legal History* (1923) . . ., and with Professor Williston when he tells us, "Uniform decisions of 300 years on a particular question may, and sometimes have been overthrown in a day, and the single decision at the end of the series may establish a rule of law at variance with all that has gone before." *Some Modern Tendencies in the Law* (1929) 125. . . .

The dangers that the majority fear, it is submitted, are more apparent than real. The doctrine of *stare decisis* tends to produce certainty in our law, but it is important to realize that certainty *per se* is but a means to an end, and not an end in itself. Certainty is desirable only insofar as it operates to produce the maximum good and the minimum harm and thereby to advance justice. The courts have been reluctant to overthrow established rules when property rights are involved for the simple reason that persons in arranging their affairs have relied upon the rules as established, though outmoded or erroneous, and so to abandon them would result sometimes in greater harm than to observe them. The question whether the doctrine of *stare decisis* should be adhered to in such cases is always a choice between relative evils. When it appears that the evil resulting from a continuation of the accepted rule must be productive of greater mischief to the community than can possibly ensue from disregarding the previous adjudications on the subject, courts have frequently and wisely departed from precedent, 14 Am. Jur., Courts, Section 126.

What then, are the relative evils in the instant case? First, we should consider the evils that will result from a perpetuation of the rule here involved. It has already been demonstrated that the rule, in each and every instance in which it is applied, results in a complete frustration of the legitimate intention of the testator. It can only operate to take property from one to whom the testator intended to give it and to bestow it upon another. . . .

Having considered the evils flowing from continuing to follow the rule, let us now inquire into the evils, if any, which might result from its rejection. It is pertinent at this point to recall the words of Mr. Justice Cardozo minimizing the effect of overruling a decision: "The picture of the bewildered litigant lured into a course of action by the false light of a decision, only to meet ruin when the light is extinguished and the decision is overruled, is for the most part a figment of excited brains." *The Nature of the Judicial Process* (1921) 122 [sic.]. The rule in question by its very nature is never relied upon by those who are seeking to make a testamentary disposition of their property, for if the rule were known to a person at the time of the drawing of his will, its operation would and could be guarded against by the choice of words appropriate to accomplish the result desired. This rule is truly subversive of the testator's intent. It is relied upon only after the testator's decease by those who seek, solely on the basis of its technical and arbitrary requirements, to profit from the testator's ignorance and to take his property contrary to his expressed desires. Certainly it is not unjust or inequitable to deny such persons resort to this rule. . . . [25]

THE COMMON-LAW TRADITION TODAY

Chief Justice Vanderbilt's dissent in *Fox* describes the essence of the common-law tradition. Judicial choices continue to change common law today. Indeed, only within the past one hundred years have judges recognized the inevitability and desirability of choice and change. Thus the full political consequences of choice and change have come sharply into focus.

Common law has in the past changed even when judges believed they merely chose the one applicable statute or line of precedents that "correctly" resolved the conflict before them. When judges think they solve problems by mechanically finding the one right solution from the past, the law develops in an almost thoughtless way. Judges do not grapple with moral and economic aspects of policy choices when they do not believe they choose policies.

But when the point of view shifts, when judges begin believing they do make policy choices, this consciousness changes the kind and quality of law that judges make in several ways.

The first of these changes we have already studied and condemned. It occurs when judges throw up their hands and say, "In a democracy, only the legislature can make new law, not the courts. We must, therefore, deliberately avoid making changes." These decisions, in spite of themselves, do make changes, of course—just as the *Fox* decision, by rejecting Vanderbilt's powerful arguments, more deeply embedded both a mechanical view of stare decisis and the rule against conditional gifts in New Jersey's law.

A second modern view of the consequences of acknowledged judicial discretion can avoid this evil. Judges, acknowledging that they can and do make law, pay closer attention, as we are about to see, to the facts and values that help them (and us) decide that some policy choices are wiser than others. Modern decisions do tend to be less mechanistic and more concerned with the consequences for the future of various alternative choices of policy. This quality, after all, gave the *Lyman* and *Hynes* cases their modern flavor.

There is, however, a third consequence of this shift in viewpoint. Judges may dramatically increase the speed of change and deliberately broaden the lengths of the legal jumps they take from old law to new. When judges realize they rightly possess authority to remake common law, they may overreact and enact what they believe are ideal legal solutions without properly honoring competing needs for stability. Similarly, they may ignore the possibility that, while both courts and legislatures share authority to make law, they do not necessarily possess identical institutional characteristics for making wise law.

---

[25] *Fox v. Snow,* 14–15, 21–27.

Some critics argue that this is just what has happened in tort law. Proponents of "tort reform" argue that judges have abused their common-law powers by adopting doctrines that allow too many plaintiffs in personal injury lawsuits to collect too much money. The media have responded to the tort reformers' claims sympathetically by publicizing bizarre or particularly controversial tort lawsuits, such as the claim that McDonald's is legally liable for making its patrons obese.[26] Tort reformers have successfully lobbied legislatures to reverse judge-made changes in tort policy and to limit the gains of personal injury lawsuits by, for example, capping the amount of damages a plaintiff can win. (Pro-plaintiff groups, meanwhile, have gone to court to argue that such legislation unconstitutionally interferes with the power of judges in common-law cases.) Tort law has thus become a battleground not just in the courts but in legislatures and popular culture.[27]

The rise of the tort reform movement demonstrates that judicial policymaking can become the object of great controversy. The potential problems posed by judicial policymaking are so central to reasoning in constitutional law that a thorough canvass of the "judicial limits" territory must be postponed until Chapter 5, which deals with reasoning in constitutional interpretation. But as the example of tort reform reminds us, these same concerns are present in common law as well.

In this perspective, consider the next case. It illustrates deliberate lawmaking. It exemplifies a dramatic expansion of common law, and it faces squarely the double problem of determining whether a given policy is wise and whether the courts were the wise place to make it. The case, *Tarasoff v. Regents of the University of California,* represented a substantial jump forward in the law of negligence and duty.[28]

Tatiana Tarasoff spent the summer of 1969 in Brazil. She had, with her parents' consent and assistance, left her home in California, in part to escape the almost fanatical affections of one Prosenjit Poddar. During her absence, Poddar kept his contact alive. He persuaded Tatiana's brother to share an apartment with him near Tatiana's home in Berkeley, California.

Tatiana returned from Brazil in October. On October 27, 1969, Poddar killed her.

In due course, Tatiana's parents learned that Poddar had, during the summer, received psychological therapy on an outpatient basis from Cowell Memorial Hospital at the University of California, Berkeley. Their further investigation uncovered these facts:

- On August 20, 1969, Poddar told his therapist, Dr. Moore, that he planned to kill his girlfriend when she returned from Brazil.

- When Poddar left, Dr. Moore felt Poddar should be committed for psychiatric examination in a mental hospital. He urgently consulted two of his colleagues at Cowell. They concurred.

- Moore then told two campus police officers that he would request commitment of Poddar. He followed up with a letter of request to the campus police chief.

- Three officers, in fact, took Poddar into custody. Poddar promised them he would leave Tatiana alone in the future. The officers believed Poddar was rational and released him.

---

[26] For two thoughtful critiques of the tort-reform movement, see Marc Galanter, "News from Nowhere: The Debased Debate on Civil Justice," 71 *Denver University Law Review* 77 (1993); and "Real World Torts: An Antidote to Anecdote" 55 *University of Maryland Law Review* 1093 (1996).

[27] Thomas F. Burke, *Lawyers, Lawsuits and Legal Rights: The Struggle Over Litigation in American Politics* (Berkeley: University of California Press, 2002); William Haltom and Michael McCann, *Distorting the Law: Politics, Media, and the Litigation Crisis* (Chicago: University of Chicago Press, 2004).

[28] *Tarasoff v. Regents of the University of California,* 551 P.2d 334 (1976).

- After this, and presumably in part because the officers released Poddar, Dr. Moore's supervisor, Dr. Powelson, asked the police to return Moore's letter. Dr. Powelson also ordered to destroy all written evidence of the affair and prohibited any further action to commit Poddar for examination or observation.

- At no point did any members of the hospital staff or the campus police attempt to notify Tatiana, her brother, or her parents of Poddar's threat.

- The staff could easily have determined Tatiana's identity as well as her location and that of her family.

The Tarasoffs sued the doctors, the officers, and the university's board of regents, claiming damages for the loss of their daughter. Among other charges, they alleged that "defendants negligently permitted Poddar to be released from police custody without 'notifying the parents of Tatiana Tarasoff that their daughter was in grave danger from Prosenjit Poddar.' "[29] They claimed, in other words, that the defendants had a duty to use reasonable care to protect Tatiana.

The California Supreme Court upheld the legality of this claim but only against the regents and the doctors. Reasoning by example played a major part in its result. The court cited precedents from California and elsewhere holding a doctor liable for the damage caused by illness contracted by people in contact with his patient if the doctor negligently failed to diagnose the disease as contagious and to isolate the patient. It also cited a case holding a doctor liable for damages where, following his negligent refusal to admit a mental patient to a hospital, the mental patient assaulted the plaintiff.

The directly relevant case law in California, however, imposed a duty only where the defendant already assumed some responsibility for the victim. If, for example, a mental hospital failed negligently to protect one patient from another's violence, the hospital became liable. In California, no law extended the duty further.

Using fact freedom, however, the court ignored the distinction. It said, "[W]e do not think that the duty should logically be constricted to such situations."[30] Let us review the majority's reasons for the conclusion.

The majority first stated a general framework for determining the existence or absence of a duty, a statement amply supported by recent California precedents. Note above all how different this statement is from earlier mechanical statements such as "duty owed to invitees but no duty owed to trespassers or licensees." The Court, quoting precedents, said the existence of a duty depends

> only upon the "balancing of a number of considerations"; major ones "are the foreseeability of harm to the plaintiff, the degree of certainty that the plaintiff suffered injury, the closeness of the connection between the defendant's conduct and the injury suffered, the moral blame attached to the defendant's conduct, the policy of preventing future harm, the extent of the burden to the defendant and consequences to the community of imposing a duty to exercise care with resulting liability for breach, and the availability, cost and prevalence of insurance for the risk involved."
>
> The most important of these considerations in establishing duty is foreseeability. As a general principle, a "defendant owes a duty of care to all persons who are foreseeably endangered by his conduct, with respect to all risks which make the conduct unreasonably dangerous."[31]

---

[29] Ibid., 341.
[30] Ibid., 344.
[31] Ibid., 342.

Having said this much, the majority then noted that at common law, a duty to warn of foreseeable harm done by a dangerous person existed only when the defendant had a "special relationship" with either the source of danger or the potential victim. The court admitted that the doctors had no special relationship to Tatiana, but it asserted that because they did have such a relationship to Poddar, they therefore owed Tatiana a duty of care.

The court cited no convincing precedent or other authority for this expansion of law, but that did not seem to bother it. The court did pay attention to the arguments sustaining and attacking the practical wisdom and effect of the new policy.

The court had to deal first with the possibility that the harm was not foreseeable in the first place. The issue was made even more difficult because only a few years earlier, the court had based an important mental health ruling on the fact that psychological and psychiatric predictions of future behavior are notoriously inaccurate.[32] To this the court responded:

> The role of the psychiatrist, who is indeed a practitioner of medicine, and that of the psychologist who performs an allied function, are like that of the physician who must conform to the standards of the profession and who must often make diagnoses and predictions based upon such evaluations. Thus the judgment of the therapist in diagnosing emotional disorders and in predicting whether a patient presents a serious danger of violence is comparable to the judgment which doctors and professionals must regularly render under accepted rules of responsibility.
>
> We recognize the difficulty that a therapist encounters in attempting to forecast whether a patient presents a serious danger of violence. Obviously we do not require that the therapist, in making that determination, render a perfect performance; the therapist need only exercise "that reasonable degree of skill, knowledge, and care ordinarily possessed and exercised by members of [that professional specialty] under similar circumstances." (*Bardessono v. Michels* (1970) 3 Cal.3d 780, 788 . . .) Within the broad range of reasonable practice and treatment in which professional opinion and judgment may differ, the therapist is free to exercise his or her own best judgment without liability; proof, aided by hindsight, that he or she judged wrongly is insufficient to establish negligence.
>
> In the instant case, however, the pleadings do not raise any question as to failure of defendant therapists to predict that Poddar presented a serious danger of violence. On the contrary, the present complaints allege that defendant therapists did in fact predict that Poddar would kill, but were negligent in failing to warn.[33]

The court then turned to the most complex policy issue of all: Will imposition of the duty to warn discourage patients from seeking the psychiatric help they need, thus preventing not only their own improvement but perhaps increasing the actual incidence of violent harm to others because people don't get help? The court insisted that such a prediction is entirely speculative. It noted that both the California code of evidence and the Principles of Medical Ethics of the American Medical Association permit a doctor to reveal information about a dangerous person if doing so could protect the patient, other individuals, or the community. The court concluded that

> the public policy favoring protection of the confidential character of patient-psychotherapist communications must yield to the extent to which disclosure is essential to avert danger to others. The protective privilege ends where the public peril begins.

---

[32] In this particular case, *People v. Burnick,* 14 CA. 3rd 306 (1975), the court held that a person could be committed to an institution for mentally disturbed sex offenders only after proof at trial beyond reasonable doubt that the defendant was, in fact, likely to repeat the offense.

[33] *Tarasoff v. Regents,* 345.

Our current crowded and computerized society compels the interdependence of its members. In this risk-infested society we can hardly tolerate the further exposure to danger that would result from a concealed knowledge of the therapist that his patient was lethal. If the exercise of reasonable care to protect the threatened victim requires the therapist to warn the endangered party or those who can reasonably be expected to notify him, we see no sufficient societal interest that would protect and justify concealment. The containment of such risks lies in the public interest.[34]

The *Tarasoff* case, like the *Hynes* case, took the common law of duty in negligence cases a large step forward. The common law does not, however, move smoothly forward in rational increments. True to its nature, the common law did much backing and filling after *Tarasoff*; indeed the false starts, contradictions, and inconsistencies generated in the 1970s only began ironing themselves out in the 1990s.

For example, in *Thompson v. County of Alameda* (614 P.2d 728, 1980), the California Supreme Court reaffirmed *Tarasoff*'s holding that one has a duty to warn only specific victims who were actually identified or were easily identifiable, as was Tatiana herself. However, the facts were different. A juvenile offender in detention told a parole officer that if he were released on furlough he would murder a child chosen at random. He was in fact released, and he did just as he predicted, but the family of the victim child lost because no specific or identifiable victim was named. Similarly in 1984, a federal appellate court affirmed that the therapist of John Hinckley, who attempted to assassinate President Reagan, was not liable for the injuries that James Brady and others suffered in the attempt because Hinckley had identified no specific or identifiable victim.[35]

The difficulty, as you may already have noted, is that such rulings contradicted California common law as it existed before *Tarasoff*. Recall that California law previously held physicians liable for the damage done by contagious patients who spread disease because they were misdiagnosed. The third-party victims in such cases were not specifically identifiable beforehand. The reality is that in some cases, we cannot reasonably expect doctors to prevent harm to a victim unless they can identify a specific victim, but in other cases we can. As the Wisconsin Supreme Court put it:

> [I]f a patient announces an intention to, for example, leave the psychotherapist's office and commit random acts of violence, the psychotherapist would be unable to warn victims of potential danger. . . . Nevertheless, notwithstanding the absence of a readily identifiable victim, warnings could, in certain instances, effectively be made to, perhaps, the patient's family or police. . . . Society must not become the victim of a dangerous patient's ambiguity.[36]

Over time new and unanticipated problems will inevitably arise, and reasoning by example will apply such precedents in new and not entirely predictable ways. Indeed this is happening with respect to potential responsibility and liability for the spread of HIV and AIDS. Consider the case of a family practitioner who treats a husband and wife and discovers that one of the two is HIV positive. Does she have a duty to warn the other, who is also her patient? Does any physician treating any married patient have an obligation to warn a

---

[34] Ibid., 347–348.

[35] And see *DeShaney v. Winnebago County Dept. of Social Services,* 489 U.S. 189 (1989).

[36] *Schuster v. Altenberg,* 424 N.W.2d 159 (1988), at 172–173.

spouse, even when the spouse is *not* her patient? Courts in many states, strongly influenced by *Tarasoff*, have ruled that doctors and other health-care workers do have such duties to third parties. Indeed, *Tarasoff* has created an entire field of law regarding the health-care worker's duty to warn.[37] Thus reasoning by example in common law marches on.[38]

ILLUSTRATIVE CASE

On September 11, 2001, terrorists hijacked four commercial jet airplanes. All four eventually crashed, two into the World Trade Center Towers in New York City, one into the Pentagon in Washington, DC, and one into a field in Pennsylvania. Victims and families of victims of this attack sued in federal court, claiming that an array of defendants, including the airlines and the designers and operators of the World Trade Center Towers, were negligent in not doing more to either prevent or mitigate the damage caused by the attack. Their argument parallels the claim made in *Tarasoff* that professionals are negligent when they fail to protect third parties—in this case those on the ground injured by the airplanes and those who survived the initial impact in the World Trade Center Towers but were unable to escape the building safely. The defendants brought a motion for "summary judgment," a motion to dismiss a lawsuit that asks the judge to declare that even if all the plaintiff's claims were proved, the plaintiffs should not prevail as a matter of law. They cited *Hamilton v. Beretta*, a case in which New York's highest court ruled that a handgun manufacturer owed no duty of care to third parties injured by its product. The defendants claimed that, like the handgun manufacturer, the defendants owed no duty to the plaintiffs under common law and that the events of September 11 were not reasonably foreseeable. The judge's ruling on this case is *not a decision about whether the plaintiff's claims are meritorious*, and a victory for the plaintiffs does not mean they will win the lawsuit; many hurdles (including a jury trial and possible appeal) remain. All a plaintiff victory means at this initial stage of the lawsuit is that the plaintiffs are entitled to go forward to try to prove their claims. As you read this case, consider the following facts: (1) Congress in the wake of the September 11 attack enacted into law a special government-budgeted Victim Compensation Fund; victims who applied to the Fund waived their right to bring a tort lawsuit like this one; (2) Congress made one major restriction for those who chose the tort option; the defendants could not be required to pay any more than their insurances covered, so that the defendants would not have to pay "out of pocket." In light of all you have read, do you find Judge Hellerstein's ruling persuasive?

---

[37] For example, after Dr. Bruce Ivins, a suspect in the frightening series of Anthrax deaths shortly after the 9/11 attacks, committed suicide in 2008, it was revealed that both his psychiatrist and his social worker had earlier reported to authorities that they believed Ivins was sociopathic and homicidal. Sarah Abruzzese and Eric Lipton, "Anthrax Suspect's Death is Dark End for a Family Man," *The New York Times*, August 2, 2008.

[38] Many state legislatures, in response to these court decisions, have in turn created statutes specifying the duties and privileges of health-care workers who treat HIV-positive patients. For a review of these developments, see Lawrence O. Gostin and James G. Hodge, Jr., "Piercing the Veil of Secrecy in HIV/AIDS and Other Sexually Transmitted Diseases: Theories of Privacy and Disclosure in Partner Notification," 5 *Duke Journal of Gender Law & Policy* 9 (1999).

In Re September 11 Litigation
280 F. Supp. 2d, 279
(S.D. N.Y., September 9, 2003)

Judge Alvin K. Hellerstein.

Plaintiffs allege that the airlines, airport security companies, and airport operators negligently failed to fulfill their security responsibilities, and in consequence, the terrorists were able to hijack the airplanes and crash them into the World Trade Center, the Pentagon, and the field in Shanksville, Pennsylvania, killing passengers, crew, and thousands in the World Trade Center and the Pentagon and causing extensive property damage. The complaints allege that the owners and operators of the World Trade Center, World Trade Center Properties LLC and the Port Authority of New York and New Jersey, negligently designed, constructed, maintained, and operated the buildings, failing to provide adequate and effective evacuation routes and plans . . .

The threshold question in any negligence action is: "does the defendant owe a legally recognized duty of care to plaintiff?" *Hamilton v. Beretta* U.S.A. Corp., 750 N.E.2d 1055, 1060, (N.Y. 2001). In New York, the existence of a duty is a "legal, policy-laden declaration reserved for judges." *Palka v. Servicemaster Mgmt. Servs. Corp.,* 634 N.E.2d 189, 192, (N.Y. 1994). The injured party must show that a defendant owed not merely a general duty to society but a specific duty to the particular claimant . . .

New York courts have been cautious in extending liability to defendants for their failure to control the conduct of others, "even where as a practical matter [the] defendant can exercise such control." *D'Amico v. Christie,* 518 N.E.2d 896, 901, (N.Y. 1987). "This judicial resistance to the expansion of duty grows out of practical concerns both about potentially limitless liability and about the unfairness of imposing liability for the acts of another." (*Hamilton*) However, courts have imposed a duty when the defendant has control over the third party tortfeasor's actions, or the relationship between the defendant and plaintiff requires the defendant to protect the plaintiff from the conduct of others. As the New York Court of Appeals ruled, "The key in each [situation] is that the defendant's relationship with either the tortfeasor or the plaintiff places the defendant in the best position to protect against the risk of harm."

. . . Ours is a complicated and specialized society. We depend on others charged with special duties to protect the quality of the water we drink and the air we breathe, to bring power to our neighborhoods, and to enable us to travel with a sense of security over bridges, through tunnels and via subways. We live in the vicinity of busy airports, and we work in tall office towers, depending on others to protect us from the willful desire of terrorists to do us harm . . .

This case is . . . distinguishable from other cases where courts did not find a duty to protect against third-party conduct. In *Waters v. New York City Housing Authority,* the court held that the owner of a housing project did not owe a duty to a passerby when she was dragged off the street into the building and assaulted. 505 N.E.2d 922, (N.Y. 1987). Imposing such a duty on landowners would do little to minimize crime, and the social benefits to be gained did not warrant the extension of the landowner's duty. Similarly, in *Hamilton,* the court held that gun manufacturers did not owe a duty to victims of gun violence for negligent marketing and distribution of firearms. The connection between the manufacturers, criminal wrongdoers, and victims was too remote, running through many links in a long chain, from manufacturer, distributor or wholesaler, retailer, legal purchasers, unlawful possessors, and finally to the victims of gun violence.

Unlike Hamilton and Waters, the Aviation Defendants could best control the boarding of airplanes, and were in the best position to provide reasonable protection against hijackings and the dangers they presented, not only to the crew and passengers, but also to ground victims. Imposing a duty on the Aviation Defendants best allocates the risks to ground victims posed by inadequate screening, given the Aviations Defendants' existing and admitted duty to screen passengers and items carried aboard.

The World Trade Center Defendants contend that they owed no duty to "anticipate and guard against crimes unprecedented in human history." Plaintiffs argue that defendants owed a duty, not to foresee the crimes, but to have designed, constructed, repaired and maintained the World Trade Center structures to withstand the effects and spread of fire, to avoid building collapses caused by fire and, in designing and effectuating fire safety and evacuation procedures, to provide for the escape of more people . . .

The duty of landowners and lessors to adopt fire-safety precautions applies to fires caused by criminals. "Landowners have a duty to protect tenants, patrons or invitees from foreseeable harm caused by the criminal conduct of others while they are on the premises." (*Hamilton*)

Plaintiffs argue that the WTC Defendants had a duty to exercise reasonable care in order to mitigate the effects of fires in the Twin Towers.[a] They allege that defendants knew about the fire safety defects in the Twin Towers, as evident by [earlier] litigation concerning inadequate fireproofing in the construction of the buildings; that defendants could have reasonably foreseen crashes of airplanes into the Towers, given the near miss in 1981 of an Aerolineas Argentinas Boeing 707 and the studies conducted during the Towers' construction reporting that the Towers would be able to withstand an aircraft crash; that defendants were aware of numerous fires and evacuations that had occurred at the World Trade Center since its creation, including arson fires in 1975 and the 1993 terrorist-caused explosion in the garage under Tower One; and that the World Trade Center continued to be a prime target of terrorists. A finding of duty does not require a defendant to have been aware of a specific hazard. It is enough to have foreseen the risk of serious fires within the buildings and the goal of terrorists to attack the building.

I hold that the WTC Defendants owed a duty to the plaintiffs, and that plaintiffs should not be foreclosed from being able to prove that defendants failed to exercise reasonable care to provide a safe environment for its occupants and invitees with respect to reasonably foreseeable risks.

---

[a] Plaintiffs concede that the WTC Defendants owed no duty to those in the Twin Towers who died upon impact of the planes.

QUESTIONS ABOUT THE CASE

1. How does Judge Hellerstein justify his decision? What social background facts and shared values does he muster in his opinion?

2. What purpose, or purposes, might a tort lawsuit such as this one serve? Is this an appropriate extension of cases such as *Tarasoff* on third-party liability? What negative consequences can you imagine might result from letting this lawsuit go forward? (Might it raise the construction cost of office buildings? Airplanes? Might it increase ticket prices and rents?)

3. Should the existence of a government fund for September 11 victims make a difference to the judge? (Has the legislature clearly spoken on this issue?)

4. Recall that on pp. 42–43, we listed the "basic features" of the common-law process. Further, recall that we illustrated these features with three cases (*Armstrong, Beck,* and *Hynes*). Those cases, like the World Trade Center lawsuit, were resolved by New York courts. Can you apply one or more of our basic common-law truths to help describe how New York tort law has evolved from the last of our three original New York cases—*Hynes,* the diving board case—to the law applied by the judge in this case?

CHAPTER 4

Statutory Interpretation

*Whoever hath an absolute authority to interpret any written
or spoken laws, it is he who is truly the Law-giver to all
intents and purposes, and not the person who first spoke
or wrote them.*

—BENJAMIN HOADLY

*It is of course dangerous that judges be philosophers—
almost as dangerous as if they were not.*

—PAUL FREUND

WHAT ARE STATUTES?

Statutes—a dusty and unromantic word. One thinks of endless rows of thick books in inadequately illuminated library stacks. The librarians have the mildew under control, but its odor remains faintly on the air.

To understand better the significance of statutory law, we must abandon our reaction to statutes as arcane words in dull and musty books; we must see them as vital forces in society. Statutes are the skeleton of the body politic. Our elected representatives officially speak to us through the statutes they enact. In political systems that honor the rule of law, statutes are the primary levers that authorize those who govern to take our property, our freedom, and our lives. Political campaigns and elections, indeed much in public life that does excite us, matter because they directly influence the making of statutory policies that can dramatically affect the quality of our lives.

When judges interpret statutes they encounter issues that differ significantly from those we discussed in the previous chapter. As we have seen, common-law judges are policymakers. They often resolve controversies where no legislature has gone before, for example, whether therapists owe a duty to warn to potential victims of their patients or whether tugboats should be required to carry AM radios. In the twentieth century, judges in common-law cases became more explicit and self-conscious about their policymaking role, and their choices have occasionally created a legislative backlash, as we saw in the case of tort reform. Judges in common-law cases, then, must wrestle with the proper balance between legislative and judicial lawmaking, but they do so knowing they are empowered to decide for themselves how to resolve public policy issues.

In statutory disputes the proper balance between legislative and judicial power is necessarily quite different. Judges who interpret statutes must remember that even in common-law

71

systems such as the United States, legislatures are the primary lawmakers, so when legislatures try to correct a problem by writing a statute, they are supreme.[1] Hence, in matters of statutory interpretation, judges must follow the legislature's policy, not their own, to resolve the case.

The history of statutory interpretation in the twentieth century is a series of attempts to respect the supremacy of legislative policymaking by devising some technique for keeping judges within their proper bounds. Statutory law has been haunted by the fear that judges might use their power over statutory interpretation to substitute their own views for those of democratically elected legislators.[2] Judges in the early twentieth century, one observer has noted, "frequently emasculated legislation designed to protect workers, children, consumers and women."[3] In the chapter on constitutional law, we will assess more carefully the claim that judicial policymaking violates fundamental principles of democracy. For now, the important point is that concerns about judicial policymaking have led legal theorists—and judges themselves—to try to find ways to limit the role of courts in interpreting statutes. In particular, judges and legal theorists have adopted several approaches to statutory interpretation aimed at neatly separating policymaking and judging.

In this chapter we argue that these approaches are misguided. Each of them involves an attempt to constrain judges by generating a single right formula by which judges can be sure that they do exactly what the law commands. But as you should see by now, law does not work that way. Legal disputes usually come to court when the law is uncertain, so that two parties have opposing interpretations of the law. No formula of interpretation can magically dissolve the ambiguities inherent in law. And statutory law, like common law, has many sources of uncertainty.

First, statutes are written in words, and as we have already seen, the words of everyday life and of law are often slippery and ambiguous. Judges who arm themselves with dictionaries and expect to find a single, unproblematic interpretation of a statute expect too much of language—and too little of themselves.

Second, the process by which legislatures make statutes is complex and multilayered. Attempts to isolate particular moments from the legislative process and glean from them a single correct answer to a statutory dispute usually do injustice to the complexity of legislating. Committee reports, floor speeches, and the rest of the legislative process may help us make sense of the law, but only the duly enacted statute has the force of law. Legislatures can communicate their chosen policies in a legally binding way only by voting favorably on a

---

[1] Legislative supremacy is taken for granted today, but until the twentieth century it was a matter of deep political controversy. Defenders of the common law argued that it embodied both natural law and the special wisdom accumulated through years of development, while legislation merely reflected the tug and pull of special interests. Common law was real "law," legislation merely politics. (Brian Z. Tamanaha, *Law as a Means to an End* (Cambridge University Press, 2006), pp. 24–52). Today the principle of legislative supremacy is well established, but it has one important exception: Courts in the United States possess the authority to reject statutory supremacy when they conclude that the enforcement of a statute would violate a legal norm expressed in or implied by the constitutions of the states or the nation. Where judges find a violation, their expression of constitutional values becomes supreme, and this political dynamic is part of the familiar set of checks and balances embedded in American government.

[2] See Samuel Popkin, *Statutes in Court: The History and Theory of Statutory Interpretation* (Durham, NC: Duke University Press, 1999).

[3] Shep Melnick, review of Samuel Popkin, *Statutes in Court: The History and Theory of Statutory Interpretation,* in *Law and Politics Book Review* (2000), available at http://www.bsos.umd.edu/gvpt/lpbr/subpages/reviews/popkin.html

written proposal. Without the vote by the legislature, no matter how forcefully individual legislators or political parties advocate a policy decision, they create no law. Judges who fruitlessly search dictionaries for a single right answer to a statutory question will be just as frustrated when they turn to the legislative process.

Third, statutes are written in general terms and so do not neatly resolve particular disputes. There are, of course, some statutes that have extremely detailed rules. Tax laws take literally thousands of pages of rules and regulations to specify how government shall raise revenues. But other statutes are incredibly general. Early antitrust statutes said that society has a problem preserving effective business competition, and so barred restraints on competition. In 1890, a nearly unanimous Congress passed with very little debate the Sherman Antitrust Act. Its first two sections state: (1) "Every contract, combination in the form of a trust or otherwise, or conspiracy, in restraint of trade or commerce among the several States, or with foreign nations, is hereby declared to be illegal"; and (2) "Every person who shall monopolize, or attempt to monopolize . . . any part of the trade or commerce among the several States, or with foreign nations, shall be deemed guilty of a misdemeanor. . . ." Such general language— Just what is "commerce"? Just what counts as a "restraint"?—leaves judges much freedom to shape and refine law.

Finally, even if they wished to make all statutes as lengthy and detailed as tax codes, legislatures could not possibly anticipate every conflict that might arise under a statute.[4] Legislators are not soothsayers, so they cannot, for example, write laws for technologies that have not yet been invented. The Congress that passed the Sherman Antitrust Law of 1890 could not possibly have conceived of the special antitrust issues posed by computer software. Yet more than a century later, judges were asked to use the Sherman Act to decide whether Microsoft's "bundling" of its Internet Explorer browser program to the Windows operating system, which for time threatened to make Microsoft dominant in the Internet software business, was illegal. Similarly, the makers of federal copyright law could not possibly have anticipated the unique issues posed by Internet "file-swapping," yet judges are being asked by music companies to use this law to decide whether college students who share copyrighted files should pay damages. In statutory law, as in common law, judges must grapple with new kinds of conflicts using old legal rules.

Given all these difficulties, how should judges decide in concrete cases what statutes mean? Because Chapters 2 and 3 have focused on the role of precedents in judging, one preliminary answer to this question should be familiar to you: Judges in statutory cases should first seek the guidance of earlier case precedents dealing with the same interpretive problem. Then, as in the common law, judges can be guided—though of course not bound—by the principle of stare decisis and by the discipline of reasoning by example.

But what if a particular kind of dispute has never arisen before? We call this *statutory interpretation in the first instance.* When judges decide what uncertain statutes "really" mean the first time, all the problems of statutory interpretation we have just sketched become particularly acute. In *McBoyle,* the airplane theft case discussed in Chapter 1 and reproduced in Appendix A, and *Caminetti,* the "weekend affair in Reno" case mentioned in Chapter 2, judges had to unravel the uncertain commands of Congress with no close precedent to guide them. Judge Richard Posner likens their challenge to that of a field commander in combat who radios his superiors for instructions. He hears the instruction, "Go . . ." but immediately

---

[4] In law, as in life, no set of rules can cover every possible situation. Chapter 6 explores this point further; see pages 141–143.

loses contact with headquarters. The field commander must decide to go forward or backward, but he knows he cannot stay where he is, even if that seems the wisest course to him.[5]

What can judges do in such a messy situation? *We argue that judges best interpret statutes when they pay attention to the purposes of legislation, an approach some scholars refer to as "purposivism."*[6] A judge must address directly such questions as these: What problem does this statute try to solve? Is the case before me an example of such a problem? If so, how does this statute tell me to solve it? These questions will not yield a single right answer to the legal problem the judge confronts, nor will they wholly eliminate the influence of the judge's worldviews on the answer she reaches. Nevertheless, the purpose-oriented approach strikes the best balance between legislative and judicial power in statutory interpretation. Judges who approach statutory interpretation as a matter of purpose acknowledge legislative supremacy, but do so in a way that does not oversimplify the complexity of legislation or the difficulty of the task before them.

Judges who approach statutes wisely know that they cannot treat the words as a series of Webster's definitions strung together. They intuitively appreciate the saying, "The greatest difficulty with communication is the illusion that it has been achieved." They know that words gain meaning not from dictionaries but from context. They realize that a sign on an outdoor escalator reading, "Dogs Must Be Carried" does not mean that everyone riding the escalator must carry a dog.[7] They know, as Judge Learned Hand has written, that the words of statutes become meaningful only when they are applied sensibly to the solution of public problems:

> . . . it is one of the surest indexes of a mature and developed jurisprudence not to make a fortress out of the dictionary; but to remember that statutes always have some purpose or object to accomplish, whose sympathetic and imaginative discovery is the surest guide to their meaning.[8]

FOUR MISGUIDED APPROACHES TO "FIRST INSTANCE" STATUTORY INTERPRETATION

We have just outlined how judges should interpret statutes in the first instance, and why we think other approaches to statutory interpretation are misguided. The rest of the chapter fills in the details. As we will demonstrate, in attempting to evade the responsibility inherent in statutory interpretation, judges not only end up on the wrong path but sometimes get downright silly.[9]

---

[5] See Posner's "Legal Formalism, Legal Realism, and the Interpretation of Statutes and the Constitution," 37 *Case Western Reserve Law Review* 179 (1986–1987), p. 189.

[6] Popkin, *Statutes in Court*, pp. 125–149.

[7] Our thanks to Professor Allan Hutchinson for this illustration.

[8] This is from Learned Hand's opinion in *Cabell v. Markham*, 148 F2d 737, 739 (1945) as quoted in Popkin, *Statutes in Court*, p. 133.

[9] The persistence of what verges on downright silliness in statutory interpretation thus illustrates a critical point made near the beginning of Chapter 2: The law's language, practices, and traditions, like those in any field of organized human action, tend to perpetuate themselves even when they no longer square well with contemporary social background facts and values; that is, they perpetuate bad legal reasoning.

Literalism: Sticking to the Words

Perhaps the most celebrated problem of statutory interpretation in American jurisprudence involves the seemingly straightforward and rather boring statutes governing inheritances. When someone with property dies with a valid will, statutes direct that the property go to the heirs named in the will. (The decision in *Fox v. Snow* in the previous chapter seems wrong in part because its result did not send Rosa's property where Rosa's will said it should go.) When a person dies without a will, statutes designate which relatives—spouses, children, parents, siblings, and so on—take priority and in what order. In Ohio, a statute made children whose parents died without a spouse and without a will the inheritors of the parents' estate. When one Elmer Sharkey murdered his mother, an Ohio court held that the law entitled him—or rather his creditors, since Ohio had already hanged Elmer—to the money because the statute did not, by its literal words, forbid murderers from inheriting from their victims. The court reviewed a New York case holding that a grandson named to inherit in his grandfather's will should, despite the law, *not* inherit after he poisoned his grandfather. The Ohio court nevertheless reasoned: "[W]hen the legislature, not transcending the limits of its power, speaks in clear language upon a question of policy, it becomes the judicial tribunals to remain silent." Is this good legal reasoning? The New York court had reasoned that it would not serve any valid statutory purpose to let someone inherit who had murdered to do so.[10]

In 1912, Lord Atkinson, speaking for the British House of Lords in its appellate judicial role, said:

> If the language of a statute be plain, admitting of only one meaning, the Legislature must be taken to have meant and intended what it has plainly expressed, and whatever it has in clear terms enacted must be enforced though it should lead to absurd or mischievous results.[11]

Lord Atkinson, no doubt, respected legislative powers and responsibilities—in this case, those of the House of Commons. The problem he presumably perceived is this: If courts can go beyond the words at all, they can go anywhere they want, setting their own limits and destroying legislative supremacy in the process. This is the classic rationale for the literal, sometimes absurd, reading of statutes.

Legislative supremacy deserves our deepest respect. But how would the good Lord react to this hypothetical statute: "A uniformed police officer may require any person driving a motor vehicle in a public place to provide a specimen of breath for a breath test if the officer has reasonable cause to suspect him of having alcohol in his body." Presumably, Lord Atkinson would not exempt women from this law just because the last sentence reads "him" rather than "him or her." The earlier use of the word "person," even to a literalist, can cover both genders. But how would Lord Atkinson handle the following argument by an equally literalistic defendant? "The statute plainly says the officer may require the specimen from a 'person driving.' I may have been slightly inebriated when the officer pulled me over, but when the

---

[10] *Deem v. Millikin*, 6 O.C.C. Rep. 357 (1892), 360, and 53 Ohio St. 668 (1895); *Riggs v. Palmer*, 115 N.Y. 506 (1889). See also Richard Posner, *The Problems of Jurisprudence* (Cambridge: Harvard University Press, 1990), pp. 105–107. For Ronald Dworkin's famous discussion of this classic problem, see his *Taking Rights Seriously* (Cambridge: Harvard University Press, 1977), pp. 23–31. And see Joel Levin's discussion of the same problem in his *How Judges Reason* (New York: Peter Lang, 1992), Chapter 6.

[11] *Vacher and Sons, Ltd., v. London Society of Compositors*, A.C. 107 (1912), 121.

officer required the specimen I was *not* 'driving a motor vehicle.' I wasn't even in my car. I was doing my imitation of a pig in the middle of the pavement when the officer requested the specimen."[12] This result is absurd, but Lord Atkinson seems willing to accept absurd results. Should he be, especially in light of the knowledge that language rarely if ever admits "of only one meaning"?

American judges have also been seduced by the appeal of adhering to the words. A Virginia statute stated: "No cemetery shall be hereafter established within the corporate limits of any city or town; nor shall any cemetery be established within two hundred and fifty yards of any residence without the consent of the owner. . . ." In 1942, after the legislature passed this statute, the town of Petersburg, Virginia, bought an acre of land within its corporate limits on which to relocate bodies exhumed during a road-widening project. The acre adjoined and would be incorporated into a long-established cemetery. A city resident well within the proscribed distance of the added acre brought suit to prevent the expansion and cited the statute.

He lost. Justice Gregory wrote for the appellate court:

> If the language of a statute is plain and unambiguous, and its meaning perfectly clear and definite, effect must be given to it regardless of what courts think of its wisdom or policy. . . .
> The word "established" is defined in *Webster's New International Dictionary,* second edition, 1936, thus: "To originate and secure the permanent existence of; to found; to institute; to create and regulate. . . ."
> Just why the Legislature, in its wisdom, saw fit to prohibit the establishment of cemeteries in cities and towns, and did not see fit to prohibit enlargements or additions, is no concern of ours. Certain it is that language could not be plainer than that employed to express the legislative will. From it we can see with certainty that . . . a cemetery . . . may be added to or enlarged without running counter to the inhibition found in [the statute]. . . . Our duty is to construe the statute as written.[13]

Judges such as Justice Gregory who cling to the literal meaning of words fail to appreciate that the Virginia legislature is filled with politicians, not dictionary writers. By sticking to the words, the judges prevent themselves from asking what problem the legislature sought to address. Just why the legislature might purposely allow *enlargement* but not *establishment* of cemeteries in cities and towns is Justice Gregory's concern. Unless he tries to solve that puzzle, we can have no confidence that he has applied the statute to achieve its purpose.

---

[12] See Sir Rupert Cross, *Statutory Interpretation* (London: Butterworths, 1976), p. 59. Or imagine a city ordinance requiring all liquor stores "to cease doing business at 10:00 P.M." Does the ordinance permit them to reopen at 10:01 P.M.?

[13] *Temple v. City of Petersburg,* 182 Va. 418 (1944), 423–424. In 1988 Congress authorized the automatic deportation of all noncitizens who were found guilty of an "aggravated felony," which Congress defined as including "crimes of violence." Did Josue Leocal, for 20 years a legal resident of the United States, commit an "aggravated felony" when he, while driving drunk, struck and injured two people? The vague words of the statute simply do not tell us. In 2004 the U.S. Supreme Court ruled that Leocal did not commit a "crime of violence" and so should not be deported. *Leocal v. Ashcroft* 543 U.S. 1 (2004). In the case featured at the end of this chapter, *Begay v. U.S.,* the Court wrestles with a similar question: Are repeated drunken driving convictions "violent felonies" under federal law?

The Golden Rule

Of course, Lord Atkinson could have solved his problem another way, by sticking to the words except when they produce absurd results. The so-called "Golden Rule" of statutory interpretation holds that judges should follow

> the grammatical and ordinary sense of the words . . . unless that would lead to some absurdity, or some repugnance or inconsistency with the rest of the instrument, in which case the grammatical and ordinary sense of the words may be modified, so as to avoid the absurdity and inconsistency, but no farther.[14]

The Golden Rule thus would solve the problem of the clever intoxicated driver. It would be absurd and possibly dangerous to require that the officer ride with him and collect the specimen while weaving down the road. But the Golden Rule, unfortunately, does not solve much more because it does not tell us how to separate the absurd from the merely questionable.

Take for example the case of Elian Gonzalez, the six-year-old Cuban boy found clinging to an inner tube in the Atlantic Ocean off the coast of Florida. Elian had been traveling by boat with his mother in an attempt to flee Cuba. When the boat capsized, 11 passengers died, including Elian's mother. Elian was brought to the United States and put in the temporary custody of his great uncle, Lazaro Gonzalez. When Elian's Cuban father requested that his son be returned to him in Cuba, Lozaro Gonzalez asked the Immigration and Naturalization Service (INS) to grant the child asylum in the United States. The INS refused, concluding that since a six-year-old is incompetent to apply for asylum on his own, only Elian's father could submit an application for him. Lazaro Gonzalez then sued the INS in federal court, claiming that he had acted at the request of Elian and noting that federal law fails to restrict asylum applications by age, providing only that "any alien . . . may apply for asylum." In a preliminary order barring the removal of Elian from the United States before a final decision in the case could be made, three federal appeals court judges ruled in favor of Lazaro Gonzalez. The judges agreed that the meaning of "any alien" is "pretty clear," and that if Congress had wanted to restrict asylum applications by age, it would not have written the statute to include "any alien":

> To some people, the idea that a six-year-old child may file for asylum in the United States, contrary to the express wishes of his parents, may seem a strange or even foolish policy. But this Court does not make immigration policy, and we cannot review the wisdom of statutes duly enacted by Congress.[15]

Is it absurd to let a six-year-old apply for asylum, or merely unwise? The Golden Rule provides no help, and so the Court simply throws up its hands.[16]

---

[14] *Grey v. Pearson*, 6 H.L. Cas. 61 (1857), 106, quoted in Cross, 15.

[15] *Elian Gonzalez v. Janet Reno*, 2000 U.S. App. Lexis 7025 (11th Circuit, April 19, 2000), at footnote 9.

[16] Two months later, the same judges decided that since "Congress has left a gap in the statutory scheme" by failing to describe *how* an alien should apply for asylum, the INS could reasonably fill that gap by deciding that a six-year-old could not go through the process of applying for asylum without the assistance of his parents. The final decision in *Gonzalez* ordered Elian to be returned to his father in Cuba. It rested on a basic principle of administrative law, deference to executive agencies. The opinion in this case concluded that the Court should not second-guess the way the INS had interpreted the statute; only if the agency's interpretation was "unreasonable" should the Court step in. *Gonzalez v. Reno* 212 F.3d 1338 (11th Circuit, June 1, 2000).

To further test the weakness of the Golden Rule, ask yourself two questions: (1) Is it absurd to allow expansion of existing graveyards while prohibiting the creation of new ones, or only questionable? (2) Is it absurd to use the Mann Act to prevent the transportation of willing girlfriends and mistresses across state lines along with unwilling "white slaves" and prostitutes, or merely questionable? The Golden Rule provides no answer.

Both the literal approach and the superficially more sensible Golden Rule fail. They deceive judges into believing that words in isolation can be and usually are clear and that the words communicate by themselves. But they don't. The word "establish" in *Temple* (the graveyard case), the phrase "immoral purpose" in *Caminetti* (the earliest of our Mann Act cases), and the word "vehicle" in *McBoyle* (the airplane theft case) simply are not clear, and no blunt assertion to the contrary will make them so. Even when words in isolation do seem unambiguous, the process of coordinating them with the facts of a particular case may make them unclear. In the Elian Gonzalez case, the words "any alien . . . may apply" seem straightforward until a judge contemplates the mental world of a six-year-old, who may not be able to understand what it means to apply for asylum, let alone fill out the application forms on his own. The judge who asserts that the words "any alien" by themselves resolve the case fails to honestly confront these difficulties. Interpreting words in isolation, then, is a danger because it leads judges to believe that they have thought a problem through to its end when they have only reached its beginning.

To summarize, words become meaningful only in each of their distinct contexts. In statutory interpretation, judges must analyze two contexts. The first is the legislative context—what general problem exists and what kind of policy response to it the legislature has created. The second is the case context—what the litigants are disputing and whether their dispute involves the problem the statute addresses. To say that words are clear or unclear depending on the context really means that the words would become clear if we could imagine a different case or context arising under each of the same statutes this book has mentioned so far. If Elian Gonzalez had been 25 years old, or if Mr. McBoyle had stolen a car rather than a plane, judges would have had no difficulty concluding that the statutory words clearly and unambiguously determine the case. Judges would similarly not have hesitated to prohibit Petersburg from opening a brand new cemetery within the city limits.

The idea that words read literally will mislead has been around a very long time. In 1615, Galileo explained in a letter to the Grand Duchess of Tuscany the same idea. After strongly affirming that "the Bible can never speak untruth," Galileo went on to write that the Bible

> is often very abstruse, and may say things which are quite different from what its bare words signify. Hence in expounding the Bible if one were always to confine oneself to the unadorned grammatical meaning, one might fall into error. Not only contradictions and propositions far from true might thus be made to appear in the Bible, but even grave heresies and follies.

Literally read, the Bible would have God forgetting the past and being clueless about the future, clearly contradictory to church teachings about the omnipotence of God. It is not too much to expect that judges learn what Galileo taught the Grand Duchess.

Canons of Statutory Construction

Judges have defended themselves against the imprecision of words by arming themselves with interpretive weapons called "canons of construction." As part of a broader interpretative approach, canons of construction can be useful. The problem comes when judges use canons as if they were mathematical equations that can provide precise answers to problems in statutory interpretation.

A canon of construction or interpretation (they are, for our purposes, the same) is really a rule for interpreting rules. These canons, developed over hundreds of years by judges in statutory cases, provide rules for resolving ambiguities in the language of laws. Take for example the *McBoyle* case. The relevant statute forbade transportation across state lines of a stolen "automobile, automobile truck, automobile wagon, motorcycle or any other self-propelled vehicle not designed for running on rails." The question raised by the case is whether an airplane is a vehicle. Can the canons help?

One of the canons of construction says:

> Where general words follow a statutory specification, they are to be held as applying only to persons and things of the same general kind or class of thing to which the specified things belong.

By invoking this canon, called *ejusdem generis* ("of the same kind"), a judge could conclude that the general words "or any other self-propelled vehicle" refer only to items *like* (in the same genus as) the objects the statute specifically mentions (the species). In this case, all the specific items run on land. Therefore, an airplane is not a vehicle.

Similarly, in *Caminetti*, Justice Day invoked the *ejusdem generis* canon in reaching the conclusion that the Mann Act did cover concubines. He said that the general words "other immoral purposes" refer only to sexual immorality because all the specific examples fit that genus. If you take your mother or a female friend across a state line to rob a bank, you will not violate the Mann Act even though the word "immoral," by its plain meaning, surely includes robbery.

Before we consider how the canons can become a vice rather than a virtue in statutory interpretation, it will help to review a few more examples from among dozens of canons that judges utilize. One frequently cited canon instructs judges to interpret criminal statutes narrowly. This means that when a judge finds that the statute does not clearly resolve his case, he should resolve it in favor of the defendant. Again *McBoyle* can illustrate. Justice Holmes wrote for the Supreme Court in that case:

> [I]t is reasonable that a fair warning should be given to the world in language that the common world will understand of what the law intends to do if a certain line is passed. To make the warning fair, so far as possible the line should be clear.

Holmes argues, in other words, that unless judges interpret criminal statutes narrowly, judges will send to jail people who had no clear notice that they had committed a crime.[17] Reflect a bit and you will see how this canon empowers judges to resist the tendency of government officials to abuse their powers.

Holmes's concern for fairness in *McBoyle* reminds us that the canons are not totally ineffective or undesirable weapons. Supreme Court Justice Felix Frankfurter said that "even generalized restatements from time to time may not be wholly wasteful. Out of them may come a sharper rephrasing of the conscious factors of interpretation; new instances may make them more vivid but also disclose more clearly their limitations."[18] Nearly every canon

---

[17] *McBoyle v. United States,* Appendix A. A narrow interpretation may produce a very different decision from that of a literal interpretation. A literal interpretation of the words "other immoral purposes" in the Mann Act would make the act cover my taking my wife to another state to rob a bank. A narrow interpretation would not.

[18] Felix Frankfurter, "Some Reflections on the Reading of Statutes," 2 *Record of the Association of the Bar of the City of New York* 213 (1947): 236.

that judges have created contains at least a small charge of sensibility. Canons exist to support each of the principles of proper interpretation that this chapter covers. For example, the canon *noscitur a sociis* ("it is known by its associates") states that words are affected by their context. One British court used this canon to confine a statute regulating houses "for public refreshment, resort and entertainment" only to places where people received food and drink and excluded musical and other theatrical places, refreshing though their shows might be. The statute bore the title Refreshment House Act.[19]

So why is it so wrong for judges to use canons as their guide to interpretation? By making disorderly words appear orderly, canons can deceive judges into thinking they have found the one correct application of the statute to the case. In fact, the canons often allow judges to evade the difficult task of untangling statutory purpose and of weighing all four elements of legal reasoning. One example of this judicial evasion of purpose occurred after Congress passed a statute in 1893 designed to promote railway safety.[20] In part, Section 2 of the statute reads:

> [I]t shall be unlawful for any . . . common carrier [engaged in interstate commerce] to haul or permit to be hauled or used on its line any car . . . not equipped with couplers coupling automatically by impact, and which can be uncoupled without the necessity of men going between the ends of the cars.

Section 8 of the Act placed the right to sue for damages in the hands of "any employee of any such common carrier who may be injured by any locomotive, car or train in use contrary to the provisions of this act. . . ." At common law, the injured employee often had no right of action against his employer; Section 8 created that right. Additionally, the act imposed criminal penalties on railroads that failed to comply.

A workman was injured while positioned between a locomotive and a car. He had tried to couple them by hand because the locomotive did not possess a coupler that coupled automatically with the car. He sued for damages and lost, both in the trial court and in the U.S. Court of Appeals, the latter holding that the statute did not require locomotives to possess the same automatic couplers. Judge Sanborn fired canon after canon in defense of his conclusion that the statutory word "cars" did not include locomotives:

- "The familiar rule that the expression of one thing is the exclusion of the others leads to [this] conclusion.

- "A statute which thus changes the common-law must be strictly construed.

- "This is a penal statute, and it may not be so broadened by judicial construction as to make it cover and permit the punishment of an act which is not denounced by the fair import of its terms.

- "The intention of the legislature and the meaning of a penal statute must be found in the language actually used."[21]

Do any of these canons convince you that this statute does not require locomotives to have automatic couplers? Again, the canons are not themselves absurd; the damage occurs when

---

[19] Cross, p. 118. The list of canons is lengthy. Karl Llewellyn cites and provides judicial citations for 56 canons in "Remarks on the Theory of Appellate Decision and the Rules or Canons about How Statutes Are to Be Construed," 3 *Vanderbilt Law Review* 395 (1950): 401–406.

[20] 27 Stat. c. 196, 531.

[21] *Johnson v. Southern Pacific Co.*, 117 Fed. 462 (C.C.A. 8th 1902). Fortunately the U. S. Supreme Court reversed, 196 U.S. 1 (1904).

they seduce judges into applying them simplistically and into thinking the canon gives *the* answer when the canon only justifies *an* answer. Does not Judge Sanborn's reasoning at least create the suspicion in your mind that he wanted, for whatever reasons, to rule for the railroads, and that the easy availability of canons only provided convenient camouflage for his personal preferences?

The vice of the canons resembles the familiar law of mechanics. For each and every canon, there is an equal and opposite canon. Llewellyn organizes 56 canons he collected into 28 sets of opposing canons: "THRUST BUT PARRY," he calls them. The judge who, for whatever reason, reaches any conclusion can find a canon to defend it.

Consider this example of Llewellyn's point: A federal statute prohibits the interstate shipment of any "obscene . . . book, pamphlet, picture, motion-picture film, paper, letter, writing, print or other matter of indecent character." One Mr. Alpers shipped interstate some phonograph records that, admitted for the sake of argument, were obscene. On the basis of the canons *ejusdem generis* ("of the same kind") and "strict construction of criminal statutes," we might expect Mr. Alpers to win his case. After all, the genus to which all the species belong is "things comprehended through sight." Instead, Justice Minton, for the Supreme Court, alluded to noscitur a sociis ("it is known by its associates"), another canon, and upheld the conviction.[22]

In short, the canons themselves are at war. In *Caminetti, ejusdem generis* pushes toward conviction, but "narrow construction" pushes toward acquittal. In the illustrative case at the end of this chapter, *Begay v. United States,* each of the three justices who wrote an opinion cites a canon in defending his interpretation of a statute, but the canons lead the justices in three different directions. Clearly canons, whatever their virtues, cannot provide the "right answer" to questions of statutory interpretation.

Legislative Intent

Another common way in which judges attempt to justify their interpretations of statutes is to try to discover what the legislature "intended" its statutory words to mean. We can define an *intention* as a conscious mental commitment to act in some specific way. Judges who use a "legislative intent" approach, then, attempt to resolve statutory conflicts by studying the intentions of legislators who voted for a statute. They try to figure out how the legislators thought the statute should apply to the case in question. We shall try in a moment to persuade you that "legislative intent" is a mirage and that the quest for it almost inevitably leads judges astray. For now, think carefully about the following use of legislative intent. How much more comfortable are you with Chief Justice Rugg's reasoning in the next case than you were with Lord Atkinson's literal approach, or Justice Gregory's reasoning in the cemetery case, or Justice Day's argument in *Caminetti?*

Shortly after it became a state, and long before the Nineteenth Amendment to the U.S. Constitution guaranteed women the right to vote, Massachusetts passed a statute providing that "a person qualified to vote for representative to the General Court [the official name of the Massachusetts legislature] shall be liable to serve as a juror." Ten years after the passage of the Nineteenth Amendment, one Genevieve Welosky, a criminal defendant, found herself facing a Massachusetts jury that excluded all women. Welosky protested the exclusion, appealed, and lost. Under the literal or Golden Rule approaches, she would surely have won, for *person* includes women, and women were "qualified to vote." Even before the days of women's liberation, we would hardly label it absurd to seat women on juries.

---

[22] *United States v. Alpers,* 338 U.S. 680 (1950).

But Massachusetts Chief Justice Rugg invoked the intent of the legislature:

> It is clear beyond peradventure that the words of [the statute] when originally enacted
> could not by any possibility have included or been intended by the General Court to
> include women among those liable to jury duty.... Manifestly, therefore, the intent of
> the Legislature must have been, in using the word "person" in statutes concerning
> jurors and jury lists, to confine its meaning to men.[23]

The legislature didn't intend women to become jurors when they passed the statute, because
at that time women could not vote. Despite the literal meaning of the words, women cannot
therefore sit on juries.

The title of this section offered the hope that judges can find statutory truth by discovering legislative intent. The Massachusetts court has identified an uncontested social
background fact—that women could not vote when the statute was passed—and concluded logically that the legislature did not intend women to sit on juries. This logic is
straightforward enough, but the *Welosky* opinion is a virtual fraud. Rugg says the simple
sequence of historical events reveals the legislature's intent; because the statute came
before the suffrage amendment, the legislature did not intend to include women. But
Rugg's first quoted sentence sends us on a wild goose chase. It is plausible that the legislature did not consider the possibility of women—or for that matter, immigrant Martians—
becoming jurors. But it is simultaneously plausible that the Massachusetts legislature
"intended" to settle the problem of who may sit as a juror once and for all by simply tying
jury service to voting eligibility, so that anyone legally entitled to vote could be called for
jury duty. A legislature that did so would hardly act absurdly. Rugg completely fails to
show that it did not so act.

Does the hope that legislative intent will reveal the meaning of statutory language hence
fail? Yes, but not because of poorly reasoned cases such as *Welosky*. The quest for legislative
intent is a search for hard evidence. It is detective work in the legal field, not Rugg's idle
armchair speculations, so we should not abandon the field of legislative intent so quickly.

Judges have many sleuthing techniques for discovering "hard evidence" of intent, of
which we now review three of the most prominent. What do you think of them?

Other Words in the Statute

The brief excerpt from the cemetery case, discussed earlier in this chapter, may have treated
Justice Gregory unfairly, for he did not simply rest his opinion on Webster's dictionary. He
continued by pointing out that another section of the cemetery statute of Virginia

> affords a complete answer to the question of legislative intent in the use of the word
> "established" in Section 56, for the former section [Section 53] makes a distinction
> between "establish" and "enlarge" in these words: "If it be desired at any time to estab-
> lish a cemetery, for the use of a city, town, county, or magisterial district, or to enlarge
> any such already established, and the title to land needed cannot be otherwise acquired,
> land sufficient for the purpose may be condemned...."
>
> The foregoing language, taken from Section 53, completely demonstrates that the
> legislature did not intend the words "establish" and "enlarge" to be used interchange-
> ably, but that the use of one excluded any idea that it embraced or meant the other.[24]

---

[23] *Commonwealth v. Welosky*, 276 MA. 398 (1931), 402–406.

[24] *Temple v. City of Petersburg*, 424.

Similarly, Justice McKenna, dissenting in *Caminetti*, found support in the official title of the Mann Act:

> For the context I must refer to the statute; of the purpose of the statute Congress itself has given us illumination. It devotes a section to the declaration that the "Act shall be known and referred to as the 'White Slave Traffic Act.'" And its prominence gives it prevalence in the construction of the statute. It cannot be pushed aside or subordinated by indefinite words in other sentences, limited even there by the context.[25]

The title of the statute tells Justice McKenna that Congress did not intend to police the activities of willing girlfriends. Willing girlfriends are not white slaves; the conclusion sounds sensible.

The Expressed Intent of Individual Legislators and Committee Reports

Like Justice Gregory, Justice McKenna, in his *Caminetti* dissent, made more than one argument to support his conclusion.[26] In fact, he went directly to the words of the bill's author and quoted extensively from Representative Mann:

> "The White Slave Trade—A material portion of the legislation suggested and proposed is necessary to meet conditions which have arisen within the past few years. The legislation is needed to put a stop to the villainous interstate and international traffic in women and girls. The legislation is not needed or intended as an aid to the states in the exercise of their police powers in the suppression or regulation of immorality in general. It does not attempt to regulate the practice of voluntary prostitution, but aims solely to prevent panderers and procurers from compelling thousands of women and girls against their will and desire to enter and continue in a life of prostitution." *Congressional Record*, vol. 50, pp. 3368, 3370.
>
> In other words, it is vice as a business at which the law is directed, using interstate commerce as a facility to procure or distribute its victims.

Judges rarely argue that the expressed views of any one legislator necessarily convey legislative intent, but they frequently cite committee reports and statements of authors as proof of intent. This is a curious practice, for it seems to allow the words of one legislator, or of a small minority, to determine what the law holds despite the fact that in a legislature, only a voting majority has the power to make law.

Other Actions, Events, and Decisions in the Legislature

To establish legislative intent, judges may also look at how the legislature handled related legislation. In *Welosky*, Chief Justice Rugg noted that the Massachusetts legislature had in 1920 changed several laws relating to women in order to make them conform to the Eighteenth and Nineteenth Amendments but did nothing about the problem of female jurors. He argued regarding the 1920 legislation:

> It is most unlikely that the Legislature should, for the first time require women to serve as jurors without making provision respecting the exemption of the considerable numbers

---

[25] *Caminetti v. United States*, 497.

[26] Appellate judges often give multiple arguments for the conclusions in their opinions, but they do not always articulate whether one argument, by itself, would justify the same result. They don't, in other words, spell out the relative importance of the arguments they use.

of women who ought not to be required to serve as jurors, and without directing that changes for the convenience of women be made in court houses, some of which are notoriously over-crowded and unfit for their accommodation as jurors.

Judges may even find in the physical evidence presented to committees the key to intent. In the 1940s, the postmaster general refused to grant the preferential lower postage rate to books, such as workbooks and notebooks, that contained many blank pages. Congress then amended the relevant statute to grant the preferential postal rates to books with space for notes. However, the postmaster general continued to refuse the rate to so-called loose-leaf notebooks with blank pages on the basis that they were not permanently bound. A shipper of such notebooks eager for the cheaper postage rate sued for an order granting the preferential rate. The opinion of Judge Groner concluded that Congress did intend to give the preferential rate to loose-leaf notebooks because the many physical exhibits placed before the committee that handled the bill included some such notebooks. Groner wrote, "[I]t follows logically that textbooks of the make and quality of those of appellant were considered and purposely included by Congress in the list of publications entitled to the book rate."[27]

The list of possibilities in this category could continue for pages. For example, judges are fond of finding legislative intent by discovering that one house's version of a bill contained a clause that does not appear in the final law, approved by both houses. They conclude from this discovery that the legislature intended that the remaining words *not* mean what the dropped clause meant. Superficially, these discoveries of "hard evidence" of legislative intent appeal to us because they seem to reveal the purpose of the statute. But comparing the examples of sleuthing with our "first principles" of statutory interpretation reveals that legislative intent fails as badly as our other two approaches. Only the statute, the words for which the majority of both houses of the legislature voted, has the force of law.

When Judge Groner concludes "logically" that the legislature intended to include loose-leaf notebooks for the preferential rate, he is logically completely incorrect. He does not give one shred of evidence that any legislator, much less the majority, actually thought about the physical exhibits when he or she voted. Of course, Representative Mann's thoughts give us some clue to his intent, but we do not know that a majority heard or read his thoughts. Even if a majority in the House and Senate did know what Mann intended, we don't know that they agreed with him. After all, the statute uses the word "prostitution" without Mann's qualifications. Maybe the majority voted for the act because they wanted a tougher response to the sex-trade problem than did Mann.

The Perils of Legislative Intent

Why then, precisely, does legislative intent fail as a tool of statutory interpretation? A legislature is an organizational unit of government. By itself, a legislature can no more intend something than can a car or an office building. *People* intend things, and, because the elected representatives in a legislature are people, they may intend something when they vote. If all members of the voting majority intended the same thing, then that might well state the purpose of the statute. However, here two difficulties fatal to the cause of legislative intent arise.

First, intent is subjective. It is usually impossible to tell with 100 percent certainty what anyone, ourselves included, intends. Thus, if a majority of legislators were fortunate

---

[27] *McCormick-Mathers Publishing Co. v. Hannegan*, 161 F.2d 873 (D.C. Cir. 1947), 875. See Arthur Phelps, "Factors Influencing Judges in Interpreting Statutes," 3 *Vanderbilt Law Review* 456 (1950).

enough to intend the same thing, it is highly unlikely that judges could actually discover what that thing was.

Second, we know enough about politics to know that in all likelihood the people making up the voting majority do not intend the same thing. Most will not have read the statute they vote on. By casting their vote, some will intend to repay a political debt, or to be a loyal follower of their party leaders, or to encourage a campaign contribution from a private source in the future. If we want to deduce collective intent on anything, we must take a poll, and the only poll we ever take of legislators is when the presiding officer of the House calls for the vote to enact or defeat a bill. "Yes" voters intend to vote yes, and "No" voters intend to vote no, but that's about all we can accurately say about their intentions.

Third, even if we somehow knew that those legislators who voted for a bill intended the same thing about a statute, it is highly unlikely, if not absolutely impossible, that they intended anything about the unique facts of the case before the court. Legislators simply do not confront the concrete and always unique case. In this sense, as former Attorney General Levi once said, "Despite much gospel to the contrary, a legislature is not a fact-finding body. There is no mechanism, as there is with a court, to require the legislature to sift facts and to make a decision about specific situations."[28] In all probability, no one in the legislature foresaw the precise problem facing the judge, and it is even less likely that the legislature consciously intended to resolve the case one way or another. Pose to the politicians who enacted the Mann Act the problems of migrating Mormons or vacationing prostitutes and you would probably get a gruff instruction to "ask a judge about the details." And if you were to somehow bring back to life the makers of the 1890 Sherman Antitrust Act to ask for their opinions about lawsuits over computer software, you would undoubtedly get blank stares.

Those are just the most basic problems with using legislative history to discern legislative intent. Consider a few more:

■ Legislators and lobbyists often "cook" legislative history, inserting comments and planting evidence in the legislative record solely for the purpose of persuading judges later on in litigation that the legislature had a particular intent. The loose-leaf notebooks that Judge Groner put so much weight on in the postal rate case might well have been planted there by a lobbyist. As long ago as 1947, Archibald Cox wrote that "it is becoming increasingly common to manufacture 'legislative history' during the course of legislation."[29]

■ The institutional dynamics of contemporary policymaking are so complex and the political cross-pressures so intense that Congress often makes garbled policy and sends conflicting messages. Indeed, judges often ignore the possibility that the lawmaking process might purposely create unclear law because legislatures *want* the courts to fill

---

[28] Edward H. Levi, *An Introduction to Legal Reasoning* (Chicago: University of Chicago Press, 1949), p. 31.

[29] Archibald Cox, "Some Aspects of the Labor Management Relations Act, 1947," 61 *Harvard Law Review* 1 (1947): 44. Justice Antonin Scalia, who describes himself as a "textualist" in the battle over statutory interpretation, has made this point one of his main arguments against legislative history. See Scalia, *A Matter of Interpretation* (Princeton, N.J.: Princeton University Press, 1997), pp. 32–36. Senators John Kyl and Lindsey Graham allegedly planted evidence in the Congressional Record to suggest that Congress intended to strip the federal courts of jurisdiction to hear cases of Guantanamo detainees under the Detainee Treatment Act. See Emily Bazelon, "Invisible Men: Did Lindsey Graham and Jon Kyl mislead the Supreme Court?" *Slate Magazine*, March 27, 2006, available at: http://www.slate.com/id/2138750/.

in the details. This may amount to buck-passing in the hope that the courts will take the pressure for an unpopular result. But legislators may also believe that case-by-case judicial action is the best way to decide precisely what the statute should include and exclude.

■ Often there is no real legislative history at all. Most state legislatures still do not produce complete documentation of proceedings that most lawyers can access. Even Congress sometimes acts without hearings or meaningful debate. In practice, a legislative aide often drafts the legislation after getting advice from a variety of members of Congress and its committees. The drafter will construct, as best he or she sees it, the language that accommodates the competing interests within Congress. Thus, practically, this drafter will be the only person who thinks fully about where the purposes of a particular piece of legislation stop. If that person is an attorney (and this is usually the case), the attorney–client privilege actually forbids communication with the courts about the actual intentions of the people whom he or she represented in the drafting process!

Much can be (and has been) said for abandoning the concept of legislative intent permanently. The ever-skeptical Holmes wrote, "I don't care what their intention was, I only want to know what the words mean." And Frankfurter added, "You may have observed that I have not yet used the word 'intention.' All these years I have avoided speaking of the 'legislative intent' and I shall continue to be on my guard against using it."[30] The candid judge looking for firm evidence of intent simply won't find it very often. A candid Rugg would, for example, have concluded, "I simply can't say whether the Massachusetts legislature thought about women becoming jurors or not." The names Holmes and Frankfurter endure more prominently than Rugg because they were especially able to make such candid judgments.[31] Given the realities of the legislative process, judges should be wary of concluding that the legislature ever collectively intended anything.

The ultimate danger in all the methods of statutory interpretation we've described—the literal and Golden Rule approaches, the use of canons, and the search for legislative intent in legislative history—is that each allows the judge to reach a conclusion without ever struggling with the fundamental question of whether one interpretation or another actually copes with social problems effectively. These methods, in other words, perpetuate decisions that may not promote law's basic goal—social cooperation. The next section describes a better way for judges to interpret statutes.

PURPOSE: THE KEY TO WISE STATUTORY INTERPRETATION

Statutory interpretation so frequently seems inadequate because judges face an unavoidable necessity. Judges must say what the law "is" in order to resolve the case before them. This is necessary because our society, our culture, believes that judges act unfairly when they do not decide on the basis of what the law says and is. Judges cannot hear a case and then refuse to

---

[30] Frankfurter, pp. 227–228.

[31] The eminent jurisprudent John Gray wrote, "The fact is that the difficulties of so-called interpretation arise when the Legislature has had no meaning at all; when the question which is raised on the statute never occurred to it. . . ." *The Nature and Sources of the Law* (New York: Macmillan, 1927), p. 173.

render a decision because they cannot determine the legal answer.[32] We do not pay judges to say, "Maybe the law is X. Maybe the law is Y. I'll guess Y. You lose!" (Or worse, "I don't care if it's X or Y. You still lose!") In order to render justice in our culture, judges must persuade us to believe with certainty that which is inherently uncertain.

Making the murky and muddled appear, within its own particular frame, *composed* (the *art* in judging and in everything else) is particularly difficult in statutory interpretation. In common law, the courts know that they have authority to make law. In these realms, judges can say, "The law ought to be X, not Y. Therefore the law is X." But legislative supremacy bars judges from interpreting statutes so boldly. They must try to make sense of the messy and often mysterious political processes in a legislature—processes in which the judges themselves did not participate. They must try to find the "oughts" somewhere in the legislative process, an uncertain and distant proceeding in which judges themselves play little part.

Judges will continue to make uncertain statutes certain in their application by creating and asserting that certainty can and does emerge from the generality, the vagueness, and the ambiguity in words, and from the disorderly world of politics. They can do so persuasively by identifying the *purpose* of the statute, the problem statutory language tries to solve.

The Centrality of Statutory Purpose

Judges should believe, almost as an article of faith, that words by themselves never possess a plain or clear or literal meaning. Statutes become meaningful only to the extent that their words fit some intelligible purpose. The problem the statute addresses always gives direction to the search for purpose. A dictionary never does.

Judges must satisfy themselves that their application of a statute to the case before them serves the statute's purpose. Sometimes a statute seems automatically to determine a case. We saw that this would occur if McBoyle had driven a stolen car across state lines rather than flying a plane. But judges must understand that no conclusion is totally automatic. We can imagine that a person could transport an automobile across state lines knowing the car to be stolen, and yet not violate the act: an FBI agent drives a recovered stolen car across a state line back to its owner, who happens to be the agent's mother. The agent does not violate the act, because he is not part of the problem the act tries to solve—he is part of the solution.

Let us explain this in a slightly different way. The questions people ask determine the answers they receive. A good answer to the wrong question should never satisfy a judge. In statutory interpretation, the right questions always begin with questions about statutory purpose: What social problems does this statute try to correct? Does the case before us in court now represent the problem the statute addresses? Think of the difference it can make in *Johnson* (the locomotive-coupling case) to ask (1) "Is a locomotive a railroad car?" versus (2) "Is protecting the safety of workers coupling locomotives to cars as well as cars to cars a sensible part of the problem this law tries to cope with?" Notice that whenever judges inquire into the purpose of the legislation, they must inevitably inquire into the social background facts in order to discover the nature of the social problems involved in the case and how the statute tries to cope with them.

To further illustrate purpose, consider an updated Mann Act. Suppose some imaginary international legislature passed a law making it a crime "to transport women or girls from one

---

[32] This is true of most formal legal systems. For example, the French Civil Code dating from 1804 states, "A judge who refuses to enter judgment on the pretext of silence, obscurity, or inadequacy of the statute is subject to prosecution for the denial of justice."

nation to another for purposes of prostitution, debauchery, or any other immoral purpose." In interpreting the purpose of such a statute, it would be entirely appropriate for courts to consider evidence that the monstrous trade in unwilling women, Representative Mann's original concern, persists to this day. Indeed, attention to the problem of international trafficking of girls and women in the sex trade has grown in recent years. National and international organizations are working to stop this trade, and Congress in 2003 passed legislation making it a crime for American citizens to travel abroad to engage in sex with children or to arrange such travel.[33] Our hypothetical law, an international Mann Act, would have to be interpreted in light of the problems it was designed to solve.

Determining Purpose: Words Can Help

It is the language of a statute that alone has the force of law. Nothing else that individual legislators and legislative bodies say and do legally binds a judge. Some legislation includes specific definitions of key words. These definitions in statutes may or may not agree with a dictionary definition, but they are law, and they bind the judge. Legislation, though lacking an internal dictionary, always contains words whose ordinary definitions unambiguously shape its purpose. By including the word "prostitution," the Mann Act unambiguously covers more than white slavery because by no ordinary definition are prostitutes necessarily any more "enslaved" in that occupation than is any worker in a dirty and dangerous job. Judges must never give words a meaning that the words, in their context, cannot bear. Except for its euphemistic title, the "White Slave Act" contains not one word to indicate that the women whose transportation it forbids must be "slaves" or, for that matter, "white." It is in this context that the word "prostitution" unambiguously shapes the Mann Act's meaning.

Context is always crucial. Some contexts require courts to decide precisely the opposite of the literal command of words. If, through some printing error, the officially published version of a statute omits a key word, judges properly include the word if the context makes such a purpose clear. Suppose that a statute prohibiting some very undesirable behavior omits in its official version the key prohibitory word "not." Although the statute would then literally permit or even require the unwarranted behavior, judges may apply the statute as if it contained the missing and critical *not*.

Canons of interpretation may help reassure judges that a given word, phrase, or sentence has a certain meaning in a specific context. They may serve as shorthand reminders of ways of thinking about purpose. But a canon should never dictate to a judge that words must have only one meaning regardless of context. The canons of *ejusdem generis* and narrow construction in criminal law may help a judge exclude airplanes and obscene records from the reach of those two statutes, but they do not compel that conclusion, as the next section illustrates.

Noscitur a sociis—it is known by its associates—can also help a judge think more clearly about statutory purpose. The context of neighboring words may crystallize the meaning of an ambiguous phrase. What, for example, is "indecent conduct"? In the abstract, we might agree that it depends on individual perceptions and moralities, and that we can't really tell what it is. But consider two statutes, one that prohibits "indecent conduct at a divine service of worship" and another that prohibits "indecent conduct at a public beach or bathing place." The contexts of worship and beach could both classify having sex in public as indecent conduct, but only one context would classify playing a game of beach volleyball in string bikinis as indecent.

---

[33] Blaine Harden, "Veteran Indicted on Sex Charges," *Washington Post*, September 25, 2003, p. A5; Barbara Ehrenreich and Arlie Russell Hochschild, eds, *Global Women: Nannies, Maids, and Sex Workers in the New Economy* (New York: Metropolitan Books, 2003).

Let us put this even more strongly. In life, as in law, things don't exist "in the abstract." In the abstract, there is no such objective thing as "indecent conduct." We might, trying to pick an extreme and hence conclusive example, say that cannibalism is automatically indecent conduct. But when the survivors of a plane crash high in the Andes consume the flesh of the dead in the hope of staying alive, does not the specific context, the specter of imminent death by starvation, change our feelings drastically about the "indecency" of cannibalism?

Determining Purpose: The Audience

Legislatures direct different statutes to different kinds of audiences. Some statutes, especially criminal statutes, communicate to the community at large. Criminal statutes thus have the purpose of communicating general standards of conduct to large populations containing people of widely varying degrees of literacy and local customs and habits. Judges properly interpret such words according to the common meanings they may expect these words to convey to this diverse population. Other perhaps highly technical laws may communicate only to special classes of people, such as radio and television stations or insurance underwriters. Here the words may assume technical meanings that only the special audience understands. Similarly, judges should hold that a statute purposely changes a long-held principle of common law or the legality of a behavior widely believed proper in the past only when they think a statute makes that purpose unambiguously clear.

Determining Purpose: The Assumption of Legislative Rationality and the Uses of Legislative History

In determining whether an issue in a lawsuit is part of the problem that a statute purposely tries to address, judges should treat the people who make laws and the process of lawmaking as rational and sensible, "reasonable persons pursuing reasonable purposes reasonably," as Hart and Sacks put it.[34] This assumption helps judges determine purpose because it forces them to determine what portion of the law, prior to the enactment of the statute, worked so poorly that a rational legislature wanted to change it.[35] Again, think about how the result in the locomotive-coupling case would differ if the court had approached the problem this way. Isn't the purpose to allow injured railroad workers to recover compensation for their on-the-job losses? Finally, what purposes would a rational legislator have for inserting the "good moral character" test in our naturalization laws? Is such a purpose well served by making moral judgments about incest or mercy killing in the abstract? (See the "Illustrative Case" section in Chapter 2.)

The judge who thinks about lawmaking as a reasonable process also recognizes that no statute exists in isolation, for rational lawmakers understand that no one act can completely define where its policy stops and another competing policy ought, instead, to govern. Members of Congress realize that state law, not federal law, assumes the major responsibility for defining and policing criminal behavior, an issue that the illustrative case at the end of this chapter squarely confronts. Knowing that state laws purposely define and prohibit sexual immorality limited the purpose the Court attributed to the Mann Act in *Mortensen* (described in Chapter 2).

---

[34] Henry M. Hart and Albert M. Sacks, *The Legal Process* (Cambridge: Harvard Law School, 1958), p. 1415.

[35] Lord Coke originated this helpful approach, sometimes labeled the mischief rule, in 1584.

Sometimes, as we have seen, no helpful legislative history exists at all. But at other times, courts can generate sensible conclusions about the purpose of statutes from the statements of legislative committees, sponsors of the bill, and so forth. This history may allow a judge to understand what aspects or consequences of prior law failed to cope with a social problem so that the legislature needed to create a new law. Legislative history may also clarify where one policy should give way to another. Legislative history relating to specific applications of the statute, as in the loose-leaf notebook case, helps the judge only to the extent that it provides good evidence of the legislation's general purpose.

Illustrations of Statutory Purpose

Two Easy Cases

You should now have little difficulty resolving some of this chapter's cases. Despite the ambiguities in the statutory language, you should not hesitate (1) to allow the officer to collect the breath specimen from a driver standing on the shoulder of the road, not while the driver weaves down the highway, and (2) to prohibit the liquor store from reopening at 10:01 (see footnote 12). The words don't require these conclusions, and judges probably lack any legislative history for these state and local laws, but judges can still reach sensible results. Notice, by the way, how the solution to both of these cases hinges on the judge's realistic assessment of the social background facts and widespread public values that bear on these cases, not merely on the rules and case facts alone.

Of course, other cases could arise under these same statutes in which the words themselves would not bear the interpretation claimed for them. Our officer cannot collect breath specimens in parking lots and driveways outside cocktail parties at midnight, even if he safely assumes that many will soon drive home and even if we believe it a highly wise social policy to prevent intoxicated drivers from driving in the first place. This action might be an effective preventive, but it is not found in the meaning and purpose of this law because the words make "driving" a prerequisite for demanding the specimen.

The Case of the Lady Jurors, or Why Legislative Intent Does Not Determine Statutory Purpose

Recall briefly Chief Justice Rugg's justification for excluding women from jury liability despite the fact that they could vote and despite the fact that the statute required jury duty of "persons" (not "men") qualified to vote. The legislature did not intend *person* to include females, because females could not then vote, Rugg said.

Like the case of the automatic couplers, *Welosky* offers a classic example of a judge reaching the right answer to the wrong question. Of course the legislature did not intend to include women, but that doesn't answer the right question. The proper question is, "What purpose is served by legislation that ties jury service to voter eligibility?"

Efficiency is one possible answer, because this policy spares the legislature from repeatedly rehashing the question of who should sit on juries. Quality is another, for this policy provides a test of qualifications that will ensure at least the same minimum degree of responsibility, competence, education, and permanence of residence for both jurors and voters. Both voting and jury duty are general civic functions of citizens, but gearing the right to practice medicine, for instance, to voting eligibility would not make much sense. Does it serve a purpose, however, to pass a statute saying, in effect, the following? "If you are qualified to vote, you are qualified to serve as a juror; however, any changes in voter eligibility hereafter enacted won't count because we haven't thought of them yet." If the legislation had this purpose, why didn't it simply list the desirable qualifications for jurors? Read the statute as Rugg did and the gearing loses purpose. Rugg did not treat the policy process as rational and sensible. He did not admit that juror qualifications could have been purposely designed to change with the times.

The difference between a search for legislative intent and a search for purpose, then, is the difference in the evidence judges seek. Judges who believe they must show intent will examine reports, speeches, and prior drafts of bills. This evidence probably won't give clear meaning to the statute, because it will contain internal inconsistencies or raise issues only in general terms. Moreover, judges who think they must find intent can fool themselves into believing that they have found it in the evidence. Judges who feel they must articulate a sensible statement of purpose, however, will necessarily search much further into dictionaries, canons, verbal contexts, and competing social policies as well as history itself. They will coordinate the materials in order to reach a confident articulation of purpose. They will perform the judicial function as Benjamin Cardozo described it (see the epigraph that opens this book). They will work harder than will judges who stop when they have found a nugget of legislative history, which is why so many judges, possessing the all-too-human tendency to laziness, are satisfied with the nugget.

Statutory Purpose in the Cases of Criminal Commerce: Caminetti, McBoyle, and Alpers

In each of these three cases, Congress, under the authority of the Commerce Clause of the U.S. Constitution, forbade citizens from moving what Congress deemed evil from one state to another. Let us assume that every state had laws to deal with each of the evil things—statutes punishing theft, prostitution, and pornography. What purpose, then, does additional *federal* legislation on these matters serve? For each of the federal statutes, we possess records of committee reports, floor speeches, and other legislative history. In no case, however, does the solid data of legislative history reveal whether the purpose of the statute does or does not include the cases of our defendants. After a delightfully detailed review of the House and Senate reports on the Mann Act and of the discussions reported in the *Congressional Record*—showing, if not total confusion about the act, at least much disagreement about its specific meaning—Levi concludes, "The Mann Act was passed after there had been many extensive governmental investigations. Yet there was no common understanding of the facts, and whatever understanding seems to have been achieved concerning the white-slave trade seems incorrectly based. The words used were broad and ambiguous."[36]

These cases resemble each other not only in their constitutional origins but also because the canons of construction could resolve each of them. The canon dictating narrow construction of criminal statutes could allow a judge to reverse the three convictions, because the law does not unambiguously apply to any of these special factual situations. A judge who adopted Holmes's belief that criminal laws must communicate to a general lay audience with a clarity the average man can understand would reach the same result. Following *ejusdem generis* ("of the same kind"), however, Mr. Caminetti, who took his girlfriend to Reno, might go to jail, but McBoyle, the airplane thief, and Alpers, the seller of obscene records, would still go free.

Despite these similarities, these cases do not come out this way. The smut peddler and the boyfriend went to jail. McBoyle went free. The three judicial opinions together articulate no coherent linkages between purposes and outcomes. To link purposes and outcomes, we must begin with the right question: Why would Congress, "reasonable persons pursuing

---

[36] Levi, p. 40, and see pp. 33–40.

reasonable purposes reasonably," pass laws making actions crimes when all the states already have, through their criminal laws, punished these same evils? Does not the purpose lie in the fact that movement from state to state makes it difficult for the states to detect or enforce the violation? A car owner who has his car stolen may have trouble tracking it in another state. The prosecutor in the state where citizens receive wanted or unwanted pornography cannot reach the man who peddles by mail from another state. Men who hustle girls far from home may make both detection and social pressure to resist prostitution impossible. Movement has consequences. It makes objects and behaviors physically harder to locate. It makes apprehension and prosecution more difficult, because police and prosecutors in one jurisdiction don't have authority in another. The presence of physical movement thus helps to reveal purpose.

In *McBoyle,* then, the proper questions ought to look something like this: (1) Do airplanes, because they are movable, complicate the task of catching the people who steal them? (2) Does it, secondarily, serve any purpose to assume that McBoyle thought flying a stolen airplane to another state was legal because of the ambiguities in the word "vehicle"? Is it, in other words, unfair to McBoyle to convict him under this act because the act does not unambiguously include airplanes? You should reach your own conclusion, but we would answer the first question with a yes, the second with a no, and respectfully dissent from Justice Holmes.

You should ask one other question about *McBoyle.* Suppose McBoyle's lawyer had argued that when the National Motor Vehicle Theft Act was passed, air travel was in such infancy that Congress probably did not intend to include airplanes. Notice that this argument should matter to you only if you think it important to ask what Congress intended. If you instead consider legislation as policy designed to adjust to future technological and other changes that lawmakers cannot in the present foresee, and if you ask instead what kind of crimes call for the kind of law enforcement help that this act provides, you would find McBoyle's lawyer's legislative intent argument trivial.

Is *Alpers* any different? It might be, particularly if you see the case as presenting a constitutional problem of free expression. The purpose of this statute might be said to be to prevent exposing children or unwilling people, people who open mail or see magazines left around, to visual pornography. Is this purpose served by prohibiting the shipment of obscene records?

Alpers is an especially difficult case. Unlike Mr. McBoyle, Mr. Alpers could reasonably have interpreted the act as not banning records for two reasons. First, the competing principle of free expression does set limits on government interference with the communication of ideas. No such principle limits governmental interference with the movement of property known to be stolen. Second, the purpose of the National Motor Vehicle Theft Act specifically seems to apply to airplanes. They are very transportable. The act's purpose may therefore especially apply to airplanes. However, one reading of the purpose of the statute in *Alpers*—visual pornography left around may offend, while a phonograph record lying around does not— reduces its applicability to *Alpers.* But, although it reduces it, it doesn't eliminate it. The recipient might play the offensive record for an unwilling person. However, would not the *McBoyle* precedent provide a strong argument for excusing Alpers? Isn't transporting stolen property at least as morally ambiguous as pornography? If Mr. McBoyle went free, why not Mr. Alpers?

Finally, consider the man who brings in a willing girlfriend from out of state for a night or for the big-game weekend. Conceivably, the Mann Act could purposely try to police all forms of sexual immorality involving, somehow, interstate transportation. But what are the probabilities that this legislation has such purpose in light of (1) the title of the act; (2) the canons of narrow construction of, and clear communication in, criminal statutes;

(3) the problem arousing public concern at the time; (4) the fact that states are just as able, if they so choose, to discover and crack down on noncommercial illegal sex as the FBI; (5) Representative Mann's report and the widespread belief that the general police powers reside in state and not federal hands?

Notice how it is only by weaving together many different techniques of interpretation that we begin to develop confidence about the purpose of the Mann Act.

A Final Complication

This summary of sensible judicial approaches to statutes may have misled you in one critical respect. You may now feel that in every case, the "right-thinking" judge will find the one "right" solution simply by uncovering a single purpose of the statute. This chapter's illustrations all make sense when we analyze them in terms of purpose. *We may, however, still honestly disagree about purpose.* The task of judging is choosing among plausible alternative possibilities, not solving an algebra problem. A purpose-oriented approach does not eliminate judicial discretion in statutory interpretation. Judges who thoughtfully and diligently consider legislative purpose may nonetheless disagree about the resolution of a specific case.

To illustrate, suppose Holmes had said in *McBoyle*:

> The purpose of this act is to permit federal assistance to states in finding easily moved and hidden vehicles. But airplanes, while easily moved, are really like trains, which the act expressly excludes, because, like trains, they are tied to places where they cannot be hidden—airports. What goes up must come down, and only in certain places. One black Ford may look like a thousand other black Fords almost anywhere, but an airplane is much more like a train in this respect. Therefore, since we believe states, not the federal government, possess primary police powers, this act does not cover airplanes.

Finally, suppose in the cemetery case Justice Gregory argued:

> Establishment and expansion of cemeteries differ because the people near an expanded cemetery are already used to its presence, but to create a new cemetery in a place where residents had not planned on seeing funeral processions and graves and other unwanted reminders of life's transience is another matter.

Whether we agree or disagree with these analyses, at least they rest on purpose. We should prefer them to the automatic citation of a canon, a quotation from a dictionary, or to any technique of interpretation that allows judges to evade the difficult task of determining statutory purpose.

STARE DECISIS IN STATUTORY INTERPRETATION

We have thus far studied an atypical occurrence in statutory interpretation, interpretation in the first instance. This may have puzzled you, for in the previous chapters we have seen that reasoning by example—using precedents as guides for resolving legal conflicts—is central to legal reasoning. So far, however, in this chapter we have not mentioned reasoning by example at all. In the interpretation of statutes in the first instance, courts by definition have no precedents with which to work. In this chapter, we have examined some methods for interpreting statutes in the first instance, but these methods do not resolve the more typical problem: Once a court has given direction and meaning to a statute by interpreting it in the first instance, when should courts in the future follow that interpretation? When, conversely, should courts prefer a different interpretation and ignore or overrule an earlier court's first effort to make sense of the statute's meaning?

Let us make this point more sharply. Assume that the *McBoyle* decision wrongly interpreted the National Motor Vehicle Theft Act because its purpose does cover the theft of airplanes. Or assume that *Caminetti* wrongly applied the Mann Act to include the transportation of girlfriends. Should a court facing a new airplane or girlfriend case feel bound to accept that interpretation? Once a precedent or series of precedents gives a clear answer on a point of law, should courts leave it to legislatures to change that questionable interpretation by statutory amendment? In what circumstances should judges adhere to stare decisis in statutory interpretation?

It might seem sensible, and indeed it *is* sensible, to answer these questions by referring to the justifications for stare decisis that appear near the end of Chapter 2. When adherence to a prior interpretation or series of cases interpreting a statute promotes stability in law, and this stability in turn allows citizens to plan their affairs by relying on specific legal rules—in short, when stability promotes the paramount social goal of cooperation—courts should not abandon stare decisis. Similarly, if a citizen now deserves to receive the same treatment a citizen in a precedent did, or if we feel stare decisis would preserve efficient judicial administration or a positive public image of justice, then courts should honor it. When stare decisis does not promote these goals, courts should freely ignore it. Thus, assuming a court felt that both *McBoyle* and *Caminetti* were wrongly decided, normal stare decisis theory would permit overruling *Caminetti* but not *McBoyle*. It injures no citizen to declare that something once held criminal is no longer so, but it does seem unfair to convict someone after declaring that his actions were not crimes.[37]

Unfortunately, some judges and legal scholars believe that judges should invariably follow the first judicial attempt to find statutory meaning even when they have doubts about the wisdom of the first attempt and, worse, when the characteristics of the problem do not call for stare decisis. We shall first review an example of this "one-shot theory" of statutory interpretation in action.[38] Then we shall evaluate its shortcomings. We shall see that, in part, it fails because it is based on myths about how legislatures operate. We shall also see in this example considerable judicial ignorance about the purposes of stare decisis.

Major League Baseball, Haviland's Dog and Pony Show, and Government Regulation of Business

The power of the federal government to regulate business derives from the constitutional clause empowering Congress to make laws that regulate commerce "among the several states." Armed with this authority, Congress has passed many statutes regulating wages,

---

[37] This very problem arose in the case of Richard Reid, the notorious mid-air "shoe bomber." Count 9 of his indictment charged him with attempting to "wreck, set fire to, and disable a mass transportation vehicle," USA PATRIOT ACT, 18 U.S.C. 1993 © (5). On June 11, 2002, the district court dismissed this count on the ground that a long history of judicial and statutory usage since *McBoyle* has distinguished between "aircraft," "vessels," and "vehicles," and that the plane that Reid tried to blow up in flight was an aircraft and therefore not a vehicle. *U.S. v. Reid*, 206 F.Supp. 2d 132 (MA. District Court, 2002). Reid eventually pled guilty to other charges in the indictment.

[38] William Eskridge calls the theory "the super-strong presumption against overruling statutory precedents." "Overruling Statutory Precedents," 76 *Georgetown Law Journal* 1361 at 1363 (1988). Eskridge's very thorough analysis agrees in nearly all respects with the position we take in this chapter. Calling the notion "a very odd doctrine," he analyzes cases from 1961 to 1987 and finds that "in only twenty-six instances (or one per term) has the Court explicitly repudiated both the reasoning and the result of a statutory precedent." (1368) He concurs with Justice Scalia's statement that "vindication by Congressional inaction is a canard." (1405n)

hours of work, safety and health standards, and other aspects of business. Such laws apply not only to businesses and businesspersons that physically cross state lines or transact business among states. They also apply to businesses operating within one state entirely, on the theory that these businesses nevertheless may compete with and affect businesses operating from other states.[39] Modern economic and political theory also suggests that the collective health of small businesses and of the work force can and does affect the national welfare.

Among the many such statutes regulating business, we shall consider only two. The more substantial of the two, the federal antitrust laws, responded to the huge cartels and monopolies that emerged in the nineteenth century by prohibiting certain activities that restrain competition in business. They authorize criminal and civil proceedings by government and by citizens privately when they feel they are damaged by anticompetitive business practices, for example, Microsoft's "bundling" of its Internet software to its Windows operating system.

The Animal Welfare Act of 1970, our second statutory example, specifies a variety of requirements for handling animals in a humane manner.[40] The statute requires "exhibitors" of animals "purchased in commerce or the intended distribution of which affects commerce or will affect commerce" to obtain an exhibitor's license. The statute explicitly includes carnivals, circuses, and zoos. It empowers the Agriculture Department to administer its regulatory provisions.

Within the context of these two statutes, we shall now observe a truly wondrous phenomenon in contemporary law. Within the past half century, courts have held: (1) that the multimillion-dollar industry of professional baseball, with all its national commercial television coverage and travel from state to state and to foreign countries, is *not* a business in interstate commerce such that the antitrust laws govern the owners of baseball clubs; and (2) that "Haviland's Dog and Pony Show," consisting of a maximum of two ponies and five dogs traveling the rural byways of the American Midwest and earning a handful of dollars weekly, is a business in interstate commerce that must therefore meet the requirements of the Animal Welfare Act.[41]

We need say little more about the *Haviland* case. Haviland refused to obtain a federally required exhibitor's license. The court held that he was wrong to refuse. Given the current legal definition of commerce, the interpretation is entirely defensible constitutionally. This interpretation and result also make sense in terms of the presumed purpose of the statute. Owners of dog-and-pony shows, we can assume, are no less likely to abuse their animals than is the staff of the San Diego Zoo; rather more likely, we would bet.

But why don't antitrust statutes regulate major league baseball? Rigid adherence to stare decisis in statutory interpretation provides the answer, as the following chronology of decisions illustrates.

1922   The "Federal Baseball Club of Baltimore," a member of a short-lived third major league, sued the National and American Leagues claiming that the two leagues had, in violation of the antitrust laws, bought out some Federal League clubs and induced other owners not to join the league at all. The Baltimore franchise found itself frozen out and sued to recover the financial losses caused by the anticompetitive practices of the other leagues. The case reached the U.S. Supreme Court, where Justice Holmes's opinion held that the essence of baseball, playing games,

---

[39] *United States v. Darby Lumber,* 312 U.S. 100 (1941), and *Wickard v. Filburn,* 317 U.S. 111 (1942).
[40] 15 U.S.C. 1 et seq. and 7 U.S.C. 2131 et seq.
[41] *Flood v. Kuhn,* 407 U.S. 258 (1972); *Haviland v. Butz,* 543 F.2d 169 (D.C. Circuit 1976).

did not involve interstate commerce. The travel from city to city by the teams, Holmes thought, was so incidental that it did not bring baseball within the scope of the act. Thus, without reaching the question whether the defendants did behave anticompetitively within the meaning of the statute, Holmes ruled that the act did not apply to professional baseball any more than it would apply to a Chautauqua lecturer traveling the circuit.[42]

Comment: We should not hastily condemn Holmes's reasoning. His opinion pre-dated by nearly 20 years the major enlargement of the Congress' commerce power that came in *U.S. v. Darby Lumber* and *Wickard v. Filburn,* so we cannot blame him for an antiquated definition. Also, to his credit, Holmes did not try to discover whether Congress intended to include baseball within the scope of the antitrust laws. There is nothing in the opinion that stamps its results with indelibility, nothing that says if the commercial character of baseball changes, baseball club owners would nevertheless remain free to behave monopolistically. For its time, *Federal Baseball* rested on defensible if not indisputable reasoning.

1923   Justice Holmes addressed the applicability of the antitrust laws in the field of public entertainment. In this case, the plaintiff, a Mr. Hart, acted as a booking agent and manager for a variety of actors. He specialized in negotiating contracts between vaudeville performers, on one hand, and large theater chains sponsoring vaudeville shows on the other. Hart sued the Keith Circuit, the Orpheum Circuit, and other theatrical chains, claiming that, in violation of the antitrust laws, they colluded to prevent any of his actors from obtaining contracts in their theaters unless Hart granted them what we would today call *kickbacks.* Holmes noted that some of these contracts called for the transportation of performers, scenery, music, and costumes. Distinguishing *Federal Baseball,* he held that "in the transportation of vaudeville acts the apparatus sometimes is more important than the performers and . . . the defendant's conduct is within the [antitrust] statute to that extent at least."[43]

Comment: Note fact freedom at work here. Holmes does not, despite vaudeville's obvious resemblance to baseball, find that the two are factually similar enough to govern vaudeville by baseball's precedent. There was, he said, a difference. Some of the disputed contracts did involve transportation itself. Holmes could have chosen to follow the previous year's precedent. The travel is still incidental to local performance of either baseball or vaudeville.

1948   Blacklisted by the major league owners because he had once chosen to play in Mexico rather than for the major leagues, an outfielder named Danny Gardella sued. The Second Circuit Court of Appeals ruled that, in part due to increased radio and television revenues, baseball was interstate commerce and subject to the Sherman Act. The court also called the major league's treatment of the players a "shockingly repugnant" form of slavery, outlawed by the Thirteenth Amendment after the Civil War.[44]

---

[42] *Federal Baseball Club of Baltimore v. National League of Professional Baseball Clubs,* 259 U.S. 200 (1922).

[43] *Hart v. B. F. Keith Vaudeville Exchange,* 262 U.S. 271 (1923), 273.

[44] See Andrew Zimbalist, *Baseball and Billions* (New York: Basic Books, 1992), p. 13. See also Stephen Jay Gould's "Dreams That Money Can Buy," *New York Review of Books,* November 5, 1992, pp. 41–45.

Question: Do you believe by now—since the business aspects of baseball had changed, since the constitutional basis for *Federal Baseball* had evaporated, and since an appellate court had ruled that the antitrust laws now govern baseball—that the baseball owners had *any* reason to rely on the *Federal Baseball* precedent?

1953   Baseball again, and once again an attempt to allege violation of the antitrust laws. The violation took the form of the well-publicized "reserve clause," or so players claimed. The players contended that the clause prevented open competition for better salaries. In *Toolson v. New York Yankees,* the Supreme Court ruled in an unsigned (*per curiam*) opinion that baseball still did not fall under the coverage of the antitrust laws. It so held despite the efforts of Justices Burton and Reed, who dissented, to marshal extensive evidence of baseball's dramatic growth since 1922. The majority opinion stated:

> Congress has had the [*Federal Baseball*] ruling under consideration but has not seen fit to bring such business under these laws by legislation having prospective effect. The business has thus been left for thirty years to develop, on the understanding that it was not subject to existing antitrust legislation. The present cases ask us to overrule the prior decision and, with retrospective effect, hold the legislation applicable. . . . Without reexamination of the underlying issues, the judgments below are affirmed on the authority of *Federal Baseball* . . . so far as that decision determines that Congress had no intention of including the business of baseball within the scope of the federal antitrust laws.[45]

Questions: Did Justice Holmes conclude in 1922 that "Congress had no intention of including the business of baseball within the scope of the federal antitrust laws"? Do you believe that because Congress has not legislated on the subject of baseball and the antitrust laws professional baseball does not fall within the act? Remember that not only had baseball become more businesslike since 1922 but the definition of commerce had also changed so that travel or movement from state to state did not have to be an essential part of a business's activities in order to put it under the act. Why is it necessary to follow the 1922 precedent? Why could not the *Toolson* opinion simply say that both the law and the sport have changed and the owners have no justified expectation to rely on an outdated judicial ruling? Do you think, in other words, that because in 1922 the Court told the established leagues they could try to prevent the formation of a third league, they therefore rightly planned in 1953 to deal with their players by contracts that prevented free competition in that business?

1955   In *United States v. Shubert,* Chief Justice Warren, speaking for the Supreme Court, upheld the government's claim that theater owners who monopolized the booking of theater attractions violated the antitrust laws.[46] The Court acknowledged *Hart,* though only in passing. It refused to follow *Toolson,* calling it "a narrow application of the rule of *stare decisis.*"

Question: One of our five principle reasons for stare decisis is to promote equality. On what basis should the law treat actors and baseball players unequally, as this case concludes the law must?

---

[45] *Toolson v. New York Yankees,* 346 U.S. 356 (1953).
[46] *United States v. Shubert,* 348 U.S. 222 (1955).

Chief Justice Warren, in a companion case to *Shubert,* held that professional boxing did fall within the scope of antitrust laws.[47] He distinguished *Toolson* for the same reasons he gave in *Shubert.*

Questions: How equally do you think baseball players felt the courts applied the law in 1955? If you had managed the Boxing Club, would you have relied on the *Toolson* decision? Would you think of boxing as any more a business than baseball? Would the new boxing decision possibly surprise you?

1957   In *Radovich v. National Football League,* the lower appellate court, mystified by the distinction between baseball and boxing that the Supreme Court had created, decided that football did not fall under the antitrust laws because football, like baseball but unlike boxing, was a team sport. The Supreme Court reversed.[48]

Comment: "A foolish consistency is the hobgoblin of little minds, adored by little statesmen . . ."—Ralph Waldo Emerson

1971   The Supreme Court held that the antitrust laws did govern professional basketball.[49]

Question: By now do you think the Court could safely overrule *Federal Baseball?*

1972   Fifty years after *Federal Baseball,* Curt Flood's challenge to the reserve clause reached the Supreme Court. After a panegyrical review of baseball's history, replete with references to Thayer's "Casey at the Bat" and a long and curious list of baseball's greats (the list includes such immortals as Three-Finger Brown and Hans Lobert but omits Stan Musial, Joe DiMaggio, Ted Williams, and Hank Aaron), Justice Blackmun refused to abandon *Toolson* or stare decisis. Flood lost. Blackmun wrote:

> [W]e adhere once again to *Federal Baseball* and *Toolson* and to their application to professional baseball. We adhere also to *International Boxing* and *Radovich* and to their respective applications to professional boxing and professional football. If there is any inconsistency or illogic in all this, it is an inconsistency and illogic of long-standing that is to be remedied by the Congress and not by this Court. If we were to act otherwise, we would be withdrawing from the conclusion as to congressional intent made in *Toolson* and from the concerns as to retrospectivity therein expressed. Under these circumstances, there is merit in consistency even though some might claim that beneath that consistency is a layer of inconsistency.[50]

Justice Douglas dissented. He wrote, "The unbroken silence of Congress should not prevent us from correcting our own mistakes."[51]

---

[47] *United States v. International Boxing Club of New York, Inc.,* 348 U.S. 236 (1955).

[48] *Radovich v. National Football League,* 352 U.S. 445 (1957).

[49] *Heywood v. National Basketball Association,* 401 U.S. 1204 (1971).

[50] *Flood v. Kuhn,* 84.

[51] The mess created by these decisions will not go away. In 1996 the Court returned to them in *Brown v. Washington Redskins,* 518 U.S. 231 (1996). See particularly Justice Stevens's dissent, in which he cites *Federal Baseball, Toolson, Radovich,* and *Flood.* The lawsuit alleged that the National Football League's unilateral arrangement to pay "taxi squad" members a flat rate of $1,000 per week violated the Sherman Antitrust Act.

Not to leave the story hanging, in 1998, Congress enacted the Curt Flood Act. (Curt Flood, alas, had died the previous year.) The Act's second section, entitled "Purpose," reads:

> It is the purpose of this legislation to state that major league baseball players are covered under the antitrust laws (i.e., that major league baseball players will have the same rights under the antitrust laws as do other professional athletes, e.g., football and basketball players), along with a provision that makes it clear that the passage of this Act does not change the application of the antitrust laws in any other context or with respect to any other person or entity.

The major league baseball owners and the players union jointly lobbied Congress for passage of this bill. Hidden in its language is this provision, which exempts all other aspects of professional baseball from antitrust laws. The statute thus protects the minor league reserve clause, issues of baseball expansion or contraction and franchise relocation, and other targets of monopolistic opportunity.[52]

What went wrong here? In the immediate case of sports and the antitrust laws, *Toolson's* utterly inaccurate insistence that *Federal Baseball* means that Congress did not intend to include baseball wreaked the most havoc. *Toolson*, to paraphrase, says, "The highest law-making body in the country, Congress, has determined that the antitrust laws should not apply to professional baseball. Therefore the owners of baseball teams have made many business arrangements in reliance on this state of the law. It would be wrong to upset these expectations legitimized by the intent of Congress." This position is pure nonsense. Congress did not intend to exclude baseball. Holmes in *Federal Baseball* never said Congress so intended. As our questions at the end of the *Toolson* excerpt imply, the baseball owners had no reason to rely on *Federal Baseball,* at least not in 1953, given intervening precedents. Stability and reliance do not in this instance require the Court to invoke stare decisis and follow *Federal Baseball*. *Toolson* reached that different result by merely saying, without supporting evidence, that Congress, in its silence, so commanded.

Unfortunately, the Supreme Court's reasoning in these cases is worse than that. At least, you might say, baseball owners probably did honestly believe that they had a good chance of escaping the antitrust laws and acted on that basis. There is some merit in the reliance argument. But if stare decisis seeks to assist people to make plans in reliance on stable law, then surely owners of football, basketball, and boxing franchises and athletes had every bit as much reason for relying on *Federal Baseball* or *Toolson* as did the baseball owners. After all, in terms of the antitrust law, there is no difference among these sports that ought to induce baseball owners to rely on the original precedent while preventing those in the other sports from doing so.

In the name of stare decisis, then, we have a series of decisions that hardly seems stable, that violates reliance expectations to the extent that there are any, and that does not treat equals equally. To complete the list of justifications for adhering to precedent, do these decisions strike you as efficient judicial administration? What image of justice do these cases flash in your mind? Crazy, perhaps?

Fortunately, we have deliberately chosen an extreme example. Faced with statutory precedents, courts do not invariably invoke stare decisis in order to wreak havoc on the very justifications for stare decisis. Nevertheless, this critical question remains: *If* a judge feels

---

[52] See http://roadsidephotos.com/baseball/curtflood.htm. See also Doug Pappas, "Time to Repeal All of Baseball's Antitrust Exemption," *Boston Baseball* (August 1998).

that an existing judicial interpretation of a statute is erroneous, and *if* the judge also feels that he may overrule it without doing violence to the five justifications of stare decisis, do *any* aspects of the court's relationship to the legislature nevertheless compel adherence to the questionable interpretation? We believe the proper answer to this question is no. However, on two analytical levels, judges and legal scholars have at times reached a different conclusion. Let us review their reasons for the one-shot theory on both levels.

The Case against Increased Adherence to Precedent in Statutory Interpretation

The first, and more superficial, analytical level holds that the legislature may take certain actions that compel the courts to adhere to precedent. In *Toolson,* for example, the Supreme Court seemed to say that since Congress had not passed a statute to cover baseball by the antitrust laws, Congress had somehow converted *Federal Baseball* into statutory law. Would any of the following events in Congress, or in any legislature, strengthen such a conclusion?

■ Many bills were introduced to cover baseball, but none of them passed.

■ Many bills were introduced to exempt baseball, but none of them passed.

■ Congress reenacted the relevant antitrust provisions, with some modifications, none of which attempted to cover or exempt baseball specifically.

■ Congress passed a statute explicitly placing, say, professional boxing prior to 1955, under the antitrust laws, and the statute makes no mention of baseball's status.

■ Congress passed a joint resolution that officially states that baseball is hereinafter to be considered "The National Pastime of the United States."

Judges often buttress their adherence to precedents on such grounds, but these grounds are insufficient. Congress possesses no power to make law other than by passing statutes. Statutes are, among other items, subject to presidential veto power. Not even joint resolutions, which escape presidential veto, therefore create law. To say that any of the legislative acts we just listed create law is to give Congress a lawmaking power not found in the Constitution.

Furthermore, consider these reasons that a legislature might not, in fact, directly respond to a judicial interpretation by law.[53]

■ Legislators never learn of the judicial interpretation in the first place.

■ Legislators don't care about the issue the interpretation raises.

■ Legislators care but feel they must spend their limited time and political resources on other more important matters.

■ Legislators like the proposed new statute or amendment but feel it politically unwise to vote for it.

■ Legislators decide to vote against the bill because they do not like another unrelated provision of the bill.

■ Legislators feel the bill does not go far enough and vote against it in hopes of promulgating more comprehensive law later.

---

[53] Hart and Sacks, pp. 1395–1396.

- Legislators don't like the bill's sponsor personally and therefore vote negatively.

- Legislators believe, in the words of Hart and Sacks, "that the matter should be left to be handled by the normal process of judicial development of decisional law, including the overruling of outstanding decisions to the extent that the sound growth of the law requires. . . ."[54]

Do not all these possibilities, especially the last, convince you that courts should not speculate about the meaning of a statutory interpretation by guessing at why the legislature didn't pass a law affecting the interpretation? Recent scholarship suggests the complexity of court–Congress interactions in statutory interpretation. Sometimes members of Congress are so outraged by a judicial decision that they immediately override it, but as John Barnes has found, there are many other possible scenarios: some overrides are matters of great controversy, with interest groups on both sides highly mobilized. Many others are quiet and consensual.[55] And most times, Congress, for a variety of reasons, does not override. Lawrence Baum and Lori Hausegger found in their study that from 1978 to 1989, Congress overrode only about 6 percent of the statutory decisions made by the Supreme Court.[56]

William Eskridge's study of 1967–1990 decisions found that most attempted overrides died in congressional committees. Eskridge coded the reasons Congress gave for overriding into such categories as bad interpretation, confusion in law, bad or outdated policy, and need to clarify law. If the courts were doing a consistently bad job of interpretation, we would expect "bad interpretation" to crop up frequently. If, on the other hand, Congress was doing a consistently bad job of writing statutes, we would expect other reasons, such as "bad policy" or "confusion," to crop up more frequently. Of the total of 311 congressional actions so coded (including overrides of lower court decisions and of multiple aspects of the same statute), only 40 actions (13 percent) cited bad or unfair interpretation as the reason. However, Eskridge lists bad or unfair policy as the reason for overriding in 240 of the 311 cases (77 percent). From this we might conclude that the courts faithfully implement a foolish policy six times more often than they interpret a statute poorly.[57]

The second analytical level is more complex. Sophisticated proponents of the one-shot theory of statutory interpretation admit that legislative silence is meaningless.[58] They worry instead about the proper apportionment of legislative and judicial responsibilities. Their argument goes this way: Legislatures deliberately use ambiguous language in statutes, not simply to bring many somewhat different specific events under one policy roof but also to allow room for the compromises necessary to generate a majority vote. Once written, the words of a statute will not change; but because they are general, vague, and ambiguous, courts will certainly have the opportunity to interpret those same words in many different ways.

---

[54] Ibid., p. 1396.

[55] John Barnes, *Overruled? Legislative Overrides, Pluralism and Contemporary Court-Congress Relations* (Palo Alto: Stanford University Press, 2004).

[56] Cited in Lawrence Baum and Lori Hausegger, "The Supreme Court and Congress: Reconsidering the Relationship," in *Putting the Pieces Together: Lawmaking from an Interbranch Perspective*, Mark Miller and John Barnes, eds. (Washington: Georgetown University Press, 2004).

[57] William Eskridge, Jr., "Overriding Supreme Court Statutory Interpretation Decisions," 101 *Yale Law Journal* 331 (1991). See more generally Eskridge's *Dynamic Statutory Interpretation* (Cambridge: Harvard University Press, 1994).

[58] See especially Levi, pp. 31–33.

If, the argument continues, words have different meanings at different times and places, the legislature's power to make law becomes pointless, or at least quite subordinated to judicial power of interpretation. Courts must find one meaning. They do so by determining legislative intent. The judiciary insults the legislature if it says that at one time the legislature intended the words to carry one meaning and at another time another meaning. To say this is to say of the legislature that it had no intent and that it did not understand its actions. That assertion would embarrass the legislature, to say the least.

The argument thus holds that part of the judicial responsibility to the legislature is to reinforce the concept that the legislature did in fact have a specific intention, because that is what the public expects of legislatures. In the first half of this chapter, we have revealed why this argument fails.

Fortunately, the argument does not stop there. Levi asserts:

> Legislatures and courts are cooperative law-making bodies. It is important to know where the responsibility lies. If legislation which is disfavored can be interpreted away from time to time, then it is not to be expected, particularly if controversy is high, that the legislature will ever act. It will always be possible to say that new legislation is not needed because the court in the future will make a more appropriate interpretation. If the court is to have freedom to reinterpret legislation, the result will be to relieve the legislature from pressure. The legislation needs judicial consistency. Moreover, the court's own behavior in the face of pressure is likely to be indecisive. In all likelihood it will do enough to prevent legislative revision and not much more. Therefore it seems better to say that once a decisive interpretation of legislative intent has been made, and in that sense a direction has been fixed within the gap of ambiguity, the court should take that direction as given. In this sense a court's interpretation of legislation is not dictum. The words it uses do more than decide the case. They give broad direction to the statute.[59]

Levi's argument cuts too deeply. Indeed, there are instances in which legislators breathe sighs of relief that courts have taken delicate political problems from them. (Curiously enough, courts most often do so by applying constitutional standards to legislation, and in this area, Levi does not demand similarly strict stare decisis.) But Levi's position is simply inaccurate in its assumption that most questions of interpretation raise highly charged public issues that legislatures ought to deal with, but won't if courts do it for them. For the most part, judicial errors in statutory interpretation involve borderline application of statutes. The interpretations may do considerable injustice to the parties who find themselves in borderline situations without, in any significant way, damaging the central purposes of the statutory policy as a whole. In the large majority of cases, then, it is wholly unrealistic to assume that either overruling or adherence will affect how legislators perform. Try to imagine, for example, how Congress would have reacted had the Supreme Court held in 1946 that the traveling bigamous Mormons did not violate the Mann Act. Probably with a yawn.[60]

---

[59] Ibid., p. 32.

[60] However, nearly three-quarters of a century after the *Caminetti* decision, Congress quietly rewrote the Mann Act with the Child Sexual Abuse and Pornography Act of 1986. The amendments eliminated the reference to white slavery, substituted *individual* for *female* and *woman or girl*, and instead of debauchery or immoral purpose, specified "any sexual activity for which any person can be charged with a criminal offense. . . ." New York Governor Elliott Spitzer was forced from office in March of 2008 after he admitted to liaisons with prostitutes who had traveled to New York from other states to tryst with him in part because he allegedly violated the Mann Act, though federal prosecutors ultimately decided not to prosecute him.

A SUMMARY STATEMENT OF THE APPROPRIATE JUDICIAL APPROACH TO STATUTORY INTERPRETATION

To conclude, notice how many of the problems that courts have created for themselves regarding the place of stare decisis in statutory interpretations would evaporate if only judges convinced themselves to seek the purpose of a statute and not to speculate about legislative intent from inconclusive legislative evidence. The inadequate conclusions that judges reach when they reason on the first and more superficial analytical level would disappear altogether. At the more sophisticated level, the concept that the courts embarrass legislatures by implying the rather obvious truth that the legislators probably had no intent regarding the precise issue before the court would also disappear. Is this truth so awful? Of course not. That statutes speak in general terms is a simple necessity in political life. Such generality explains and justifies the existence of courts.

Judges should follow precedents when one or more of the five justifications for stare decisis so dictate (see pp. 32–33). Their primary obligation to the legislature is to apply the statutes it creates so as to achieve, as best judges can determine it, the intelligible solution of problems the statute exists to solve. Judges should try to determine purpose accurately, but they will err from time to time. It is no embarrassment to the legislature for judges to admit that they erred in determining statutory purpose and in properly applying it to cases before them. They should therefore give stare decisis no special weight in statutory interpretation. They should do so with the confidence that, to the extent that they can predict legislative behavior at all, they can predict that the legislature is no less likely to correct them if they err today than if they erred yesterday. Of course, legislation needs judicial consistency. Affixing proper legislative responsibility will occur only when courts sensibly articulate statutory purposes.

ILLUSTRATIVE CASE

After a night of heavy drinking, Larry Begay first threatened his aunt and then his sister with an unloaded rifle. Begay's possession of the rifle violated federal statutory law because he was a convicted felon; he had been convicted a dozen times for driving under the influence (DUI), and under New Mexico law, the fourth and all succeeding DUI convictions are punishable as felonies. Ordinarily Begay would have received 10 years for possessing a gun, but a federal judge sentenced him under the Armed Career Criminal Act, which imposes a mandatory 15-year sentence on an offender who has had three prior convictions for a "violent felony or a serious drug offense."

The Act defines a "violent felony" as "any crime punishable by imprisonment for a term exceeding one year" that

(i) has as an element the use, attempted use, or threatened use of physical force against the person of another; or

(ii) is burglary, arson, or extortion, involves use of explosives, or otherwise involves conduct that presents a serious potential risk of physical injury to another.

Begay appealed his sentence, arguing that his DUI convictions did not fall under either of the two specified descriptions of a "violent felony."

Begay v. United States 553 U.S. _____ (2008)

(routine citations omitted)

Justice Breyer delivered the opinion of the Court:

. . . In our view, the provision's listed examples—burglary, arson, extortion, or crimes involving the use of explosives—illustrate the kinds of crimes that fall within the statute's scope. Their presence indicates that the statute covers only *similar* crimes, rather than *every* crime that "presents a serious potential risk of physical injury to another." (ii). If Congress meant the latter, *i.e.*, if it meant the statute to be all-encompassing, it is hard to see why it would have needed to include the examples at all. Without them, clause (ii) would cover *all* crimes that present a "serious potential risk of physical injury." Additionally, if Congress meant clause (ii) to include *all* risky crimes, why would it have included clause (i)? A crime which has as an element the "use, attempted use, or threatened use of physical force" against the person (as clause (i) specifies) is likely to create "a serious potential risk of physical injury" and would seem to fall within the scope of clause (ii) . . .

These considerations taken together convince us that, " 'to give effect . . . to every clause and word' " of this statute, we should read the examples as limiting the crimes that clause (ii) covers to crimes that are roughly similar, in kind as well as in degree of risk posed, to the examples themselves . . . Of course, the statute places the word "otherwise," just after the examples, so that the provision covers a felony that is one of the example crimes "or *otherwise* involves conduct that presents a serious potential risk of physical injury." (ii) [emphasis added]. But we cannot agree with the Government that the word "otherwise" is *sufficient* to demonstrate that the examples do not limit the scope of the clause. That is because the word "otherwise" *can* (we do not say *must* (Scalia, J., concurring in judgment)) refer to a crime that is similar to the listed examples in some respects but different in others—similar say in respect to the degree of risk it produces, but different in respect to the "way or manner" in which it produces that risk. Webster's Third New International Dictionary 1598 (1961) (defining "otherwise" to mean "in a different way or manner") . . .

In our view, DUI differs from the example crimes—burglary, arson, extortion, and crimes involving the use of explosives—in at least one pertinent, and important, respect. The listed crimes all typically involve purposeful, "violent," and "aggressive" conduct. See *Taylor v. United States*, 495 U.S. 575, 598 (1990) ("burglary" is an unlawful or unprivileged entry into a building or other structure with "intent to commit a crime"); ALI Model Penal Code §220.1(1) (1985) ("arson" is causing a fire or explosion with "the purpose of," *e.g.*, "destroying a building . . . of another" or "damaging any property . . . to collect insurance"); *id.*, §223.4 (extortion is "purposely" obtaining property of another through threat of, *e.g.*, inflicting "bodily injury"); *Leocal v. Ashcroft*, 543 U.S. 1, 9 (2004) (the word " 'use' . . . most naturally suggests a higher degree of intent than negligent or merely accidental conduct" which fact helps bring it outside the scope of the statutory term "crime of violence"). That conduct is such that it makes more likely that an offender, later possessing a gun, will use that gun deliberately to harm a victim. Crimes committed in such a purposeful, violent, and aggressive manner are "potentially more dangerous when firearms are involved." And such crimes are "characteristic of the armed career criminal, the eponym of the statute."

By way of contrast, statutes that forbid driving under the influence, such as the statute before us, typically do not insist on purposeful, violent, and aggressive conduct;

rather, they are, or are most nearly comparable to, crimes that impose strict liability, criminalizing conduct in respect to which the offender need not have had any criminal intent at all . . .

When viewed in terms of the Act's basic purposes, this distinction matters considerably. As suggested by its title, the Armed Career Criminal Act focuses upon the special danger created when a particular type of offender—a violent criminal or drug trafficker—possesses a gun. . . . In order to determine which offenders fall into this category, the Act looks to past crimes. This is because an offender's criminal history is relevant to the question whether he is a career criminal, or, more precisely, to the kind or degree of danger the offender would pose were he to possess a gun.

In this respect—namely, a prior crime's relevance to the possibility of future danger with a gun—crimes involving intentional or purposeful conduct (as in burglary and arson) are different than DUI, a strict liability crime. In both instances, the offender's prior crimes reveal a degree of callousness toward risk, but in the former instance they also show an increased likelihood that the offender is the kind of person who might deliberately point the gun and pull the trigger. We have no reason to believe that Congress intended a 15-year mandatory prison term where that increased likelihood does not exist . . .

Scalia, concurring:

. . . the problem with the Court's holding today is that it is not remotely faithful to the statute that Congress wrote. There is simply no basis (other than the necessity of resolving the present case) for holding that the enumerated and unenumerated crimes must be similar in respects *other than the degree of risk that they pose.*

The Court is correct that the clause "otherwise involves conduct that presents a serious potential risk of physical injury to another" signifies a similarity between the enumerated and unenumerated crimes. It is not, however, *any* old similarity, such as (to take a random example) "purposeful, 'violent,' and 'aggressive' conduct." Rather, it is the *particular* similarity specified after the "otherwise"—i.e., that they all pose a serious potential risk of physical injury to another. They need not be similar in any other way. As the Court correctly notes, the word "otherwise" in this context means "in a different way or manner." Webster's New International Dictionary 1729 (2d ed. 1957) ("in another way or in other ways"). Therefore, by using the word "otherwise" the writer draws a substantive connection between two sets only on one specific dimension—i.e., whatever follows "otherwise." What that means here is that "committing one of the enumerated crimes . . . is *one way* to commit a crime 'involv[ing] a serious potential risk of physical injury to another'; and that *other ways* of committing a crime of that character similarly constitute 'violent felon[ies].'

The Court rejects this seemingly straightforward statutory analysis, reading the residual clause to mean that the unenumerated offenses must be similar to the enumerated offenses not only in the degree of risk they pose, but also "in kind," despite the fact that "otherwise" means that the *common* element of risk must be presented " 'in a *different* way or manner.' . . .

The Court supports its argument with that ever-ready refuge from the hardships of statutory text, the (judicially) perceived statutory purpose. According to the Court, because the Armed Career Criminal Act is concerned with "the special danger created when a particular type of offender—a violent criminal or drug trafficker—possesses a gun," the statutory purpose favors applying [the statute's] enhanced penalty only to those criminals "who might deliberately point the gun and pull the trigger." I cannot possibly infer that purpose from the statute. For all I know, the statute was meant to punish those who are indifferent to human life, or who are undeterred by the criminal penalties attached to the commission of other crimes (after all, the statute enhances penalties for drug traffickers). While the Court's asserted purpose would surely be a reasonable one, it has no more grounding in the statutory text than do these other possibilities. And what is more, the Court's posited purpose is positively contradicted by the fact that one of the enumerated crimes—the unlawful use of explosives—may involve merely negligent or reckless conduct. See ALI, Model Penal Code §220.2(2) (1985) ("A person is guilty of a misdemeanor if he recklessly creates a risk of catastrophe in the employment of fire, explosives or other dangerous means"); ("A person is guilty of criminal mischief if he . . . damages tangible property of another purposely, recklessly, or by negligence in the employment of fire, explosives, or other dangerous means") . . .

Under my interpretation of [the statute], I must answer one question: Does drunk driving pose at least as serious a risk of physical injury to another as burglary? From the evidence presented by the Government, I cannot conclude so. Because of that, the rule of lenity requires that I resolve this case in favor of the defendant . . .

Alito, dissenting:

The Court holds that an offense does not fall within the residual clause unless it is "roughly similar, in kind as well as in degree of risked posed," to the crimes specifically listed in [the statute] i.e., burglary, extortion, arson, and crimes involving the use of explosives. These crimes, according to the Court, "all typically involve purposeful, 'violent,' and 'aggressive' conduct."

This interpretation cannot be squared with the text of the statute, which simply does not provide that an offense must be "purposeful," "violent," or "aggressive" in order to fall within the residual clause. Rather, after listing burglary, arson, extortion, and explosives offenses, the statute provides (in the residual clause) that an offense qualifies if it "otherwise involves conduct that presents a serious potential risk of physical injury to another." Therefore, offenses falling within the residual clause must be similar to the named offenses in one respect only: They must, "otherwise"—which is to say, "in a different manner," 10 OED 984 (def. B(1)); see also Webster's 1598—"involve[] conduct that presents a serious potential risk of physical injury to another." Requiring that an offense must also be "purposeful," "violent," or "aggressive" amounts to adding new elements to the statute, but we "ordinarily resist reading words or elements into a statute that do not appear on its face." *Bates* v. *United States*, 522 U. S. 23, 29 (1997) . . .

The Court defends its new statutory element on the ground that a defendant who merely engages in felony drunk driving is not likely to be "the kind of person who might deliberately point the gun and pull the trigger." The Court cites no empirical support for this conclusion, and its accuracy is not self-evident . . .

Justice Scalia, like the Court, does not follow the statutory language. The statute says that offenses falling within the residual clause must present "a serious potential risk of physical injury to another." The statute does not say that these offenses must present at least as much risk as the enumerated offenses . . .

QUESTIONS ABOUT THE CASE

1. What purpose does Breyer's opinion see in the statute? That is, what problem does Breyer think this statute aims to solve, and why does Breyer conclude that Mr. Begay is not part of the problem? What evidence does Breyer use to convince us that his reading of statutory purpose is plausible?

2. Besides statutory purpose, a theme of this chapter, this case also involves *criminal purpose*, or the intent behind various criminal acts. How does Breyer use criminal purpose to distinguish DUI from burglary, arson, and extortion?

3. Scalia criticizes Breyer's purposive approach. Why? Do you agree with his criticisms? What approach to interpreting the statute does Scalia use?

4. On what basis does Alito disagree with Breyer's purposive interpretation of the statute? With Scalia's non-purposive interpretation?

5. If Scalia and Alito see no purpose in the statute, how do they make sense of it? For example, imagine that Begay had no history of drunk driving but had been repeatedly ticketed for speeding so far above the limit as to constitute the felony of reckless driving. How would Scalia and Alito apply the statute to that case? (Keep in mind that, as the common phrase has it, "speed kills.") Don't we have to figure out the purposes of statutes before we can make sense of them?

6. Each of the justices uses a canon of statutory construction, but the canons lead the justices in different directions. What canon of statutory interpretation does Breyer cite? (Hint: Holmes used it in interpreting the National Motor Vehicle Theft Act.) What canon of statutory interpretation does Scalia cite? (Hint: He calls it the "rule of lenity.") What canon of statutory construction does Alito cite? (Hint: He draws it from *Bates v. U.S.*) Does the simultaneous firing of three canons in three different directions suggest that canons are useless as tools of statutory interpretation?

7. The interpretation of Just one sentence in a federal statute split the Court into three contending groups. What exactly made this sentence so befuddling to the Court? After reading the opinions, do you believe that one interpretation is "correct" and the others "wrong"? If not, do you nonetheless believe one of the justices nonetheless did a better job of writing a persuasive opinion? Why?

CHAPTER 5

Interpreting the United States Constitution

*We are under a Constitution—but the Constitution is what
the Judges say it is.*

—CHARLES EVANS HUGHES

*I look forward to seeing my plays staged so that I can find
out what they mean.*

—TOM STOPPARD, PLAYWRIGHT

Chapter 1 described legal reasoning as a shorthand term for evaluating the fairness by which courts and judges exercise political power. Our argument has proceeded in four steps. First, in a political system committed to the rule of law, the law must in fact rule—people must act consistently with the law. Second, courts have unquestioned power to interpret what the law means in legal cases. Third, rules of law are often unclear when applied to specific cases, so cases are constantly appealed on points of law and judges must choose what the law means. But now the obvious question arises: How can judges follow the law if at the same time they choose what the law means? Hence the fourth step: Judges who exercise political power under the rule of law must justify their choices. In common-law nations, judges do this through the medium of legal reasoning, which requires them to render decisions that fit together, or harmonize, rules of law, facts of cases, social background facts, and widespread social values. (This is not an expectation in civil-law nations such as France, where judges do not give extensive justifications for their decisions.)

In constitutional law, the third and final type of law this text examines, we encounter what we conventionally think of as the most truly political part of law. Political science has historically paid close attention to constitutional law but has largely ignored common law and statutory law. It has also largely ignored state constitutions, though all 50 states have them, and though they also play a role in some important political controversies. Why should this be so?

The U.S. Constitution does two important things. First, it allocates specific powers both among the branches of the national government and between national and state governments. (Only the national government may coin money; the states have primary but not exclusive power over alcohol regulation.) Second, the Constitution declares rights over which no branch of government at any level can exert power—freedom of speech or the free exercise of religion, for example. But state constitutions simultaneously convey powers and provide rights. Indeed, recent decisions on the rights of lesbians and gays to marry have been based on state constitutional law.[1] What makes the U.S. Constitution uniquely important?

THE SUPREME LAW OF THE LAND

The short answer is that the Constitution of the United States declares itself, in Article VI, to be "the supreme law of the land." If the Constitution is supreme, it presumably overrides all state constitutions and all statutes and common-law rulings. In other words, when a legal rule is inconsistent with the Constitution, the rule has got to go.

The "supremacy clause" is the constitutional equivalent of the familiar saying, "The buck stops here." Since, as we have seen, rules of law do not provide one and only one demonstrably correct answer to concrete legal conflicts, and since only the scarcity of time and money curb the ingenuity of lawyers in creating legal arguments, virtually every question of governmental operation and of civil rights and liberties can become a constitutional question.

Newspapers put major constitutional decisions on their front pages. But every year, countless other constitutional issues, less headline-worthy but of deep importance to somebody, also arise. Here are three recent examples:

■ Police clocked Victor Harris driving 73 miles per hour in a 55-mile-per-hour zone, but when they flashed their lights at him, Harris sped up and committed several other traffic violations. An officer attempted to stop Harris by ramming his car, but the bump caused Harris to crash, paralyzing him. Was the officer's decision to use potentially deadly force to stop a traffic scofflaw justified, or did it violate the Fourth Amendment's prohibition against "unreasonable" seizures?[2]

■ A website, Wikileaks, posts anonymously leaked documents that purportedly reveal abuses by governmental, corporate, and religious organizations. In 2008, it posted account information from a bank in the Cayman Islands that the leakers claimed were evidence of money laundering and tax evasion. The bank, contending that some of the information was confidential and some was false and libelous, sued the website in federal court. Lacking any way to locate those responsible for publishing the lead— the creators of Wikileaks remained anonymous—the bank asked a federal judge to issue an injunction closing the whole Web site down. Should Wikileaks remain on the Web, even if some of the information it provides infringes state and federal laws?

---

[1] The California Supreme Court ruled on May 15, 2008, that laws defining marriage as between a man and a woman violated state constitutional guarantees of privacy, equality, and due process. *In Re Marriage Cases,* 43 Cal.4th 757 (Cal. S. Ct., 2008) that decision was, however, overturned later in 2008 by Proposition 8, a ballot measure that amended the California Constitution to specify that marriage was restricted to opposite-sex couples. The California decision followed that of the Massachusetts Supreme Judicial Court, which in 2003 ruled that state constitutional guarantees of due process and equal protection gave same-sex couples the right to marry. *Goodridge v. Dept. of Public Health,* 440 MA. 309 (MA. S. Jud. Ct., 2003).

[2] The Supreme Court ruled 8-1 that the officer did not violate the Fourth Amendment. *Scott v. Harris* 550 U.S. 372 (2007).

Does shutting the Web site down under such circumstances violate freedom of the press as guaranteed by the First Amendment?[3]

■ A Georgia law restricts convicted sex offenders from living within 1,000 feet of schools, churches, or any other place that children might congregate. Anthony Mann, a convicted child molester, owned a home that was outside this prohibited zone. When a day-care center opened up within 1,000 feet of his house, Mann was told he would have to vacate his home. Mann argued that there was no place in the state where he could buy a home without the threat of ejection looming over him any time a child-related organization moved to his neighborhood. Should a sex offender be asked to leave his own property whenever a child-related concern locates nearby? Does the Georgia law deprive Mann of his property rights without due process of law?[4]

All of these constitutional questions, if fully litigated, end up in one place—the federal judicial system. The Constitution in Article III gives the U.S. Supreme Court, and all federal courts, jurisdiction to hear cases "arising under this Constitution." In the famous case of *Marbury v. Madison* in 1803, Chief Justice John Marshall, a lifetime appointee from the repudiated Federalist Party government of John Adams, put the jurisdiction clause and the supremacy clause together and announced that the federal courts could declare the acts of democratically elected Congress—in 1803, a very decidedly pro-Jefferson Republican Congress—null and void. We call this process "judicial review."

Judicial review of constitutionality puts courts in a uniquely strong position. Legislatures, as previous chapters demonstrated, can overturn both common law and statutory judicial decisions. In constitutional interpretation, no such democratic backstopping exists. Those who oppose a constitutional ruling must either persuade the Court to change its mind or amend the Constitution. But a constitutional amendment requires approval of two-thirds of both houses of Congress and three-fourths of the states.[5] Therefore, relatively small minorities can block a proposed amendment's passage. Only two of the eleven amendments ratified in the twentieth century (the Sixteenth Amendment, authorizing a federal income tax, and the Nineteenth, granting women's suffrage) can be said to have corrected controversial Supreme Court readings of the Constitution. To a large extent, then, the Constitution really is, as Justice Charles Evans Hughes put it in this chapter's epigraph, "what the Judges say it is."[6]

---

[3] Federal Judge Jeffrey S. White issued the injunction but withdrew it a month later, citing First Amendment concerns. The judge noted as well that the purpose of the injunction had been defeated as other Web sites had simply reposted the bank account information. Jonathan D. Glater, "Judge Reverses His Order Disabling Website," *The New York Times*, March 1, 2008.

[4] The Georgia Supreme Court concluded that the rule as applied violated Mann's constitutional right to just compensation for the taking of property. *Mann v. Georgia Department of Corrections*, 282 Ga. 754 (Ga. S. Ct., November 21, 2007).

[5] Article V of the Constitution provides a second route to amending the Constitution: Two-thirds of the state legislatures can call for a constitutional convention, at which one or more amendments could be considered. Any amendments approved by the convention, however, would require ratification by three-quarters of the states. This second route to amending the Constitution has never been used.

[6] H.J. Powell "Constitutional Virtues," *9 Green Bag* (2006) 379–389, quoting Charles Evans Hughes, *Addresses of Charles Evan Hughes* (1916), p. 185. Hughes in fact did not literally believe that the Supreme Court controlled the meaning of the Constitution and came to regret the way this famous quotation was used. Recent scholarship has questioned the Court-centric approach to constitutional interpretation, see footnote 65.

Interpretations of the Constitution are at the center of many of our most urgent political controversies. Based on their reading of the Constitution, courts tell cities what rules they can make to regulate guns. Courts strike down some laws prohibiting abortion and uphold others. Courts tell the federal government what it can and can't do to regulate the Internet. Courts reverse the convictions of killers because of what some critics call "technicalities." Courts decide which affirmative action programs can be operated and which cannot.

Why, in a democracy, should decisions such as these be made by judges who do not subject themselves to the rigors of the electoral process? As we shall see, that question has created an entire academic industry of legal theorists and social scientists who have attempted to square judicial review with democratic theory. Even more than statutory law, the subject of the previous chapter, scholarship on constitutional law is haunted by the fear that judges, insulated from the people, will use their position to remake society according to their own visions. Yet, when disputes arise over what the Constitution requires, some group or individual must settle them. And, as more and more of the nations of the world are deciding, courts are appropriate institutions for that task.[7]

The desire for an authoritative interpretation of constitutional language is especially acute in the United States because of the "openness" of our Constitution. The Constitution speaks in some instances with considerable clarity but in many others only generally, ambiguously, and vaguely. As you would expect, the clear parts of the Constitution rarely create much dispute. For example, the Constitution says that the president must be 35 years old. While we can imagine hypothetical cases—an 18-year-old guru claims to be reincarnated and is "really" 105—in fact no one has ever litigated that clause.[8] But the Constitution's most frequently litigated clauses do little more than command the courts to *care* about basic political and governmental values without specifying with any precision the values or the problems to which the provisions apply:

- "Care," says the First Amendment, "that government not take sides on religious matters. Care that it not constrain religious freedom, or speech, or the press, unduly. But it's up to you to define 'religion,' 'speech,' and 'the press' and to decide when government action can limit them."

- "Care," say the Fourth, Fifth, Sixth, and Eighth Amendments, "that government not become too zealous in fighting crime. Respect people's homes and property. Give them a fair chance to prove their innocence in court and do not punish the guilty too harshly. In short, be fair. But it's up to you to decide what's fair."

- "People must be able to trade effectively," says Article I's commerce clause and the contract clause. "Work it out so they can."

---

[7] On the growing importance of judicial review around the world, see Tom Ginsburg, *Judicial Review in New Democracies* (New York: Cambridge University Press, 2003), Ran Hirschl, *Towards Juristocracy* (Cambridge, MA: Harvard University Press, 2004), Patricia J. Woods, *Judicial Power and National Politics* (Albany, New York: State University of New York Press, 2008), and Alex Stone Sweet, *Governing with Judges: Constitutional Politics in Europe* (New York: Oxford University Press, 2000).

[8] There was some minor discussion about whether presidential candidate John McCain was a "natural born citizen" as the Constitution requires of presidents. This is because "natural born" is a much more ambiguous concept than "35." The "natural born" provision bars Americans who were born outside the United States and subsequently became citizens from the presidency. McCain was born on a military base in the Panama Canal Zone, not within the boundaries of the United States, raising concerns about his eligibility. Carl Hulse, "McCain's Canal Zone Birth Prompts Queries About Whether That Rules Him Out," *The New York Times*, February 28, 2008.

The Constitution omits references to some rights that the structure of our government seems to require. For example, the Constitution contains no guarantee of a right to vote. Obviously the Constitution's framers could not anticipate some violations of liberty and privacy, such as thermal imaging or surveillance by airplanes, or wiretapping, the subject of the case featured at the end of this chapter.[9] Conversely, the Constitution omits reference to some rights that we assume the framers knew about and took for granted—rights that are so much a part of our liberty as to "go without saying." The right to marry may well fall in this category. Thus to interpret the Constitution only according to what its words actually say seems to defeat its purpose. And once we accept that there are some liberties that the Constitution protects yet never specifically mentions, someone has to decide where to draw the line.[10]

The Supreme Court has declared the right to choose whether to carry a fetus to term to be an unspecified liberty. Similarly, the Court declared in 2000 that parents had a constitutional right to raise children as they wish, though no provision in the Constitution mentions child rearing.[11] In 2003 the Supreme Court declared that the right of persons to freely associate with each other, another unspecified right, made Texas's law banning homosexual sodomy unconstitutional.[12] The scope of the right of privacy, or of the right to raise children without interference from the state, or of the freedom of association, is unclear. So, even if we could assume that every governmental representative—whether a legislator before voting for a statute or a police officer before deciding to arrest—stopped and made a conscientious determination of the constitutionality of a decision, under our Constitution, we would still need a constitution-interpreting organization such as the courts. The Constitution is so vague, general, and ambiguous that people with the best of intentions do not necessarily reach the same interpretation.

Federalism also seems to require a Supreme Court to interpret the Constitution. We have one national constitution but many state constitutions. If we take its legal status seriously, then the Constitution should mean the same everywhere, just as the Mann Act should not have one meaning in Utah and another in the District of Columbia. If we lived under a unitary government, then maybe (but only maybe) we could count on a conscientious Congress to determine uniform constitutional applications. Under our Constitution, however, Congress is neither structured nor empowered to review the constitutionality of the actions of state and local governments.

For all these reasons—the finality of the Supreme Court, the importance of constitutional issues, the inconclusiveness of the Constitution's text, and the need for constitutional uniformity—we might expect the Supreme Court to take particular care to honor the conventional formulas for good legal reasoning in order to persuade us that justice is done. The bulk of this chapter explains why just the opposite happens, and why the practice of justification in constitutional law differs from the practices of legal reasoning described in previous chapters.

Readers will have to put up with a higher level of abstraction in this chapter than in Chapters 3 and 4. In part, it is necessary to move toward the general and the abstract in order to say anything at all about such an immense subject, one on which books about the

---

[9] Jeffrey Rosen, *The Unwanted Gaze: The Destruction of Privacy in America* (New York: Random House, 2000).

[10] See Judge Richard Posner's case against "strict constructionism," aptly titled, "What Am I? A Potted Plant?" *New Republic*, September 28, 1987, pp. 23–25.

[11] *Troxel v. Granville*, 530 U.S. 65 (2000).

[12] *Lawrence v. Texas*, 539 U.S. 558 (2003).

Supreme Court, the judicial selection process, and constitutional interpretation itself flow steadily forth.[13] But there is a much more profound reason for the abstraction to follow, and the reason itself will seem difficult and abstract at first: Because the Constitution is supreme and because we believe we should follow it, we have throughout the many turbulent changes in our history worked very hard to make the Constitution fit and harmonize with what we do and what we believe. Bruce Ackerman's *We the People: Foundations* emphasizes that the United States has had—under one written document—two constitutional revolutions, the Civil War and the New Deal, both of which radically transformed American government. Though we have not changed many of the Constitution's words, we have profoundly altered its meaning.[14]

Constitutional law, then, is abstract because most of the Constitution's meaning is symbolic rather than specific. We need the security of believing we are one political community with a continuous history, so we say we are living under one Constitution when in fact we work hard to change our interpretations of it to legitimate contemporary realities. Recall, however, that the common-law tradition is also built on continuous legal change and adaptation.

CONVENTIONAL LEGAL REASONING IN CONSTITUTIONAL INTERPRETATION

The Court's unique political position, we shall now see, makes it unwise to use the conventional techniques of legal reasoning that might normally apply in common and statutory law. You might well think that the factors described in the last section—the inconclusiveness of the constitutional text, the centrality of constitutional issues in American politics, and the need for uniform constitutional meaning both within the national government and among all the states—call for especially stable and clear patterns of legal reasoning and justification. This is, however, precisely what 200 years of constitutional interpretation has never achieved, and for good reason. As in statutory interpretation, the formulas (literalism and intent, for example) that some judges use in a vain attempt to avoid making public policy are doomed to fail. But in constitutional law, the more open-ended, purpose-oriented techniques we recommended for interpreting statutory commands fall short as well. Let us see why.

Words as Channels of Meaning

Four words drawn from the Constitution loomed over the battle over the impeachment of Bill Clinton: high crimes and misdemeanors, the Constitution says, are impeachable offenses. But what exactly are "high crimes and misdemeanors"? Naturally, Republicans and Democrats in Congress had different views. Democrats argued that even if Bill Clinton lied

---

[13] Here is a small sampling of recent books on the subject: Walter Murphy, *Constitutional Democracy: Creating and Maintaining a Just Political Order* (Baltimore, MD: Johns Hopkins University Press, 2007); Sandy Levinson, *Our Undemocratic Constitution: Where the Constitution Goes Wrong (And How We the People Can Correct It)* (New York: Oxford University Press, 2006); Jeffrey Toobin, *The Nine* (New York: Doubleday, 2007); Sotirios A. Barber and James E. Fleming, *Constitutional Interpretation: The Basic Questions* (New York: Oxford University Press, 2007); Mark A. Graber, *Dred Scott and the Problem of Constitutional Evil* (New York: Cambridge University Press, 2006); Keith E. Whittington, *Political Foundations of Judicial Supremacy* (Princeton, NJ: Princeton University Press, 2007); and Richard Davis, *Electing Justice: Fixing the Supreme Court Nomination Process* (New York: Oxford University Press, 2006).

[14] Bruce Ackerman, *We the People, Vol. 1: Foundations* and *Vol. 2: Transformations* (Cambridge: Belknap Press of Harvard University Press, 1991 and 1997).

in a deposition about his sexual relationship with Monica Lewinsky, this did not relate closely enough to his performance in office to qualify as "high crimes and misdemeanors." Republicans, however, believed that Clinton had broken the law, betrayed the trust of the American people, and demeaned the office of the presidency, a combination that amounted to "high crimes and misdemeanors." As usual in constitutional conflicts, the language divided rather than united.[15] Similarly in 2008, the Supreme Court fought over the language of the Second Amendment, which speaks both of the states' need to maintain a "well regulated militia" and the "right of the people to keep and bear arms." One side argued that the Amendment grants a person a right to own and carry firearms, while the other concluded that it simply protected the right of states to organize their armed militias as they see fit.[16]

Constitutional language by itself rarely resolves disputes that reach the Supreme Court. As in statutory law, many cases turn on arguments about the meaning of key terms—"due process," "establishment of religion," "cruel and unusual punishment," and so forth. These symbolic phrases are broad and general, making literalism a particularly unsatisfactory method of constitutional interpretation.

Yet, in constitutional law, the Supreme Court sometimes ignores even *specific and unambiguous language*. For example, Article I, Section 10 of the Constitution prohibits the states from engaging in certain activities altogether. It prohibits them from making treaties, coining money, or keeping a state militia during times of peace without congressional permission. The section also includes these words: "No state shall . . . pass any . . . law impairing the obligation of contracts."

Debts provide the best example of the kind of contract the state may not impair under the contract clause. In the typical case of such a contract—"executory" contracts in legal language—Pauline borrows money, say from a bank, and promises to pay the money back some time in the future. Until she pays the money back (and at the stated time), she has a contractual obligation to do so. The contract clause prevents the state from impairing Pauline's "obligation" to repay. In short, the state can't pass a law saying people don't have to pay back what they owe, even if a popularly elected legislature voted to do so. Thus the word "impairing" would seem to prevent the state from allowing Pauline to forget about paying the interest or to pay back years later than she promised.

During the Great Depression, a number of states passed laws allowing owners of homes and land to postpone paying their mortgage payments as the mortgage contracts required. These statutes forbade banks and other mortgage holders from foreclosing. The depression, of course, destroyed the financial ability of hundreds of thousands of "Paulines" to repay mortgages on time, but these mortgage moratorium laws spared the Paulines from this peril by impairing the bank's ability to recover the debt. Yet the Supreme Court ruled, in *Home Building and Loan Association v. Blaisdell,* that these laws did not violate the contract clause.[17]

---

[15] For a provocative analysis of the impeachment battle, see Richard A. Posner, *An Affair of State: The Investigation, Impeachment and Trial of President Clinton* (Cambridge: Harvard University Press, 1999); for an equally provocative rebuttal, see Ronald Dworkin, "Philosophy and Monica Lewinsky," *New York Review of Books,* March 9, 2000. Impeachment, we should add, is one instance in which the Supreme Court clearly does not have the final say on the meaning of constitutional words.

[16] The "individual" view of the Second Amendment prevailed, and by a 5-4 vote, the Supreme Court struck down a District of Columbia handgun ban as unconstitutional. *District of Columbia v. Heller* 554 U.S. ____ (2008).

[17] *Home Building and Loan Association v. Blaisdell,* 290 U.S. 398 (1934). See also *East New York Savings Bank v. Hahn,* 326 U.S. 230 (1945) and *El Paso v. Simmons,* 379 U.S. 497 (1965).

The political context of Minnesota's moratorium statute was volatile. In Brest and Levinson's words, "angry farmers denounced and in some instances forcibly stopped foreclosure of their farms. In Iowa, a local judge who refused to suspend foreclosure proceedings was dragged from a courtroom and had a rope put around his neck before the crowd let him go."[18] Yet surely the Supreme Court should not decide cases simply to minimize violence. That only invites constitutional blackmail.

We *can*, however, defend this decision, even though it ignores the words of the Constitution. Just as in nature, survival of economic and political values depends on adaptation, on change, and on the ability to reevaluate policies in light of new information. The Supreme Court rejected the contract clause's words and upheld the depression's mortgage moratorium laws because these laws were based on economic knowledge not fully available to the framers. In the forced-panic sale of land following massive numbers of foreclosures of mortgages, what would happen to the price of land? Supply and demand analysis predicted that the price would drastically decline—quite possibly to the point where the creditors, the bankers, as well as the debtors, the farmers, would both lose because the land could be sold for only a fraction of what the banks had originally loaned on it. The Court upheld the law as a defensible method for attempting to prevent further collapse of the economy. Indeed, more than 70 years later, in 2008, policymakers, facing another plunge in housing prices that threatened to spiral out of control, once again considered loan moratoriums to forestall foreclosures.[19]

A decision in the monumental school desegregation cases provides another example of prudent judicial flight from constitutional words. In its celebrated decision, *Brown v. Board of Education*, the Court held that the equal protection clause of the Fourteenth Amendment prohibited laws and policies designed to maintain segregation in public schools of the then 48 states.[20] A case decided the same day as *Brown*, *Bolling v. Sharpe*, concerned the problem of segregation of schools in the nation's capital. The Fourteenth Amendment's sentence containing the equal protection clause begins with the words "no state shall." It does not govern the District of Columbia. The original Bill of Rights does govern the national government and hence the District, but it contains no equal protection clause. Nonetheless, the Court in *Bolling* forbade segregation in the District's public schools by invoking the due process clause of the Fifth Amendment.[21] The Court did this even though the due process clause does not address the problem of equality. Its words—"No person shall . . . be deprived of life, liberty, or property, without due process of law . . ."—seem to address the problem of the fairness of procedures, the "due process," in the courts. The Fourteenth Amendment contains both due process and equal protection clauses, which further suggests that they convey different messages.

---

[18] Paul Brest and Sanford Levinson, *Processes of Constitutional Decisionmaking*, 3rd ed. (Boston: Little, Brown & Co., 1992), p. 352.

[19] As in the Great Depression, housing prices beginning in 2006 began a sharp decline. People who had taken out "teaser loans," home mortgage loans with low initial payments but much higher charges in later years, found themselves unable to make payments or to get a new loan on more favorable terms. As a result, foreclosures spiked, pushing home prices down. The Bush administration proposed, much as Minnesota had done in the 1930s, to postpone mortgage payments to try to avoid a deluge of home foreclosures. See Michael Grynbaum, "Plan to Aid Borrowers is Greeted by Criticism," *The New York Times*, February 13, 2008, p. C4.

[20] *Brown v. Board of Education*, 347 U.S. 483 (1954).

[21] *Bolling v. Sharpe*, 347 U.S. 497 (1954). See also *Hirabayashi v. United States*, 320 U.S. 81 (1943).

Yet the Court was right to go beyond the words of the Fifth and Fourteenth Amendments. If the Constitution denies government the power to segregate schools by race, it would be absurd to permit segregation only in the national capital. It is proper to say in this instance that the due process clause of the Fifth Amendment does address this problem of equality despite its words. Sometimes, even when the words of a constitutional provision are clear, the Supreme Court must pay attention instead to "the felt necessities of the time," as Justice Holmes famously put it.

Original Intent and Purpose

In 1985, Attorney General Edwin Meese called for a style of constitutional interpretation derived from the original understandings of the framers of the Constitution.[22] "Originalism" has become a rallying cry for conservative critics of the judiciary, but as an approach to constitutional interpretation it is deeply problematic. Searching for the actual intent of the framers of the original Constitution (or of its later amendments) proves just as frustrating as searching for legislative intent. The processes of constitution- and statute-making are equally political. People make arguments they don't fully believe in order to win support. Others do not express what they do believe in order to avoid offending. The painful process of negotiation and accommodation that produced the Constitution in 1787 left many questions unresolved. Most confounding of all, the framers could have had no intent in relation to the new facts that have surfaced since their work concluded.[23]

Originalists in recent years have turned from "intent" to an "original meaning" approach in which the words of the Constitution are understood not in terms of specific intentions of the framers, but in light of common usage at the time of the founding. The Court has, however, often ignored original meaning. Indeed, the Court has on occasion even ignored the clear *purpose* behind provisions in the Constitution. The Court ignored the original purpose of the Sixth Amendment's command when it expanded the right to counsel. This amendment states in part that "In all criminal prosecutions, the accused shall enjoy the right . . . to have the assistance of counsel for his defense." The framers who drafted it sought to alter the common-law rule that prohibited accused felons from having any lawyer at all. They wanted to stop the government from preventing the accused from bringing his lawyer to court with him. The amendment makes no reference to the problem that a man's poverty may stop him from hiring a lawyer. Yet in 1938, the Court held that these words required the federal government to provide lawyers for the poor, and the Court has since expanded the right to protect those accused of felonies and misdemeanors in state and local courts.[24]

And consider again the mortgage moratorium laws of the Great Depression. If we examine the purpose of the contract clause from the framers' viewpoint, we discover that they feared excessive democracy—they worried that popularly elected legislators would enact the "selfish" interests of the masses. The masses contain more debtors than creditors, and it was

---

[22] Edwin Meese III, "Toward a Jurisprudence of Original Intention," 45 *Public Administration Review* 701–704 (1985).

[23] For further elaboration, see Lief Carter, *Contemporary Constitutional Lawmaking: The Supreme Court and the Art of Politics* (Elmsford, NY: Pergamon Press, 1985), pp. 52–55. For a thorough review of the intellectual history of the founding period, see Jack N. Rakove, *Original Meanings* (New York: Alfred A. Knopf, 1996).

[24] *Johnson v. Zerbst,* 304 U.S. 458 (1938); *Gideon v. Wainwright,* 372 U.S. 335 (1963); *Argersinger v. Hamlin,* 407 U.S. 25 (1972). For a persuasive defense of this shift, see Anthony Lewis's classic, *Gideon's Trumpet* (New York: Random House, 1964).

precisely in economically difficult times that the framers most feared that debtors would put irresistible pressure on legislators to ease their debts. Hence the Court in *Home Building and Loan* rejected more than constitutional words and more than the specific intent of some individual framers: It arguably rejected the purpose of the provision. But the Court did so wisely because it understood, as presumably the framers did not, how postponing mortgage foreclosures could benefit creditors and debtors alike.

Finally, H. Jefferson Powell has shown two reasons why the leading figures of the founding period would have rejected the idea that their own actual hopes and expectations of the Constitution would dictate legal conclusions in the future. First, at common law, the reading of texts such as wills and contracts rejected actual intent in favor of giving words their "reasonable," "grammatical," or "popular" meaning. Second, the framers, as members of the Protestant tradition, believed that texts ought to speak for themselves, unmediated by church or scholarly authority. They believed each person should be free to interpret biblical texts for himself or herself and that complex scholarly interpretations—interpretations imposed by experts such as officials within the Catholic Church—had no presumptive authority.

Powell describes how George Washington required in his will the nonlegal arbitration of any ambiguity in administering its provisions precisely in order that the decisionmaker might consider Washington's actual intent in the matter. None of the debaters in Philadelphia acknowledged that his words might shape the future, and James Madison believed that usage ("usus") and the lessons learned from political practice should override any "abstract opinion of the text." Thus, though Madison had thought the First U.S. Bank was unconstitutional, he signed the Second Bank Bill because the people had approved of the bank and it had worked.[25]

In this historical evidence, we find the beginnings of America's major contribution to Western philosophy—pragmatism.[26] Despite the way it is sometimes used in everyday discourse, *pragmatism* does not refer to an unprincipled, selfish attempt to "do whatever it takes to win." Pragmatism holds that our attitudes and choices should follow primarily from the lessons experience teaches us about what works, not from abstract rules or theories. The "radicalism of the American revolution," as Gordon Wood calls it, succeeded in implanting a democracy that made a pragmatic move away from the values and beliefs of the framers inevitable. Wood quotes a political leader of the generation that followed the framers:

> "We cannot rely on the views of the founding fathers anymore," Martin Van Buren told the New York convention in 1820. "We have to rely on our own experience, not on what they said or thought." "They had many fears," said Van Buren, "fears of democracy, that American experience had not borne out."[27]

In constitutional law, as in statutory law, "intent" is a muddled concept. We have argued in favor of a purpose-oriented approach to statutory interpretation, acknowledging that it often leaves some discretion to judges to pick among competing purposes. But in constitutional law, even when "purpose" is relatively clear, judges must sometimes ignore it.

---

[25] H. Jefferson Powell, "The Original Understanding of Original Intent," 98 *Harvard Law Review* 885 (1985). Compare Richard Kay, "Adherence to the Original Intentions in Constitutional Adjudication: Three Objections and Responses," 82 *Northwestern University Law Review* 226 (1987).

[26] For a wonderful intellectual history of the origins of pragmatism in the United States, see Louis Menand, *The Metaphysical Club* (New York: Farrar, Straus and Giroux, 2001).

[27] Gordon Wood, *The Radicalism of the American Revolution* (New York: Alfred A. Knopf, 1992), pp. 368–369.

Stare (In) Decisis

In 1940, the Supreme Court held that a public school could require all children—including Jehovah's Witnesses, whose religious convictions forbade it—to salute the flag each day. In 1943, the Court overruled itself and held the opposite.[28] In 1946, the Court refused to require state legislatures to make electoral districts roughly equal in population, but in 1962, the Court ruled that the Constitution requires just that.[29] In 1986 the Supreme Court declared that laws against sodomy were constitutional; in 2003 the Court found that such laws violate the Fourteenth Amendment.[30]

While the justices sometimes make stare decisis a primary rationale for their decisions,[31] they have also from time to time recognized reasons to ignore precedents in constitutional law. After all, no legislature sits mainly to update constitutional policy in light of new conditions. It is not simply that the Court should correct its own mistakes—that, as we have argued in the previous chapter, is always wise policy. It is also that wise policy at one time is not necessarily wise policy at another. If we take seriously the idea that the Constitution is law and so ought to have teeth, then the courts must do the updating. As Justice William O. Douglas once said:

> The place of *stare decisis* in constitutional law is . . . tenuous. A judge looking at a constitutional decision may have compulsions to revere past history and accept what was once written. But he remembers above all else that it is the Constitution which he swore to support and defend, not the gloss which his predecessors may have put on it. So he comes to formulate his own views, rejecting some earlier ones as false and embracing others. He cannot do otherwise unless he lets men long dead and unaware of the problems of the age in which he lives do his thinking for him.[32]

Of course people rely on constitutional decisions. Teachers in 1943 believed they could require all students—regardless of their individual beliefs—to salute the flag. State judges in 1963 did not believe they had to appoint counsel in all felonies. The Texas police officers who arrested John Lawrence in 2003 for engaging in anal intercourse believed that laws against sodomy were constitutionally valid. The point is that constitutional values may be important enough to override reliance on past policy.

JUDICIAL REVIEW AND DEMOCRATIC THEORY

If neither the conventions of legal justification nor the backstop of legislative correction of judicial decisions limits the Supreme Court's power and discretion, then what does? This question has preoccupied constitutional scholarship for nearly a century. The great constitutional theorist Alexander Bickel coined the phrase "the Countermajoritarian Difficulty" to summarize the problem: How could a democracy empower unelected judges to make

---

[28] *Minersville School District v. Gobitis*, 310 U.S. 586 (1940), and *West Virginia State Board of Education v. Barnette*, 319 U.S. 624 (1943).

[29] *Colegrove v. Green*, 328 U.S. 549 (1946), and *Baker v. Carr*, 369 U.S. 186 (1962).

[30] *Bowers v. Hardwick*, 478 U.S. 186 (1986), and *Lawrence v. Texas*, 539 U.S. 558 (2003).

[31] One such instance was *Planned Parenthood v. Casey*, as discussed in Chapter 2 on pp. 29–30.

[32] William O. Douglas, "Stare Decisis," 4 *Record of the Association of the Bar of the City of New York* 152 (1949): 153–154.

decisions about many of the nation's most important controversies, sometimes against the wishes of the majority of the people?[33]

This issue surfaced in the 2000 presidential debates. When George W. Bush was asked what kind of judges he would pick for the Supreme Court, he contended that, unlike his opponent, he would appoint competent judges who would not seek to use their position to "write social policy":

> I believe that the judges ought not to take the place of the legislative branch of govern-
> ment, that they're appointed for life and that they ought to look at the Constitution as
> sacred. They . . . shouldn't misuse their bench. I don't believe in liberal activist
> judges. . . .[34]

We have argued that in constitutional law, as in statutory and common law, judges can-
not help but write social policy. Another problem with Bush's position, though, is that it's not clear that judges can avoid being "activists," whether of the conservative, liberal, or moderate varieties. This is because activism has several dimensions, and a decision that is inactivist on one dimension may be activist on others. Professor Bradley C. Canon suggests six such dimensions:

1. Majoritarianism—Does the decision nullify an act of an elected legislature?
2. Interpretive stability—Does the decision overrule prior court precedent?
3. Interpretive fidelity—Does the decision contradict the manifest intent of the framers?
4. Substance—Does the decision make new basic policy for the society (as, for example, *Brown v. Board of Education* began a new policy of school desegregation)?
5. Specificity—Does the decision require people to follow specific, court-created rules?
6. Availability of political alternatives—Are other political institutions equally able and willing to formulate effective policy in the area the decision touches?[35]

In this light, consider *Planned Parenthood v. Casey*, the Supreme Court's 1992 decision reaffirming the right to an abortion that we discussed in Chapter 2. By striking down part of a Pennsylvania law restricting abortions, the Supreme Court overturned the policy choice of an elected legislature (though not necessarily the policy choice of the majority of Americans) and so according to dimensions 1 and 6 was being activist. But notice that if the Supreme Court had decided in favor of Pennsylvania, it also would have been activist, this time according to dimension 2 and perhaps 4 (since the Court would be approving a new policy regarding abortion). Moreover, the decision the Court did make in *Casey* seems to be "nonactivist" according to dimension 5 (since the Court did not announce a detailed set of rules for abortion regulation), and to 3 (since it's doubtful any of the framers had any intent about the constitutionality of abortion, much less a "manifest" one).

As this example suggests, activism is a much more complex concept than politicians such as George W. Bush typically acknowledge. And yet Bush's comments do point to an

---

[33] Alexander Bickel, *The Least Dangerous Branch: The Supreme Court at the Bar of Politics,* 2nd ed. (New Haven: Yale University Press, 1986), p. 16.

[34] "The 2000 Campaign: Transcript of Debate Between Vice President Gore and Governor Bush," *The New York Times,* October 4, 2000, p. A30.

[35] Bradley C. Canon, "A Framework for the Analysis of Judicial Activism," in *Supreme Court Activism and Restraint,* Stephen Halpern and Charles Lamb, eds. (Lexington, MA: Lexington Books, 1982), Chapter 15.

oft-voiced concern about the Supreme Court's role in American democracy. That concern is underlined when we realize that the Court has (rightly, we have argued) at times ignored the clear words of the Constitution, the clear intent of the framers, and the clear purposes of constitutional provisions. How can we keep unelected judges from misusing their power to interpret the Constitution?

Theories of Judicial Self-Restraint

Academic legal sleuths have been on the case for more than a century now. They seek a theory of constitutional justification that would constrain the justices and thus resolve the countermajoritarian difficulty. Their concern is not merely "academic," for the Supreme Court has time and time again misused its power. In the late nineteenth and early twentieth centuries, for example, the Supreme Court tried to proclaim itself the final arbiter of social and economic policy and of political morality. It actively thwarted economic and social reforms at all levels of government, based on its own philosophy, which held that most forms of economic regulation were illegitimate.

So in *U.S. v. E.C. Knight* (1895), the Court aggressively reduced national power over commerce by defining the commerce power (contrary to precedents going back to John Marshall) to cover only the physical movement of goods among the states.[36] In 1905, in *Lochner v. New York*, the Court struck down statutory protections against harsh working conditions in bakeries by creating, under the Fourteenth Amendment's due process clause, a constitutional right to individuals' freedom to make any contracts they chose subject only to the "reasonable" exercise of the state's police power. The Court decided what was reasonable.[37] In 1918, Congress forbade the shipment in interstate commerce of goods made with child labor. Although the statute seemed to honor restrictions on the commerce power set in *E.C. Knight,* the Court struck down this statute because there was nothing inherently harmful about the goods shipped.[38]

The Court was operating under a philosophy in which any regulation that had the effect of redistributing income or power from one group to another was automatically suspect.[39] Thus, Justice David Brewer in 1893 told the New York Bar Association that strengthening the judiciary was necessary to protect the country "against the tumultuous ocean of democracy!" He believed that

> the permanence of government of and by the people . . . rests upon the independence and vigor of the judiciary, . . . to restrain the greedy hand of the many from filching from the few that which they have honestly acquired. . . .[40]

This claim to unlimited judicial power, and the political controversy it created, prompted a search for theories that would constrain the judiciary in its interpretation of the Constitution.

The first of these theories, authored in 1893 by James B. Thayer of the Harvard Law School, attempted to reaffirm the representative nature of American constitutional government. All acts

---

[36] 156 U.S. 1.

[37] 198 U.S. 45.

[38] *Hammer v. Dagenhart,* 247 U.S. 251.

[39] Howard Gillman, *The Constitution Besieged: The Rise and Demise of Lochner Era Police Powers Jurisprudence* (Durham, N.C.: Duke University Press, 1993).

[40] David Brewer, "The Movement of Coercion," 16 *Proceedings of the New York State Bar Association* 37 (1893).

of elected bodies carry a heavy presumption of constitutionality. The courts may properly overturn legislation only on a showing that the legislature has made a very clear mistake.[41]

Thayer's thesis proved unsatisfactory for two reasons. First, like the "golden rule" of statutory interpretation, it contained no standards for determining what counted as a clear mistake. From the perspective of Justice David Brewer (and Justice Field, who thought the income tax marked the beginning of a war waged by the poor against the rich), economic regulation was a clear mistake. Thayer's position left to courts the responsibility for doing the extralegal analysis necessary to decide what counts as a clear mistake: "The ultimate arbiter of what is rational and permissible is indeed always the courts, so far as litigated cases bring the question before them."[42]

Second, if Thayer's theory did nudge the Court into a posture of judicial self-restraint, the Court would then lack power to protect violations of civil liberties. Yet before the final collapse of the Court's economic activism in 1937, it had begun to move into the civil liberties area. In 1931, in *Near v. Minnesota,* the Court struck down a Minnesota law permitting prior censorship of the press.[43] In a 1932 case, *Powell v. Alabama,* it reversed the death sentences of six black defendants sentenced to death after a one-day trial in Scottsboro, Alabama, in which the six were denied adequate representation of counsel.[44]

The synthesis of the two extremes—the theory that justified judicial abstinence from evaluating the rationality of economic policy without curtailing its power to protect civil liberties—appeared quietly (and in the most obscure legalese possible) in the fourth footnote to a 1938 case, in which the Court upheld congressional authority to regulate the ingredients in milk products processed for interstate commerce. This now-famous "*Carolene* footnote four" reads:

> There may be narrower scope for operation of the presumption of constitutionality when legislation appears on its face to be within a specific prohibition of the Constitution, such as those of the first ten amendments, which are deemed equally specific when held to be embraced within the Fourteenth. . . .
>
> It is unnecessary to consider now whether legislation which restricts those political processes which can ordinarily be expected to bring about a repeal of undesirable legislation, is to be subjected to more exacting judicial scrutiny under the general prohibitions of the Fourteenth Amendment than are most other types of legislation. . . .
>
> Nor need we inquire whether similar considerations enter into the review of statutes directed at particular religious . . . or national . . . or racial minorities . . . whether prejudice against discrete and insular minorities may be a special condition, which tends seriously to curtail the operation of those political processes ordinarily to be relied upon to protect minorities, and which may call for a correspondingly more searching judicial inquiry. . . .[45]

The first paragraph justified cases such as *Near* because the First Amendment guarantees a free press—and *Powell* because the Fifth and Sixth Amendments guarantee a fair trial. In such cases, the Court deemed that the Fourteenth Amendment's due process clause applied these federal restrictions to state and local governmental actions.

---

[41] James B. Thayer, "The Origin and Scope of the American Doctrine of Constitutional Law," 7 *Harvard Law Review* 129 (1893).

[42] Ibid., p. 152.

[43] *Near v. Minnesota,* 283 U.S. 697.

[44] *Powell v. Alabama,* 287 U.S. 45.

[45] *United States v. Carolene Products Co.,* 304 U.S. 144 (1938), at 152–153.

The note's second paragraph explained why the Court need not intervene in economic policy: Fights over allocation of economic resources—like the debate over the working conditions in bakeries in *Lochner*—are usually waged by well-organized groups on various sides of the issue. The political compromises among those interests may not equate with a professional economist's definition of rationality, but they are legally acceptable because all sides participate in the process. But if the electoral machinery itself breaks down so as to bias the messages policymakers receive, the Court may intervene, for example, as in the reapportionment cases.[46]

The footnote's third paragraph suggests that even when the machinery of electoral politics works properly, prejudice against racial, religious, or other minorities (including people accused of serious crimes such as murder, rape, and robbery) may prevent them from being heard. The Court's leadership regarding racial segregation took place at a time when blacks in the deep South were systematically denied the chance to organize and vote. These racist policies arguably violated all three parts of the *Carolene* theory.

In 1980, John Hart Ely and Jesse Choper developed the details of these theories.[47] To the three *Carolene Products* points, Choper added a fourth: The Court should avoid upsetting political decisions about the balance of power between national and local government. The fact that state and local parties and elections select the members of Congress and that reelection depends on satisfying local demands ensures a rough balance of state and local power without help from the Supreme Court.

Many more scholarly theories of the Court's role have emerged since 1937. Herbert Wechsler, for example, has advocated that the Court decide cases only on the basis of "neutral principles," rules that future courts can apply in cases with very different partisan or political alignments. A principle protecting those who demonstrate for racial justice must be articulated in such a way as to protect demonstrating members of the American Nazi Party.[48]

Wechsler, Choper, and Ely are among a vast array of constitutional theorists who seek to find a place for judicial review in democratic theory. But despite the scholarly elegance of each of the theories, they do not answer our fundamental question. We seek legal and political dynamics that actually do limit the constitutional power of the Supreme Court—not merely a resolution of an academic debate about what might, in theory, limit the Court. We seek an understanding of the Court's actual practices that can assure us that its justifications are good—and the fact of the matter is that, in practice, the Court does not consistently follow these theories any better than it follows more conventional methods of legal reasoning.

Consider the Court's decision in *Griswold v. Connecticut*, in which the Court struck down state laws prohibiting the distribution of contraceptives. The "right of privacy" created by the Court to justify the result is hardly a "specific prohibition" in the Bill of Rights, and the people it protects—women and men both—are as far from an insular and discrete minority as we could imagine.[49] The Court's extension of the principle of privacy in the abortion case—including the right of a single female—might seem to practice Wechsler's neutral principles concept but for the fact that the Court also ruled that the Constitution

---

[46] *Baker v. Carr,* 369 U.S. 186 (1962), and see *Reynolds v. Sims,* 377 U.S. 533 (1964).

[47] John Hart Ely, *Democracy and Distrust: A Theory of Judicial Review* (Cambridge: Harvard University Press, 1980); and Jesse Choper, *Judicial Review and the National Political Process: A Functional Reconsideration of the Role of the Supreme Court* (Chicago: University of Chicago Press, 1980).

[48] Herbert Wechsler, "Toward Neutral Principles of Constitutional Law," 73 *Harvard Law Review* 1 (1959).

[49] *Griswold v. Connecticut,* 381 U.S. 479 (1965).

permits government to deny funds for abortion to the indigent who are otherwise qualified to receive them.[50] Indeed Justice Stone, the coauthor of *Carolene Products'* footnote four, voted (perhaps for Bickelian reasons) against allowing the Court to intervene in legislative reapportionment, in direct contradiction to his note's second paragraph.[51]

We have already seen that a precedent does not dictate how a judge applies it. (If it did, a case that cited the precedent would usually not reach the appellate courts in the first place, as the two conflicting parties would be able to predict how the appellate judge would rule.) Just as "fact freedom" allows different judges to apply the same precedents in opposite ways, so each constitutional theory does not dictate or constrain. The history of judicial review, starting with *Marbury v. Madison*,[52] more resembles a tool bench, where the judge decides how the case ought to come out and then chooses whatever tool seems handiest to get the job done. All abstract theories about the Supreme Court's role fail to answer our question. But perhaps the political role of the Supreme Court makes theoretical consistency both impossible and unnecessary. We explore that possibility next.

Political Constraints on the Court

Grand theories of constitutional lawmaking of the sort we have just reviewed have dominated the academic discussion of constitutional law for decades. The main problem with these grand theories is that Supreme Court justices in practice neither care much about them nor make decisions consistent with them.[53] Political scientists have instead looked for constraints on the Supreme Court in the practical operation of politics itself.

This resolution of the constitutional paradox was expressed most pithily in 1901 by Finley Peter Dunne's satirical character, Mr. Dooley: "th' supreme coort follows th' iliction returns." Martin Shapiro, a leading figure in political jurisprudence, put it this way:

> No regime is likely to allow significant political power to be wielded by an isolated judicial corps free of political restraints. To the extent that courts make law, judges will be incorporated into the governing coalition, the ruling elite, responsible representatives of the people, or however else the political regime may be expressed.[54]

Subject to a few historical exceptions, particularly the Court's dogmatic opposition to economic regulation during the early New Deal, the theory holds that the Court rarely strays far enough from dominant popular opinion to worry about checking it through legal doctrine or theories of judicial review.[55] This approach combines historical observations of instances in which presidential selections of justices have steered the Court onto more popular courses with analyses of the structural and procedural characteristics of the Court's work that make it politically responsive. The rest of this subsection weaves the important threads of this perspective together.

---

[50] *Roe v. Wade*, 410 U.S. 113 (1973), but see *Harris v. McRae*, 448 U.S. 297 (1980).

[51] *Colegrove v. Green*, 328 U.S. 549 (1946).

[52] *Marbury v. Madison*, 5 U.S. 87 (1803).

[53] See generally, Lief Carter, *Contemporary Constitutional Lawmaking*. Also Mark Graber, "Constitutional Politics and Constitutional Theory: A Misunderstood and Neglected Relationship," 27 *Law and Social Inquiry* 309 (2002).

[54] Martin Shapiro, *Courts: A Comparative Political Analysis* (Chicago: University of Chicago Press, 1981), p. 34.

[55] See Robert Dahl, "Decision-Making in a Democracy: The Supreme Court as National Policy Maker," 6 *Journal of Public Law* 294 (1958).

Many constitutional decisions do not invalidate the work of popularly elected legislators in the first place. They set aside—as in the decisions regarding search and seizure of
criminal evidence and of interrogation of suspects—decisions of nonelected administrative
personnel who are, like judges, only indirectly affected by electoral politics. Where the work
of elected representatives is concerned, the Court has found constitutional defects in only a
tiny fraction of all statutes passed by Congress since World War II. In nearly all of these
instances, the Court has invalidated not an entire statutory scheme or policy but only an
offending clause or provision.[56] The most activist of courts touches only a tiny fraction of
the democratic work of Congress. Elected officials do not vote according to the "majority
will," because on most policy issues before a legislature, the public has no opinion whatsoever. The benefit of elections in the daily operation of politics comes from the fact that
elected politicians listen to interest groups and individual citizens because they need as
many votes from as many different sources as possible. Elections tend to overcome the
natural inertia of all organized human effort. The legal process has a different but equally
effective method for forcing judges to listen: Anyone can file a lawsuit about anything, and
judges must hear that suit at least long enough to determine that it alleges no legal injury.

The president fills a vacancy on the Supreme Court on the average of slightly less often
than once every two years. The system of presidential appointment usually means that
changes in the composition of the Court, admittedly in a very rough way, track the outcome
of national elections, and thus of public opinion. George W. Bush had fewer opportunities to
appoint justices than this average, but his two appointees, Samuel Alito and Chief Justice
John Roberts, clearly reflected Bush's conservative philosophy. Bill Clinton, a Democrat,
appointed two moderate liberals, Ruth Bader Ginsburg and Stephen Breyer, who as expected
voted in ways that tempered the conservative tendencies of the Rehnquist Court. Similarly,
just as President Nixon's "law and order" campaign had pledged, his appointees stalled the
expansion of the liberal Warren Court's protection of the rights of the accused.[57] In part
because of this electoral connection, Supreme Court decisions often line up fairly closely
with public opinion. For example, Justices O'Connor, Souter, and Kennedy voted to follow
the *Roe v. Wade* abortion precedent at a time (1992) when popular opinion seemed to favor
just that result. Indeed, Jeffrey Rosen has argued that the judiciary today is "the most democratic branch" because it is more regularly in sync with public opinion than the other
branches.[58]

As we saw regarding the case of the sunken barges in Chapter 3, courts process information very much as other decisionmakers do. The sides present positions. Lawyers file
briefs containing abundant factual as well as legal assertions. They criticize the positions
their opponents take. The capacity of judges to understand information is based on two
things. First, does the issue really depend on the intelligent digestion and interpretation of a
complex body of facts at all? Many of the most dramatic civil rights questions depend so
extensively on moral rather than factual reasoning that the technical competence of judges
really does not seem relevant. The decision to forbid mandatory flag salutes does not depend

---

[56] Through the year 2001, the Supreme Court had invalidated portions of 162 acts of Congress and
1,270 state laws and local ordinances. The Rehnquist Court (1994-2005) was unusually tough on Congress,
overturning 29 federal statutes in the 6 years between 1995 and 2001, but even so it overturned more state
and local acts—37. Thomas Keck, "Activism and Restraint on the Rehnquist Court," *Polity 35* (2002):
Tables I and II, p. 128–129.

[57] For an argument favoring independent Senate screening of the president's judicial appointments, see Laurence Tribe, *God Save This Honorable Court* (New York: Random House, 1985).

[58] Jeffrey Rosen, *The Most Democratic Branch* (New York: Oxford University Press, 2006).

on scientific analysis of data revealing the beneficial and harmful consequences of such practices. Second, when the issue does depend on an understanding of facts, then judges should have the capacity to understand the facts before they proceed. Judges must understand the language through which the problem expresses itself. Most judges are well equipped to understand the dimensions of a right-to-counsel issue. Most judges are not equipped to understand the econometric analysis on which the Federal Reserve Board determines its national monetary policy. The problem must not be of the sort in which part of the information is necessarily hidden from judges, as it is in many foreign-policy matters because the information is secret or because the only people who possess it do not live or work within reach of the court's jurisdiction. Finally, if a given decision generates feedback information that will produce improved policy, the courts should have access to that information in the course of further litigation.[59]

Constitutional decisions possess all the characteristics of the common-law tradition. No one decision permanently sets the course of law. The process is a thoroughly incremental one in which, case by case, new facts and new arguments pro and con repeatedly come before the courts. The law can change and adjust to new facts and conditions. A judicial commitment to protecting liberties does not require the courts to articulate a complete theory of equal protection or due process.[60]

For the most part, the Court has avoided creating legal doctrine that appeared to "take sides" along popular partisan lines. Decisions defending the freedom of civil rights activists to organize and demonstrate also protect antiabortion activists. The Vinson Court, though it had four appointees from the Truman administration, nonetheless ruled that President Truman's attempt to avert a work stoppage by seizing the nation's steel mills was illegal. The Burger Court, loaded with Nixon appointees, denied President Nixon's claim of executive privilege in the Watergate crisis.

The main thrust of the Madisonian constitutional scheme works to prevent too much power from accumulating in one place. The dispersion of power takes place more through the sharing than the separating of power. Different institutions must compromise because none can act effectively without cooperating with the others. Perhaps, therefore, the indeterminacy of constitutional theory is a blessing in disguise, a measure of the success of Madison's vision.[61]

These indisputable characteristics of American politics may help us to answer the challenge posed by Bickel's countermajoritarian difficulty. American government is not constructed to be purely majoritarian, but instead to be a system of separated institutions sharing power. The courts are typically the least majoritarian of these institutions, but they do not usually fall very far out of line with the dominant political opinions of the time. As Alexander Hamilton said in defending the federal judicial structure in *Federalist Papers #78*, the judiciary is the "least dangerous branch" because it has the power of neither "purse nor

---

[59] Lief H. Carter, "When Courts Should Make Policy: An Institutional Approach," in *Public Law and Public Policy*, John A. Gardiner, ed. (New York: Praeger, 1977), pp. 14–157; Donald L. Horowitz, *The Courts and Social Policy* (Washington, D.C.: The Brookings Institution, 1977); Gerald Rosenberg, *The Hollow Hope: Can Courts Bring About Social Change?* (Chicago: University of Chicago Press, 1991).

[60] Felix Cohen, "Transcendental Nonsense and the Functional Approach," 35 *Columbia Law Review* 809(1935). See also Martin Shapiro, "Stability and Change in Judicial Decision Making: Incrementalism or Stare Decisis?" 2 *Law in Transition Quarterly* 134 (1964). And see Janet S. Lindgren, "Beyond Cases: Reconsidering Judicial Review," *Wisconsin Law Review* 583 (1983).

[61] See Walter Murphy, James Fleming, Sotirios Barber, and Stephen Macedo, *American Constitutional Interpretation*, 3rd ed. (Mineola, NY: Foundation Press, 2003), Chapters 1–4, especially pp. 79–89.

sword." It has neither the staff nor the budget to implement its own decisions, so it must rely on others, especially the other branches of government, to put its rulings into effect.[62] No wonder then, that the Court rarely takes on the branch most connected to the people, Congress, in a major dispute.

Taken together, these facts about the role of courts within American government answer the democracy question that Bickel and others have posed. But do all these facts provide an acceptable substitute for persuasive legal justification? Do they obviate the need for good legal reasoning in constitutional law?

Two lines of reasoning indicate that they do not. First, although these factors do suggest no cause for immediate alarm about the Supreme Court's political role, they completely sidestep the original question. Legal reasoning ought to provide standards of satisfactory justification for specific case decisions. The political factors do not guide judges in the crafting of actual opinions. The political environment may reassure the average voter, but it will hardly satisfy a losing litigant in a concrete case to learn that the president might appoint a more sympathetic justice a year or two later.

Second, the reassuring argument may prove too much. The Constitution in part seeks to protect individuals from what Alexis de Tocqueville called "the tyranny of the majority."[63] If the judiciary tracks public opinion too closely, it will not reliably provide this protection. The unpopular speaker and the deviant religious belief may thrive only if the courts are *not* politically responsive. If we must sustain the belief that the Constitution is a central source of political structure and communal values—if we need to believe in it—then conventional political jurisprudence provides no satisfying solution to our problem.

THE TURN TO INDIVIDUAL DIGNITY AND CONSTITUTIONAL DIALOGUE

One important movement in legal theory—"Critical Legal Studies"—recognized the two reservations just described. Beginning in the mid-1970s, Duncan Kennedy, Roberto Unger, Mark Tushnet, Robert Gordon, Paul Brest, John Henry Schlagel, and other law professors who came of professional age during the antiwar movement of the 1960s began in their writings to assert that the political culture constrains court and legislature alike from protecting individual dignity adequately. But they also recognized that the solution lay in changing not legal doctrine but the political culture itself. The negative side of the movement articulated a powerful case for abandoning the search for any doctrinal solution to constitutional interpretation.[64]

The positive contribution of Critical Legal Studies was less clear or convincing, in part because the very success of the movement's critique of doctrine makes a case that no doctrinal solution is possible. Nevertheless, Critical Legal Studies seemed to move toward endorsing the idea that constitutional goodness depends on the Court's enhancing our capacity to converse about the moral or normative quality of our communal life. To achieve this, the Court

---

[62] *The Federalist Papers* (New York: Mentor, 1961), pp. 464–472. For a study of the limits of the judiciary in implementing its rulings, see Gerald Rosenberg, *The Hollow Hope: Can Courts Bring About Social Change?* (Chicago: University of Chicago Press, 1991).

[63] Alexis de Tocqueville, *Democracy in America*, George Lawrence, trans., J. P. Mayer, ed. (New York: Harper and Row, 1969), p. 250.

[64] Lief Carter has discussed Critical Legal Studies in more depth in his *Contemporary Constitutional Lawmaking*, especially pp. 98–101 and 127–133.

must do more than protect First Amendment freedoms or individual privacy. It must protect individual integrity and dignity so that people feel empowered to participate in political life. To accomplish that task, the Court must in turn model good conversation. It must speak candidly about the world that law, politics, science, economics, and religion all inhabit.

In recent years, legal scholars have largely abandoned the attempt to find a grand theoretical solution to the problem of judicial review. Instead they have sought to make constitutional discourse both more realistic and more principled. One group of scholars has attempted to validate and reinvigorate discussion about constitutional issues outside the judiciary, "popular constitutionalism," arguing that courts must share responsibility for resolving difficult legal issues with the people.[65] Another group has urged judges to write "minimalist decisions," opinions that don't sweep too far beyond the facts of the case, so as to facilitate learning from later cases that arise, and from dialogue with the other branches of government.[66] Both perspectives remind us that courts are enmeshed in a larger system of separated powers, challenging the notion that courts by themselves can protect individual freedoms. Recent constitutional scholarship focuses not on finding the "right answer" to difficult constitutional issues but instead on improving the process by which we arrive at our judgments. This focus reflects the constitutional aspiration to form "a more perfect union." We, being imperfect, will never fully achieve it, but it is essential that we not abandon our effort to combine the lessons of the past with our experience in the present to define what is politically good.

The final chapter presents this book's theory of justification in all areas of law, one that flows from this goal of political goodness. For now, the lesson is that a preoccupation with doctrine may do more harm than good. The judge or scholar who insists on a doctrinally elegant legal resolution of a case may shut herself off from the cares and aspirations of the litigants themselves. The people whose lives the courts shape will not likely have doctrinal elegance at the top of their list of priorities. Perhaps this is what Justice Harry Blackmun meant in a 1983 interview:

> "Maybe I'm oversensitive," Justice Blackmun says, "But these are very personal cases. We're dealing with people—the life, liberty, and property of people. And because I grew up in poor surroundings, I know there's another world out there we sometimes forget about."[67]

ILLUSTRATIVE CASE

The following case illustrates a fundamental problem in constitutional law, how to interpret a provision of the Constitution in light of new social developments. In this case the development was technological: The Supreme Court for the first time, in 1928, considered the

---

[65] Mark V. Tushnet, *Taking the Constitution Away from the Courts* (Princeton, N.J.: Princeton University Press, 2000); Larry D. Kramer, *The People Themselves: Popular Constitutionalism and Judicial Review* (New York: Oxford University Press, 2005); and George Thomas, *The Madisonian Constitution* (Baltimore: Johns Hopkins University Press, 2008).

[66] Cass R. Sunstein, *One Case at a Time: Judicial Minimalism on the Supreme Court* (Cambridge, MA: Harvard University Press, 2001). We thank Keith Bybee for his guidance in helping us to understand trends in constitutional scholarship.

[67] John Jenkins, "A Candid Talk with Justice Blackmun," *New York Times Magazine*, February 20, 1983, pp. 23–24.

wiretapping of phones. As you read the case, pay attention to the techniques of constitutional interpretation used by Taft in his majority opinion and Brandeis in his dissent. How do they differ? Which do you find more convincing, and why? Controversy over wiretapping has been reignited in recent years by the Bush administration, which without judicial authorization wiretapped phones and searched e-mails between the United States and other nations. This was the background to the "hospital story" that began Chapter 1 of this book, in which members of the administration attempted to get Attorney General John Ashcroft to certify the legality of a program of surveillance from his hospital bed. We further examine the Bush administration's program of surveillance in the next chapter and in Appendix B of this book. As you read this case, though, think about what principles might guide you in deciding whether the Bush administration's surveillance program violated the Fourth Amendment, and what facts you might take into account in forming your judgment.

Olmstead v. New York
277 U.S. 438 (1928)

(routine citations omitted)

Chief Justice Taft delivered the opinion of the Court:

The petitioners were convicted in the District Court for the Western District of Washington of a conspiracy to violate the National Prohibition Act by unlawfully possessing, transporting and importing intoxicating liquors and maintaining nuisances, and by selling intoxicating liquors. Seventy-two others, in addition to the petitioners, were indicted. Some were not apprehended, some were acquitted, and others pleaded guilty.

The evidence in the records discloses a conspiracy of amazing magnitude to import, possess, and sell liquor unlawfully. It involved the employment of not less than 50 persons, of two sea-going vessels for the transportation of liquor to British Columbia, of smaller vessels for coastwise transportation to the state of Washington, the purchase and use of a branch beyond the suburban limits of Seattle, with a large underground cache for storage and a number of smaller caches in that city, the maintenance of a central office manned with operators, and the employment of executives, salesmen, deliverymen dispatchers, scouts, bookkeepers, collectors, and an attorney. In a bad month sales amounted to $176,000; the aggregate for a year must have exceeded $2,000,000.[68]

The information which led to the discovery of the conspiracy and its nature and extent was largely obtained by intercepting messages on the telephones of the conspirators by four federal prohibition officers. Small wires were inserted along the ordinary telephone wires from the residences of four of the petitioners and those leading from the chief office. The insertions were made without trespass upon any property of the defendants. They were made in the basement of the large office building. The taps from house lines were made in the streets near the houses.

---

[68] This amounts to about $25 million in 2008 dollars if calculated using the consumer price index as a measure of the declining purchase power of the dollar (calculated by the authors).

The Fourth Amendment provides:

The right of the people to be secure in their persons, houses, papers, and effects, against unreasonable searches and seizures, shall not be violated, and no warrants shall issue, but upon probable cause, supported by oath or affirmation, and particularly describing the place to be searched, and the persons or things to be seized.

. . . The Fourth Amendment may have proper application to a sealed letter in the mail, because of the constitutional provision for the Post Office Department and the relations between the government and those who pay to secure protection of their sealed letters. See Revised Statutes, 3978 to 3988, whereby Congress monopolizes the carriage of letters and excludes from that business everyone else, and Section 3929 (39 USCA 259), which forbids any postmaster or other person to open any letter not addressed to himself. It is plainly within the words of the amendment to say that the unlawful rifling by a government agent of a sealed letter is a search and seizure of the sender's papers or effects. The letter is a paper, an effect, and in the custody of a government that forbids carriage, except under its protection.

The United States takes no such care of telegraph or telephone messages as of mailed sealed letters. The amendment does not forbid what was done here. There was no searching. There was no seizure. The evidence was secured by the use of the sense of hearing and that only. There was no entry of the houses or offices of the defendants. By the invention of the telephone 50 years ago, and its application for the purpose of extending communications, one can talk with another at a far distant place.

The language of the amendment cannot be extended and expanded to include telephone wires, reaching to the whole world from the defendant's house or office. The intervening wires are not part of his house or office, any more than are the highways along which they are stretched.

This court, in *Carroll v. United States,* 267 U.S. 132, 149, declared:

The Fourth Amendment is to be construed in the light of what was deemed an unreasonable search and seizure when it was adopted, and in a manner which will conserve public interests, as well as the interest and rights of individual citizens.

Justice Bradley, in the *Boyd* Case, and Justice Clarke, in the *Gouled* Case, said that the Fifth Amendment and the Fourth Amendment were to be liberally construed to effect the purpose of the framers of the Constitution in the interest of liberty. But that cannot justify enlargement of the language employed beyond the possible practical meaning of houses, persons, papers, and effects, or so to apply the words search and seizure as to forbid hearing or sight.

. . . Congress may, of course, protect the secrecy of telephone messages by making them, when intercepted, inadmissible in evidence in federal criminal trials, by direct legislation, and thus depart from the common law of evidence. But the courts may not adopt such a policy by attributing an enlarged and unusual meaning to the Fourth Amendment. The reasonable view is that one who installs in his house a telephone instrument with connecting wires intends to project his voice to those quite outside, and that the wires beyond his house, and messages while passing over them, are not within the protection of the Fourth Amendment. Here those who intercepted the projected voices were not in the house of either party to the conversation.

Neither the cases we have cited nor any of the many federal decisions brought to our attention hold the Fourth Amendment to have been violated as against a defendant, unless there has been an official search and seizure of his person or such a seizure of his papers or his tangible material effects or an actual physical invasion of his house 'or curtilage' for the purpose of making a seizure.

We think, therefore, that the wire tapping here disclosed did not amount to a search or seizure within the meaning of the Fourth Amendment.

Justice Brandeis, dissenting:

The government makes no attempt to defend the methods employed by its officers. Indeed, it concedes that, if wire tapping can be deemed a search and seizure within the Fourth Amendment, such wire tapping as was practiced in the case at bar was an unreasonable search and seizure, and that the evidence thus obtained was inadmissible. But it relies on the language of the amendment, and it claims that the protection given thereby cannot properly be held to include a telephone conversation.

"We must never forget," said Mr. Chief Justice Marshall in *McCulloch v. Maryland,* 17 U.S. 316, "that it is a Constitution we are expounding." Since then this court has repeatedly sustained the exercise of power by Congress, under various clauses of that instrument, over objects of which the fathers could not have dreamed. We have likewise held that general limitations on the powers of government, like those embodied in the due process clauses of the Fifth and Fourteenth Amendments, do not forbid the United States or the states from meeting modern conditions by regulations which "a century ago, or even half a century ago, probably would have been rejected as arbitrary and oppressive." *Village of Euclid v. Ambler Realty Co.,* 272 U.S. 365, 387; *Buck v. Bell,* 274 U.S. 200. Clauses guaranteeing to the individual protection against specific abuses of power, must have a similar capacity of adaptation to a changing world. It was with reference to such a clause that this court said in *Weems v. United States,* 217 U.S. 349, 373:

> Legislation, both statutory and constitutional, is enacted, it is true, from an experience of evils, but its general language should not, therefore, be necessarily confined to the form that evil had theretofore taken. Time works changes, brings into existence new conditions and purposes. Therefore a principal to be vital must be capable of wider application than the mischief which gave it birth. This is peculiarly true of Constitutions. They are not ephemeral enactments, designed to meet passing occasions. They are, to use the words of Chief Justice Marshall, "designed to approach immortality as nearly as human institutions can approach it." The future is their care and provision for events of good and bad tendencies of which no prophecy can be made. In the application of a Constitution, therefore, our contemplation cannot be only of what has been but of what may be. Under any other rule a Constitution would indeed be as easy of application as it would be deficient in efficacy and power. Its general principles would have little value and be converted by precedent into impotent and lifeless formulas. Rights declared in words might be lost in reality.

When the Fourth and Fifth Amendments were adopted, "the form that evil had theretofore taken" had been necessarily simple. Force and violence were then the only means known to man by which a government could directly effect self-incrimination. It could compel the individual to testify-a compulsion effected, if need be, by torture. It could secure possession of his papers and other articles incident to his private life-a seizure effected, if need be, by breaking and entry. Protection against such invasion of "the sanctities of a man's home and the privacies of life" was provided in the Fourth and Fifth Amendments by specific language. *Boyd v. United States*, 116 U.S. 616, 630. But "time works changes, brings into existence new conditions and purposes." Subtler and more far-reaching means of invading privacy have become available to the government. Discovery and invention have made it possible for the government, by means far more effective than stretching upon the rack, to obtain disclosure in court of what is whispered in the closet. Moreover, "in the application of a Constitution, our contemplation cannot be only of what has been, but of what may be." The progress of science in furnishing the government with means of espionage is not likely to stop with wiretapping. Ways may some day be developed by which the government, without removing papers from secret drawers, can reproduce them in court, and by which it will be enabled to expose to a jury the most intimate occurrences of the home. Advances in the psychic and related sciences may bring means of exploring unexpressed beliefs, thoughts and emotions. "That places the liberty of every man in the hands of every petty officer" was said by James Otis of much lesser intrusions than these. To Lord Camden a far slighter intrusion seemed "subversive of all the comforts of society." Can it be that the Constitution affords no protection against such invasions of individual security?

A sufficient answer is found in *Boyd v. United States*, a case that will be remembered as long as civil liberty lives in the United States. This court there reviewed the history that lay behind the Fourth and Fifth Amendments. We said with reference to Lord Camden's judgment in *Entick v. Carrington*, 19 Howell's State Trials, 1030:

> The principles laid down in this opinion affect the very essence of constitutional liberty and security. They reach farther than the concrete form of the case there before the court, with its adventitious circumstances; they apply to all invasions on the part of the government and its employee of the sanctities of a man's home and the privacies of life. It is not the breaking of his doors, and the rummaging of his drawers, that constitutes the essence of the offense; but it is the invasion of his indefeasible right of personal security, personal liberty and private property, where that right has never been forfeited by his conviction of some public offense-it is the invasion of this sacred right which underlies and constitutes the essence of Lord Camden's judgment. Breaking into a house and opening boxes and drawers are circumstances of aggravation; but any forcible and compulsory extortion of a man's own testimony or of his private papers to be used as evidence of a crime or to forfeit his goods, is within the condemnation of that judgment. In this regard the Fourth and Fifth Amendments run almost into each other.

In *Ex parte Jackson*, 96 U.S. 727, it was held that a sealed letter intrusted to the mail is protected by the amendments. The mail is a public service furnished by the government. The telephone is a public service furnished by its authority. There is, in essence, no difference between the sealed letter and the private telephone message. As Judge Rudkin said below:

> True, the one is visible, the other invisible; the one is tangible, the other intangible; the one is sealed, and the other unsealed; but these are distinctions without a difference.

The evil incident to invasion of the privacy of the telephone is far greater than that involved in tampering with the mails. Whenever a telephone line is tapped, the privacy of the persons at both ends of the line is invaded, and all conversations between them upon any subject, and although proper, confidential, and privileged, may be overheard. Moreover, the tapping of one man's telephone line involves the tapping of the telephone of every other person whom he may call, or who may call him . . .

Time and again this court, in giving effect to the principle underlying the Fourth Amendment, has refused to place an unduly literal construction upon it. This was notably illustrated in the *Boyd* Case itself. Taking language in its ordinary meaning, there is no "search" or "seizure" when a defendant is required to produce a document in the orderly process of a court's procedure. "The right of the people of be secure in their persons, houses, papers, and effects, against unreasonable searches and seizures," would not be violated, under any ordinary construction of language, by compelling obedience to a subpoena. But this court holds the evidence inadmissible simply because the information leading to the issue of the subpoena has been unlawfully secured. *Silverthorne Lumber Co. v. United States*, 215 U.S. 385. Literally, there is no "search" or "seizure" when a friendly visitor abstracts papers from an office; yet we held in *Gouled v. United States*, 255 U.S. 298, that evidence so obtained could not be used. No court which looked at the words of the amendment rather than at its underlying purpose would hold, as this court did in *Ex parte Jackson*, 96 U.S. 727, 733, that its protection extended to letters in the mails . . .

. . . The makers of our Constitution undertook to secure conditions favorable to the pursuit of happiness. They recognized the significance of man's spiritual nature, of his feelings and of his intellect. They knew that only a part of the pain, pleasure and satisfactions of life are to be found in material things. They sought to protect Americans in their beliefs, their thoughts, their emotions and their sensations. They conferred, as against the government, the right to be let alone—the most comprehensive of rights and the right most valued by civilized men. To protect, that right, every unjustifiable intrusion by the government upon the privacy of the individual, whatever the means employed, must be deemed a violation of the Fourth Amendment . . .

. . . Experience should teach us to be most on our guard to protect liberty when the government's purposes are beneficent. Men born to freedom are naturally alert to repel invasion of their liberty by evil-minded rulers. The greatest dangers to liberty lurk in insidious encroachment by men of zeal, well-meaning but without understanding.

QUESTIONS ABOUT THE CASE

1. Taft uses a literalist approach to the Constitution. How does that lead him to his conclusion? On what bases does Brandeis reject the literalist approach?

2. Taft also employs an original intent approach to interpreting the Constitution. What does Brandeis say against original intent? What approach to constitutional interpretation does Brandeis take? Does the distinction we drew in Chapter 4 between interpreting law in terms of guesses about what its makers actually intended, on one hand, versus thinking about a law's purposes—the "good" it seeks to do for society—help explain the difference between Taft's and Brandeis's conclusions about wiretapping?

3. Brandeis quotes Chief Justice John Marshall's famous statement in *McCulloch v. Maryland* that "we must never forget . . . that it is a Constitution we are expounding." What do you think Marshall meant by this, or Brandeis meant in quoting it? How is constitutional interpretation different from, say, statutory interpretation? How is constitutional interpretation different from decision-making in common law?

4. The ruling in *Olmstead* that judicially unauthorized wiretapping is not a violation of the Fourth Amendment was eventually overturned in *Katz v. United States*, 389 U.S. 347 (1967). Justice Hugo Black, however, dissented, arguing in part that wiretapping is not unlike eavesdropping, and that eavesdropping is clearly not outlawed by the Fourth Amendment. Do you agree? How would you analyze Black's argument?

5. Does not this case also raise echoes of the main theme in Chapter 3's discussion of common law, namely that law evolves to parallel changes in the "real world"? There, we saw how the practical meaning of the concept of trespass and its legal consequences changed over time as strangers became more inevitably intertwined with each other in day-to-day living. In a sense, the wiretapping case is really a trespass case in which the majority says wiretapping is not a trespass. Note here a seeming contradiction: In tort law, trespass law has changed so as to *narrow* the obligation not to interfere with someone else's person or property, but in constitutional law, which now follows more Brandeis than Taft, one's legal right not to be trespassed against seems to have *expanded*. How might the materials in this book explain and justify why the law should operate with seeming contradictions like this?

CHAPTER 6

Law and Politics

The ultimate goal is to break down the sense that legal argument is autonomous from moral, economic and political discourse.

—DUNCAN KENNEDY

When judges make law and scholars propose rules of law, they necessarily rely on their vision of society as it is and as it ought to be. If law is to be made well, those visions must be accurate and attractive.

—MARK TUSHNET

THE RULE OF LAW

On the night of July 31, 2001, Roy Moore, the elected Chief Justice of the Alabama Supreme Court, had a 5,280-pound granite monument placed in the rotunda of the state's Judicial Building in Montgomery. Chief Justice Moore did so without the knowledge or consent of the other eight justices on the court. The monument depicted a book, presumably the Holy Bible, open to two pages on which the stonemason had carved the King James translation of the Ten Commandments. A private evangelical group, Coral Ridge Ministries, paid the costs of the project. Within days, Stephen Glassroth, a Jewish attorney practicing in Montgomery, sued to have the monument removed.

In the summer of 2003, after Moore lost both at trial and on appeal, federal district court judge Myron Thompson commanded Moore to remove the display. Refusal would subject the state of Alabama to a fine of $5,000 a day for contempt of court. The federal courts cited precedents that, under the "establishment clause" of the First Amendment, prohibited schools from posting the Ten Commandments in classrooms and prohibited courthouses from displaying the Commandments unless accompanied by other secular historical examples of the sources of American law. Moore had specifically refused one request to place in the Judicial Building's rotunda a plaque containing the words of Martin Luther King, Jr.'s "I Have a Dream" speech, and another request to put an atheist symbol there. On August 26, the eight remaining justices of the Alabama Supreme Court, who by then had voted to suspend Moore from his office for refusing to comply with the court order to remove the monument, hired a moving company in Georgia (no Alabama company would take the job) and moved "Roy's Rock" from the rotunda to a courthouse area not open to the public.

In an essay in the *Wall Street Journal,* titled "In God I Trust," Chief Justice Moore wrote, "Today, I argue for the rule of law, and against any unilateral declaration of a judge to ban the acknowledgment of God in the public sector." His defense of the display included the following legal arguments:[1]

- The constitution of the State of Alabama specifically invokes "the favor and guidance of Almighty God."

- As the state's chief justice, "I am entrusted with the scared duty to uphold the state's constitution. I have taken an oath before God and man to do such, and I will not waver from that commitment."

- In preventing Moore from complying with his sacred duty, the federal court has "violated the rule of law."

- The founding fathers were greatly influenced by William Blackstone, who stated that judges have no power to make laws, only interpret them. "No judge has the authority to impose his will on the people of a state. . . ."

- If the federal courts had ordered "the churches of my state to be burned to the ground," the Alabama courts would rightly refuse to enforce the order, and the same principle applies here.

- The "separation of church and state" in the First Amendment of the U.S. Constitution endorses "the legitimate jurisdictional separation between church and state," not the "separation of God and state."

- Literally read, the First Amendment's language—"Congress shall make no law respecting the establishment of religion . . ."—obviously does not apply here, since Congress has not made a law requiring a display of the Ten Commandments in courthouses.

Moore concluded:

Not only does Judge Thompson put himself above the law, but above God, as well. I say enough is enough. We must "dare to defend our rights," as Alabama's state motto declares. No judge or man can dictate what we believe or in whom we believe. The Ninth and Tenth Amendments are not a part of the Constitution simply to make the Bill of Rights a round number. The Ninth Amendment secured our right as a people. The 10th guaranteed our right as a sovereign state. Those are the rules of law.[2]

At the core of Roy Moore's bold political action, which made front-page stories around the country, lies a political debate about the issues you have studied so far in this book. In a nutshell, that debate and this book ask, "What is the rule of law?" We could, of course, analyze the Roy Moore story as just another political power struggle, another case of ambition countering ambition, as James Madison put it in *The Federalist Papers.*[3] Moore claims that the

---

[1] Roy Moore, "In God I Trust," *Wall Street Journal,* August 25, 2003, p. A10.

[2] The Ninth Amendment reads, "The enumeration in the Constitution, of certain rights, shall not be construed to deny or disparage others retained by the people." The Tenth reads, "The powers not delegated to the United States by the Constitution, nor prohibited by it to the States, are reserved to the States respectively, or to the people."

[3] Writing in defense of the separation of legislative, judicial, and executive powers from one another in the U.S. Constitution, Madison wrote, "Ambition must be made to counteract ambition" so that no one faction could gain tyrannical control over government. "Federalist Papers #51" in *The Federalist Papers,* Isaac Kramnick, ed. (New York: Penguin, 1987), p. 319.

people of Alabama have elected him to his judicial post. He, having taken an oath to defend the Alabama constitution, is just doing his job. The federal court judges, appointed to their posts for life, represent a different and more national constituency; therefore, they reach a different conclusion. Perhaps because William Pryor, Alabama's attorney general, agreed that the federal court order was valid and had to be enforced, federal power out-muscled Roy Moore's power in this struggle.[4]

This book suggests another way to frame the Roy Moore story. Recall our basic definition of law: Law is a language used to prevent or resolve conflicts using rules made by the state as a starting point. We call this language "legal reasoning." Legal reasoning, when done well, helps reassure communities that judges resolve disputes with integrity and respect. Legal reasoning contains too many sources of generality, vagueness, and ambiguity to generate objectively correct answers to legal questions. Nevertheless, just as we can tell better performances of Beethoven's Fifth Symphony or of Twisted Sister's *We're Not Gonna Take It* from worse ones, so can we tell good legal reasoning from bad.

We shall apply the four elements of legal reasoning to Moore's argument later in this chapter. For the moment, we return to the analysis in Chapter 1 of the critical importance of judicial impartiality (starting on p. 5). There, we made the following argument: Judicial impartiality plays a major role in maintaining peaceful and progressive political regimes. It does so because the existence of a neutral third-party judge, a triadic process of conflict resolution as we have called it, keeps conflicts from turning into two-against-one power struggles. The presence of a third-party referee allows the loser of a conflict to accept the loss without feeling wronged or worse, humiliated, and hell-bent on revenge.

THREE THREATS TO THE RULE OF LAW

Examples of successful triadic dispute resolution are all around us. The decisions of referees and umpires, for example, are routinely accepted as tolerably fair in all kinds of organized sports and games. (If you think that sports and games don't involve significant stakes, think again. A professional league championship in the United States brings literally millions of dollars to the winning team.) But though triadic dispute resolution is common, threats to this process, and thus to the rule of law, are common as well. Consider three such threats.

Democracy

You may be startled to see democracy listed first as a threat to the rule of law, but you should not be. If by democracy we mean "a government created by elections in which every adult citizen could vote," then we must confront a difficult fact.[5] Democracies can elect racist and fascist governments that trample the rule of law. Hitler rose to power democratically. The leaders of Israel and Palestine hold power through elections, but wage constant war on one another. Democratic politics in India, which began as a secular nation, has led some Indian parties to mobilize along pro-Hindu, anti-Muslim lines, thus exacerbating divisions in society.

As Fareed Zakaria points out in *The Future of Freedom,* we unthinkingly use democracy as the only test of good government. Zakaria reminds us that the best test of good government, confirmed by the qualities of stable and peaceful regimes in the developed world, is not

---

[4] In February 2004, President Bush, unable to secure Pryor's Senate confirmation to the federal bench, made Pryor a "recess appointee," giving him the right to serve until 2005. In 2005 Pryor was confirmed by the Senate to a permanent position.

[5] Fareed Zakaria, *The Future of Freedom* (New York: Norton, 2003), p. 13.

elections but the liberalism (in the classical philosophical sense) of governmental institutions and practices. Liberal government, which is not necessarily democratic by his definition, secures individual freedom. It does so by protecting the formal equality of the parties before the law and by providing judges who are independent and nonpartisan.[6] These features help insulate the triadic dispute-resolution process from the illiberal aspects of democracy.

Elections make sense as a mechanism for selecting most government officeholders. Electoral pressures to win and keep a job do motivate public officials to respond, if crudely, to public demands and public criticisms. But judges are not like other officeholders; to do their job well, judges must be impartial—and impartiality coexists uneasily, if at all, with democratic responsiveness. To illustrate, imagine a world in which the professional baseball team owners, or perhaps the players themselves, voted on competing slates of umpires each season. If you held a job paying roughly $100,000 a year as a Major League Baseball umpire because you were elected by, say, the "Batters' Party," instead of the "Pitchers' Party," and you wanted to keep your job, might your calls tend to slant toward batters or instead of toward pitchers? In fact, in the real world, umpires are separately schooled and trained and evaluated on merit.

Most of the world's legal systems train and supervise judges from law school onward, much as we do with our umpires. American systems of judicial selection, by contrast, largely fail to train judges or insulate them from partisan pressures. In 43 states, judges on the highest level courts are elected or must face retention elections after an initial appointment. In eight states, these elections are partisan, so judges run as members of the Democratic or Republican parties.[7] In many state elections, judges receive campaign contributions to help them get reelected, and the main source of financing are lawyers' groups and businesses—organizations that have a strong interest in cases those same judges will hear. In 2004, for example, state supreme court candidates raised nearly $47 million in campaign funds, an average of more than $400,000 per candidate, much of which was spent on television ads.[8] In the aftermath of the "Ten Commandments" struggle in Alabama, the League of Christian Voters targeted Jean Brown, an Associate Justice who had supported removal of the Moore monument. Tom Parker, running as a "pro-life leader" and "conservative Christian," unseated Brown.[9] In 2006, Parker ran for a promotion to Chief Justice of the Court, arguing in television commercials that the incumbent chief had voted against the death penalty for a convicted murderer-rapist. Parker was unsuccessful, but the incumbent was defeated by another candidate. Judges facing reelection know that unpopular votes can cost them their jobs.[10]

Federal judges, unlike most state judges, are appointed rather than elected, and most federal judges serve for life. Congress may impeach and remove them from office, but this

---

[6] Zakaria, pp.19–20.

[7] Robert A. Carp and Ronald Stidham, *Judicial Process in America*, 5th ed. (Washington, D.C.: CQ Press, 2001), Table 9-2, p. 273.

[8] Deborah Goldberg, Sarah Samis, Edwin Bender, and Rachel Weiss, *The New Politics of Judicial Elections 2004* (Washington, D.C.: Brennan Center for Justice and the Institute for Money in State Politics, 2005), available at http://www.justiceatstake.org/contentViewer.asp?breadcrumb=3,570,633, Fig. 9, p. 14 and Fig. 11, p. 16.

[9] Ibid., pp. 32–33.

[10] James Semple, Lauren Jones, and Rachel Weiss, *The New Politics of Judicial Elections 2006* (Washington, D.C.: Justice at Stake Campaign, 2007), available at http://brennan.3cdn.net/49c18b6cb 18960b2f9_z6m62gwji.pdf. On judicial elections generally see Matthew J. Streb, ed., *Running for Judge: The Rising Political, Financial, and Legal Stakes of Judicial Elections* (New York: New York University Press, 2007).

happens so rarely that it does not systematically coerce judges to abandon sound legal positions. These facts mean that federal judges are more insulated from democratic pressures than the average state judge. Still, the federal judicial selection system also has a partisan component because presidents normally nominate judges from their own party, and most of the nominees are active in party affairs.[11] For this reason, partisan battles have regularly erupted whenever the Senate, which must confirm the president's nominees, is controlled by a party different from that of the president. Until recently, nominations below the Supreme Court level rarely resulted in a fight. Beginning in the late twentieth century, however, that began to change, and today, lower court nominations are a major battleground in the Senate.[12]

Despite these signs of increasing partisanship, federal judges still remain relatively insulated from partisan pressures. Once federal judges get on the bench, after all, they cannot easily be removed, unlike many of their colleagues in the state judiciary. In the Roy Moore case, federal judges made a decision that was quite controversial in Alabama but faced no major repercussions. Federal judges have promoted equality before the law and have enforced the separation of church and state in ways that, as the example of Alabama suggests, can be perilous for elected officials.

Attacks on Judicial Legitimacy

Judicial authority, like the authority of referees and umpires, requires both the litigants and the observers of the process to understand and accept the role and function of judges in the game. When people, for whatever reasons, come to see judges, referees, and umpires as no longer legitimate deciders of the fortunes of others, the system breaks down.

This suggests another problem with American systems of judicial selection—they can be delegitmizing. Highly funded, media-saturated judicial election campaigns seem almost designed to lower respect for judges. As money pours into these elections, mostly from business groups but also from personal injury lawyers who have strong interests in the cases that come before the judges, citizens are left to ponder the effects. Candidates running for seats on the Alabama Supreme Court raised $13.4 million (and exposed Alabama voters to nearly 18,000 television campaign ads) in 2006. In the campaign for Alabama chief justice, one side accused the other of being funded by gambling organizations and personal injury lawyers; the other accused its opposition of being in the pocket of oil and insurance interests.[13] In the Nevada court system, according to a *Los Angeles Times* report, lawyers say that campaigns contributions are required for favorable treatment from judges. Contributions "get you juice

---

[11] Jeffrey Toobin's *The Nine* describes the process by which the George W. Bush administration screened judicial candidates. Bush, Toobin writes, "did not want a process like the one that led his father to nominate David Souter," a deep disappointment to conservatives because of Souter's votes on abortion and gay rights. "George W. Bush didn't want any surprises," Toobin reports. See *The Nine: Inside the Secret World of the Supreme Court* (New York: Random House, 2007). Through 2002, 83 percent of George W. Bush's nominees to federal district courts and 81 percent of his nominees to appeals courts were Republicans; more than half of his nominees had a record of party activism. This record is roughly comparable with the nominees of previous presidents Clinton, George H.W. Bush, Ronald Reagan, and Jimmy Carter. See Sheldon Goldman et al., "W. Bush: Remaking the Judiciary: Like Father Like Son?" 86 *Judicature* 6 (May–June 2003): Tables II and IV, pp. 304, 308.

[12] Nancy Scherer, *Scoring Points* (Palo Alto, CA: Stanford University Press, 2005).

[13] James Semple et al., *The New Politics of Judicial Elections 2006*, pp. 4–5.

with a judge—an 'in,'" said one.[14] Seventy-five percent of those surveyed in a 1999 poll agreed or strongly agreed with the statement "Elected Judges are influenced by having to raise campaign funds."[15]

The American legal system is also facing a delegitimating attack in the media. Media coverage of one aspect of the legal system—civil litigation—is scornful of both judges and juries. As William Haltom and Michael McCann have argued in their book *Distorting the Law*, simplistic and often factually wrong coverage of legal events misinforms the public about the legal system and thus erodes legal legitimacy.[16] The authors analyze closely the "McDonald's Coffee Case" and note the wide gap between the actual facts of the case and media's conversion of these facts into a gripping story. An Associated Press headline captured the public story: "Woman Burned by Hot McDonald's Coffee Gets 2.9 Million."[17] As the tale spread through popular culture, the struggles of a low-income, elderly woman badly burned in an accident became a "personification of runaway litigiousness" and the subject of a "pithy homily condemning individual recklessness, blame avoidance, and greed."[18] The public story, then, suggested that an out-of-control legal system produced a very unfair award. The legal story was less dramatic, less personal, and less sellable, however; the media's version of it was in many ways flat wrong.

We cannot retell the entire legal story here, but here are some of the case and social background facts that the media ignored or downplayed:

- Stella Liebeck, a 79-year-old woman, was a passenger in a car driven by her grandson. She purchased a cup of coffee with her breakfast at a McDonald's drive-through. After her grandson had parked at the curb, she spilled the coffee in her lap while trying to get the cup's lid off to add cream and sugar. She screamed in pain. Within minutes, her grandson perceived that she was going into shock. He took her to one hospital that refused to admit her, then to a second hospital that did admit her and determined that she had suffered third-degree burns to her thighs, buttocks, genitals, and groin area.[19]

- The McDonald's manual directs its coffee to be made at temperatures between 195 and 205 degrees and served at temperatures between 180 and 190 degrees. Burn experts testi-fied that liquids at such temperatures can cause third-degree burns in from 2 to 7 seconds. Home coffeemakers hold coffee temperatures between 150 and 157 degrees.[20]

- In the previous decade, McDonald's had received more than 700 complaints for harm done by hot coffee and had paid out nearly $750,000 in settlement of the claims.[21]

- The coffee cup did contain a warning, "CAUTION: CONTENTS HOT," but the warning was the same color and size as the ornamental trim on the cup and not easily noticeable.

---

[14] Michael J. Goodman and William C. Rempel, "In Las Vegas, They're Playing With a Stacked Judicial Deck," *The Los Angeles Times,* June 8, 2006.

[15] National Center for State Courts, "How the Public Views the State Courts: A 1999 Survey," presented at the National Conference on Public Trust and Confidence in the Judiciary, May 14, 1999, Washington, D.C.

[16] William Haltom and Michael McCann, *Distorting the Law: Politics, Media and the Litigation Crisis* (Chicago: University of Chicago Press, 2004).

[17] Ibid., p. 183.

[18] Ibid., p. 184.

[19] Ibid., pp. 185–186.

[20] Ibid., pp. 189–190.

[21] Ibid., p. 190.

■ Ms. Liebeck brought her lawsuit against McDonald's only after McDonald's had refused her first offer, which comprised three requests: (1) to check the coffee machine at that particular McDonald's to see if it was faulty; (2) to reevaluate its temperature standards for brewing coffee; (3) to reimburse her for her direct and indirect expenses totaling about $20,000. McDonald's refused the first two requests and offered her $800 in settlement.

■ After Ms. Liebeck's attorneys filed her complaint for negligence in trial court, McDonald's refused to negotiate a settlement in court-ordered mediation.[22]

■ After a trial jury found for Ms. Liebeck and awarded compensatory and punitive damages, the trial judge reduced the jury award for punitive damages from nearly 2.7 million dollars to $480,000. At this point, McDonald's settled for an undisclosed amount. Ms. Liebeck never "got" 2.9 million dollars.

Return to the principles of common-law liability we discussed in Chapter 3. McDonald's clearly owes a duty not to harm its own customers. There is no doubt that the hot coffee injured Ms. Liebeck. McDonald's' own manual demonstrates that it knew that it brewed and served coffee at temperatures that could cause third-degree burns. Is it foreseeable that people in cars occasionally spill hot coffee trying to remove the lid from their cup? But the popular press did not tell this story. It regularly does not tell accurate legal stories because they do not make dramatic news. In "Java Jive," the authors conclude that the media also lost an opportunity to tell a different and more political story:

> For example, the injuries suffered by Ms. Liebeck and her frustrated resort to litigation could instead have highlighted the need for better consumer protection standards, better regulatory oversight, the need for expanded medical benefits for the elderly, the inadequate medical insurance options for most citizens in the United States, or the lack of workplace leave compensation policies to deal with family emergencies.[23]

The authors raise the disturbing possibility that the combination of the moralistic elements in pop culture, the profit motive in the media, and behind that, the drive of corporations to try to use the media to protect themselves from legitimate lawsuits for damages, may indeed threaten the ability of the legal system to check, as liberal government requires, the abuse of power in the system.[24]

National Crises

The need for a neutral, dispassionate triadic dispute resolver is greatest when disputes are most intense and when the legal decision will have a major impact on the lives of many people. That is often the case during a period of national crisis, such as a war, when concerns about national security often lead government officials to curtail civil liberties. Unfortunately, it is in just such times that judges are most tempted to relinquish their role as neutral decision makers and bend to popular sentiments and perceived needs. American history is replete with examples in which courts succumbed to public pressure, or "followed the election returns." When, for example, the administration of President Franklin

---

[22] Ibid., pp. 186–187.
[23] Ibid., p. 226. Ms. Liebeck's daughter had to take unpaid leave from her job to care for her mother.
[24] See generally Haltom.

Delano Roosevelt sent thousands of Japanese Americans to concentration camps during World War II, federal courts offered only feeble resistance.[25]

Worse yet, the normal impulse during periods of national crisis emboldens leaders to forgo the legal system altogether and operate outside the rule of law. There are certainly moments when a true emergency makes normal legal processes inappropriate. In the heat of the Civil War, Abraham Lincoln suspended habeas corpus and locked up war resisters without benefit of a legal proceeding, even after the Supreme Court had ruled his actions unconstitutional.[26] Historians continue to argue over whether Lincoln's actions were justified. But making exceptions to the rule of law—even those that seem amply justified at the time—is dangerous. Post 9/11, the Bush administration argued that because of the necessity of stopping terrorism, it was not bound by laws restricting surveillance of international communications, detention of "enemy combatants," or even torture. Appendix B analyzes the Bush administration's claims, and argues that its actions violated the rule of law.

Thus 9/11, like previous national crises, has demonstrated that threats to national security also pose dangers for the rule of law. Yet, despite all the dangers we have outlined, the American legal system operates fairly and impartially most of the time. And so we return to the main theme of the book: We, legal professionals and laypeople alike, possess standards for telling fair and impartial judicial actions from suspicious ones. The rule of law will remain alive and well as long as we don't abandon these standards. Many historical stories, for example the collapse of the Roman Republic and the rise of Nazi Germany, tell us how easy it is for civilized peoples to stray from the rule of law. As these examples suggest, judges are just one of many social actors whose actions can sustain or undermine the rule of law. Nonetheless, in the United States the quality of judges' legal reasoning is an important determinant of the health of our legal culture.

THE RULE OF LAW AS LIBERAL JUSTIFICATION

A Recap

Did you notice one remarkable feature of Roy Moore's argument for placing the Ten Commandments in the Alabama courthouse? He insisted that he was merely following the rule of law. The rule of law is so central to our political culture that political activists across the spectrum invoke it. Below is a recap of some reasons why this is so.

Communities are groups of people who seek to work and play cooperatively and productively together. Communities come in all sizes, from families and clusters of "good neighbors" to states and nations—communities of strangers. Sometimes, and particularly in small groups with long histories, cooperation comes easily. People know the customs that bind each other. They trust each other not to cheat, and so they trust the economic and social trades they make with each other. But as communities get larger, some people must rule others. Someone must use power to coerce those who have not cooperated either to become cooperative or to get out of the group. Here formal political institutions emerge— leaders with weapons, codes of rules and courts to enforce them, and so on.

---

[25] Peter Irons, *Justice at War: The Story of the Japanese American Internment Cases* (Berkeley: University of California Press, 1983). See also Greg Robinson, *By Order of the President: FDR and the Internment of the Japanese Americans* (Cambridge: Harvard University Press, 2001).

[26] See William Rehnquist, *All the Laws But One: Civil Liberties in Wartime* (New York: Knopf, 1998). Daniel Farber's study of Lincoln in wartime also mostly sides with the president. See Farber, *Lincoln's Constitution* (Chicago: University of Chicago Press, 2003).

Liberal political systems try to minimize the harm that rulers do to the ruled by imposing on the powerful the obligation to justify their use of power based on community norms and understandings. We have an expectation, for example, that presidents will not simply make decisions, but explain and justify their decisions to the public, through speeches, press conferences, and writings.

Here enters legal reasoning, which is also a kind of explanation and justification. Our political system generates an immense quantity of legal texts—statutes, regulations, constitutional provisions, and the prior judicial opinions that we call *precedents*. These texts represent attempts to give communities rules by which people can live together. Yet inevitably from time to time, these attempts fail, and social cooperation falters. Families of victims of September 11 hold the airlines and the designers of the World Trade Center responsible for their losses, but the airlines and designers disagree. Federal agents think they can wiretap phones without a warrant, but a convicted bootlegger argues that this violates the Fourth Amendment. Roy Moore insists that the Fourteenth Amendment does not prevent him from placing the Ten Commandments in his courthouse, but some Alabama residents disagree. When conflicts such as these arise, the parties may call on judges to the dispute. And because we insist on justification in our legal culture, we do not simply permit judges to exercise their power by declaring their decisions. They must justify what they have done.

The judge's resolution of the conflict uses the legal texts as a starting point but not, as we have shown, the ending point. This is partly because words are ambiguous, and in a diverse society, people can understand them differently. But it's also because in law, as in life, no set of rules can cover every possible situation. To understand this point better, consider an analogy literary theorist Stanley Fish makes to the game of basketball:

> Suppose you were a basketball coach and taught someone how to shoot baskets and how to dribble the ball, but had imparted these skills without reference to the playing of an actual basketball game. Now you decide to insert your student into a game, and you equip him with some rules. You say to him, for instance, "Take only good shots." "What," he asks reasonably enough, "is a good shot?" "Well," you reply, "a good shot is an 'open shot,' a shot taken when you are close to the basket (so that the chances of success are good) and when your view is not obstructed by the harassing efforts of opposing players." Everything goes well until the last few seconds of the game; your team is behind by a single point; the novice player gets the ball in heavy traffic and holds it as the final buzzer rings. You run up to him and say, "Why didn't you shoot?" and he answers, "It wasn't a good shot." Clearly, the rule must be amended, and accordingly you tell him that if time is running out, and your team is behind, and you have the ball, you should take the shot even if it isn't a good one, because it will then *be* a good one in the sense of being the best shot in the circumstances. (Notice how both the meaning of the rule and the entities it covers are changing shape as this "education" proceeds.) Now suppose there is another game, and the same situation develops. This time the player takes the shot, which under the circumstances is a very difficult one; he misses, and once again the final buzzer rings. You run up to him and say, "Didn't you see that John (a teammate) had gone 'back door' and was perfectly positioned under the basket for an easy shot?" and he answers "But you said. . . ." Now obviously it would be possible once again to amend the rule, and just as obviously there would be no real end to the sequence and number of emendations that would be necessary. Of course, there will eventually come a time when the novice player (like the novice judge) will no longer have to ask questions; but it will not be because the rules have finally been made sufficiently explicit to cover all cases, but because explicitness will have been rendered unnecessary by a kind of knowledge that informs rules rather than follows from them.[27]

---

[27] Stanley Fish, *"Fish v. Fiss,"* 36 *Stanford Law Review* 1325 (1984): 1329–1330.

Legislatures, constitution makers, and judges who set precedents are each in the position of Fish's basketball coach, unable to anticipate every possible dispute that may arise under the rules they propound. That's why, as we have argued, judges must look beyond the words of legal texts in order to implement the law wisely. And that's also why judges must justify their decisions rather than simply announcing them.

Judges justify their decisions in the language of legal reasoning. This book argues that when a judicial opinion fits the four elements of legal reasoning plausibly together, the judicial writer has met his or her obligation to use judicial power the way our political culture expects. By implication, we have argued as well that when judges harmonize the four elements—the facts of cases, the official legal texts, social background facts about the world in which we live, and norms widely shared in our polity—they *necessarily* create an image of a viable community. It is the job of this final chapter to explain why you should believe this.

Impartiality and Trust

Governing a large community, a group of total strangers who happen to live—often by the millions—in one city, state, or nation, is a difficult business. It is more difficult than, say, running Microsoft or the Seattle Symphony for several reasons.

■ The government's rules speak to the public, to the community, to everyone, in a way that Microsoft's rules (or for that matter, the pope's rules) do not.

■ The community is the greatest source of disruption and uncertainty in our lives because it exposes us to the work of strangers that we individually cannot control. The community is the place where people's psychological need for confidence in structure is greatest, for it is the one place that binds everyone, and beyond it, we will find no social structure at all. The rules that the *government* makes and enforces must maintain confidence in structure—confidence that even strangers can share values.

■ People need to maintain this confidence even when they cannot express precisely the "right" limit or value by which to judge a concrete situation.

The judicial process and legal reasoning therefore play a major part in preserving the confidence that the community can reconcile rules, facts of disputes, social conditions, and ethics. Our confidence does not rest entirely or immediately on the quality of legal reasoning, but the language of legal justification is one important means by which those who govern can reassure us that our communal life is "accurate and attractive." Unlike other social processes in and out of government, courts must make *some* decision—reach some closure on the problems litigants bring to them. Like game umpires and referees, they cannot just walk away and refuse to decide. Regardless of the wisdom of the solution, we need to believe that our community contains forums in which decision and action replace indecision and drift. In this book, we have criticized many conventional practices, habits, and assumptions in legal reasoning precisely because good legal reasoning is so vital to the flourishing of communities. Reason in law must, as Duncan Kennedy put it in one of the epigraphs of this chapter, "break down the sense that legal argument is autonomous from moral, economic, and political discourse," or it will ultimately destroy our confidence in community.

Thus, the ethical view of the legal process holds that, despite its potentially infinite complexity and uncertainty, law must contain a method of applying the abstractions of law to human affairs. This does not require finding the perfect solution. It is much more important that the process attempt to reach acceptable reconciliations of facts, social conditions, laws, and ethical values. For this process to succeed, judges must speak for the community and not simply for the profession or their political beliefs, or to ensure that one side or another always wins. We must therefore shift our attention to the concepts of trust, impartiality, and judgment.

Impartial Judgment

Imagine yourself in each of these three situations:

1. *A midsummer afternoon in Wrigley Field.* The Cubs versus the Cardinals. You are calling balls and strikes behind home plate.

2. *A late Saturday night in Atlantic City in September.* You are judging the finals of the Miss America Pageant.

3. *Eight-thirty in the evening, in the home of your young family.* The children are squabbling. They appeal to you for judgment.

   Laurie: Daddy, Robbie bit me!

   Robbie: I did not!

   Laurie: You did too! Look! Tooth marks!

   Robbie: But Dad! Laurie took my dime!

   Laurie: I took your dime cuz you stepped on my doll and broke it.

   Robbie: But it was an accident, dum-dum.

   Laurie: I am not a dum-dum, you fathead!

Each of these situations calls for judgment. Each judge makes decisions that affect the claims of others, and he decides before an audience that has some expectations about how the judge should decide. Without necessarily determining what the judge should conclude, the audience knows what the judge should look at and will test the judgment against these expectations. Even a child seeking justice from a parent does so.

To judge is to decide the claims of others with reference to the expectations of an audience that define the process of decision. We shall see shortly where this definition leads in law. For the moment, consider what these three nonlegal judging situations do and do not have in common.

First and most important, notice that the three are not equally reasoned. Reasoning—defined as a choice that depends on calculations about future consequences—influences the umpire calling balls and strikes only indirectly. Occasionally, he may reflect on the fact that if he calls a pitch wrong, angry fans may pitch obscenities at him. Basically, however, he simply tries to fit physical—visual—evidence to a category, ball or strike, predetermined by some formula. He judges because the audience (baseball fans) has (have) specific expectations of how umpires should behave. At the other extreme, in most households, the parent cannot escape from making some calculation about the effects of his decision on the children, or at least on his own sanity.

The second difference is that rules do not equally affect all three situations. On the one hand, the umpire works with an elaborate set of written rules about baseball, most of which he commits to memory. He decides most questions literally in a second or less by applying the rules to the facts. In baseball, time is of the essence, which is why its rules are so elaborate. Additionally, baseball allows for precise rules because, as in most sports, we can pinpoint what matters to us in time and space.

On the other hand, we cannot define male or female beauty so precisely. Beauty contest judges exercise more discretion because their rules do not so precisely tell them what to seek.[28] Finally, the squabbling children may invoke no family rule at all. The family may have no regulation forbidding or punishing Robbie's toothy assault on his sister and his lie, and no conventions governing Laurie's theft or the children's gratuitous exchange of insults. But even in the absence of a family rule, the children need their parents to pass judgment.

Third, these three kinds of judges have different opportunities to make rules for the future. The parent can explicitly respond to the squabble by announcing what is right and wrong and declaring his official policy for the future. Such a setting of limits may be precisely what the children hope the judge will do. But beauty contest judges may do so only informally and the umpires hardly at all, given audience's expectations of their roles.

This definition and discussion of the nature of reason makes clear that not all reasoning is legal reasoning. Legal reasoning involves judgment—deciding the claims of others in front of some audience, before a "public." We have also seen, from the example of the home plate umpire in baseball, that not all judgment involves reason. Law therefore employs reasoned judgment, and we shall develop that concept momentarily. First, however, we must pin down that quality inherent in all judging, whether reasoned or not: impartiality.

Impartiality is not a mysterious concept. The *American Heritage Dictionary* defines *partial* as "pertaining to only part; not total; incomplete." To decide impartially is to leave the final decision open until all the relevant information is received. It means that the information—the placement of the pitch, the beauty contestant's stage performance, and the children's actual behavior—rather than a personal affection or preference for one "party" determines the result.[29]

While "impartiality" is not itself a difficult concept—we have all judged and been judged in our lives—it is often difficult for audiences to satisfy themselves that judges actually decide impartially. Initially a judge may succeed if her mistakes cancel out, if her decisions randomly favor both sides equally. But the loser, being the loser, will probably not take a balanced count of errors. The judge's only long-range security, therefore, is to care about and try as best she can to *fulfill the expectations of judgment that the audience imposes.*

To judge is to be judged. The argument assumes, of course, that audiences can, in fact, distinguish their expectations of the process of decision from their hopes that one side—their side!—will win. Your authors are convinced that people can do so, though we rely more on our experiences as sports fans, employees, teachers, and family members than we do on psychological experimentation. Teams can lose championships; employees can receive

---

[28] There is another interesting difference: With rare exceptions, such as when he calls the game on account of rain or ejects an ornery manager or player, the umpire has minimal control over who wins. But the beauty contest judges *declare* the winner. This differential effect on the outcome explains why we have only one home plate umpire but several judges in contests of beauty and on our appellate courts. (Notice that when the umpire does make discretionary calls, he is also more likely to consult other umpires than when he calls balls and strikes.)

[29] Empirical research on how jurors in trials think builds on a very similar definition of impartiality. These studies document the frequency with which jurors close their minds and refuse to admit new facts, sometimes long before a trial ends. These jurors don't come to court biased for one side. They simply jump to a conclusion and thereafter don't listen to the other parts of the argument. They are partial in just that sense. Effective trial lawyers know how to keep minds open: They tell stories. Jurors then have a framework for knowing what facts are missing, just as all of us do when we read or hear a story and stay alert waiting for the final clues to fall into place. A jury trial, then, becomes a contest between two competing narratives, two stories. See Neil Vidmar and Valerie Hans, *American Juries: The Verdict* (New York: Prometheus, 2007).

poor assignments; students can receive disappointing grades; and children can be ordered to wash the dishes, all without doubting that the judges have decided impartially.

Professor Robert Cover has written:

> The critical dimension of the rule of law is not the degree of specificity with which an actor is constrained, but the very fact that the actor must look outside his own will for criteria of judgment. There is a difference—intelligible to most pre-adolescents—between the directions "Do what you want" and "Do what you think is right or just."[30]

To "look outside his own will for criteria of judgment": If we have any single key to legal judgment, it is here.

To judge is to decide the claims of others before an audience. The judgmental decision need not be reasoned, as the umpire's calling of pitches reveals. But judgmental decisions must be impartial, which means in the end they must, to appear impartial, conform to audience expectations of the process of decision.

In law, as in all contexts in which judging takes place, the audience can never know for sure why the judge decided as he did. It cannot see inside a judge's head. That is why the legal audience is so concerned with the way an appellate judge justifies her decision, because it is the only visible evidence of the judge's impartiality. What criteria will a legal audience use to assess the impartiality of an appellate judge? To answer that question, we must determine the legal audience's expectations of the appellate process.

We believe, as we have argued, that the audience for law expects the process to reconcile and harmonize case facts, legal rules, social background facts, and shared values. This is the test of judicial impartiality, and hence of reason in law. When judges justify the result they reach in a case, they must attempt to convince readers that the result does *not* depend on inaccurate characterization of the facts in the case, does *not* depend on false assumptions about social conditions, does *not* depend upon a tortured reading of a rule, and does *not* depend on a value judgment that the community of readers would reject. The result need not please everyone, but that is not the point. Judges cannot and need not discover one right solution that everyone somehow believes best. They convince us of their impartiality as long as they convince us that they have attempted to describe these four elements accurately. We expect law judges, unlike umpires, to engage in *reasoned* judgment when they do so.

Let us here anticipate a problem that often bothers alert readers (including Sanford Levinson, the author of our Foreword) at this stage of the argument: Only an infinitesimal number of people in a state or nation read appellate opinions. How can we argue that judges must build and maintain trust and impartiality by performing for an audience that is by definition very large and almost totally ignorant of the very performances we're talking about? Doesn't history show us that the actual political reaction to controversial cases depends on whose ox was gored?

We have two responses to this troublesome problem. First and foremost, judges must try to persuade the parties, and particularly the losers, that the results are impartial. But these parties do come from, and share understandings of facts and values in common with,

---

[30] Robert Cover, book review of R. Berger's *Government by Judiciary, New Republic,* January 14, 1978, p. 27. Two essays in which judges vigorously defended the impartiality of the appellate courts are Harry T. Edwards's "Public Misperceptions Concerning the Politics of Judging," 56 *Colorado Law Review* 619 (1985), and Patricia Wald's "Thoughts on Decisionmaking," 87 *West Virginia Law Review* 1 (1984). And see the Australian film *Breaker Morant,* a powerful essay on the politicization of the judicial process.

the larger audience. In writing for "the people," judges will more likely write persuasively for the parties when they avoid obscure legalese and write opinions that non-lawyers can understand. Second, over time on issues that concern many, the word tends, slowly, to get out. Anthony Lewis's now-classic book, *Gideon's Trumpet*,[31] did much to explain and justify the reasoning behind extending constitutional protections to the accused. Conversely, *Roe*, the first abortion case, which was widely criticized for its unconvincing reasoning, might have forestalled so much of the subsequent litigation had it constructed a clearer and more coherent statement of what the right of privacy did and did not entail and why. The Supreme Court's legal reasoning in *Bush v. Gore*, the 2000 presidential election case, was the stuff of television talk shows and newspaper headlines. When judges write decisions in these landmark cases, they know that the audience goes far beyond the parties and lawyers in the dispute.[32]

The Value of Impartiality

What evidence might confirm that lawyers and judges value impartiality in the ways we have suggested? In a fascinating assessment of the 1992 U. S. Supreme Court term, Linda Greenhouse of the *New York Times* identified the unassuming Justice David Souter as the emerging leader of the coalition of justices at the center of the Court. She explained his leadership this way:

> Court observers on both ends of the political spectrum have noted that Justice Souter, much more than most judges, tends to acknowledge the weight of opposing arguments and to discuss and defend his own choices from among competing rationales.[33]

According to Greenhouse, David Souter's trustworthiness, not the political acceptability of his results, accounted for his leadership. More importantly, this is just as it should be. If legal reasoning matters politically because it convinces us that we and the judge belong to the same community, then legal reasoning should build trust in the integrity of leaders, not conviction about the correctness of the outcome.

---

[31] Anthony Lewis, *Gideon's Trumpet* (New York: Random House, 1964).

[32] The quality of the legal reasoning of *non-judges* can also at times have immediate and weighty historical consequences. In *The Terror Presidency* (New York: Norton, 2007), Jack Goldsmith describes how the legal reasoning of Robert Jackson, Franklin Roosevelt's Attorney General, shaped the outcome of World War II. Roosevelt wanted to help Great Britain withstand Germany's attacks but felt legally blocked by an isolation-leaning Congress. Jackson wrote a very careful and narrow legal justification of Roosevelt's proposed "lend-lease" program that found a path around some very tricky legal obstacles, allowing Roosevelt to go ahead with his plan to supply Britain with naval destroyers. Jackson's memo did not "approve one thing more than it needed to" (p. 198), and its tight legal reasoning persuaded Roosevelt that he was on firm legal grounds with the deal, which Roosevelt described as the most important action to defend the United States since the Louisiana Purchase. Goldsmith contrasts Jackson's memo with the legal reasoning of lawyers in the Bush administration on national security issues, which was riddled with costly legal and political errors. Goldsmith got a firsthand view of those errors when he was appointed to the Office of Legal Counsel in the Bush administration. The Bush administration's legal reasoning in several policy areas is examined in Appendix B.

[33] Linda Greenhouse, "Souter Anchoring the Court's New Center," July 3, 1992, A1 and A12. Souter's reclusive and scholarly lifestyle has been compared with that of Benjamin Cardozo. See Richard Posner, *Cardozo: A Study in Reputation* (Chicago: University of Chicago Press, 1990). Also linking candor and trustworthiness, see David L. Shapiro, "In Defense of Judicial Candor," 100 *Harvard Law Review* 731 (1987) and Ruth Bader Ginsburg, "Remarks on Writing Separately," 65 *Washington Law Review* 133 (1990).

Ronald Dworkin criticizes Justice Scalia's failure to build trust in the judiciary. Dworkin argues that Justice Scalia's dissenting reasoning in *Casey*, the case in which the majority reaffirmed the basic holding in *Roe*, loses our trust precisely because he fails to harmonize the four elements of legal reasoning effectively:

> Scalia, in his own partial dissent, makes even plainer his contempt for the view that the Constitution creates a system of principle. He reaches the conclusion that abortion is not a liberty protected by the Constitution, he says, "not because of anything so exalted as my views concerning the 'concept of existence, of meaning of the universe, and of the mystery of human life'" but "because of two simple facts: (1) The Constitution says absolutely nothing about it, and (2) the long-standing traditions of American society have permitted it to be legally proscribed." Scalia's flat assertion that the Constitution says nothing about abortion begs the question, of course. The Fourteenth Amendment does explicitly forbid states to abridge liberty without due process of law, and the question, in this case as in any other case involving that clause, is whether the state legislation in question does in fact do exactly that. If it does, then the Constitution does say something about it: the Constitution forbids it. The majority argues that if we accept the principles that underlie past Supreme Court decisions everyone accepts, we must also accept that forbidding abortion before viability denies liberty without due process. Scalia says nothing at all that undermines or even challenges that claim.
>
> So Scalia's entire argument depends on his assertion that since a majority of states had outlawed abortion before the Fourteenth Amendment was adopted, it would be wrong to interpret the due process clause as denying them the power to do so now. He refuses to consider whether laws outlawing abortion, no matter how popular they were or are, offend other, more general principles of liberty that are embedded in the Constitution's abstract language and in the Court's past decisions. He disdains inquiries of that character because, he says, they involve "value judgments." Of course they do. How can any court enforce the abstract moral command of the Constitution that states may not violate fundamental liberties, without making judgments about "values"? Judges have had to make such judgments since law began.[34]

Justice Scalia's opinions, though elegant, often seem bitter and dismissive. Not only is the other side wrong, he seems to say, but its view is utter nonsense, unworthy of any consideration. Though Scalia's style amuses those who come to his opinions already in agreement with him, it is unlikely to reassure the losing party of his impartiality.

Here is another example of the importance of the legal audience in judging. Justice Stephen Breyer, appointed by President Clinton to the Supreme Court in the summer of 1994, has received very positive "reviews" from both the bar and the popular press. A self-described nonideological pragmatist, Breyer believes passionately in his responsibility to communicate clearly. Not long after he first took a lower position on the federal bench, he decided never to use footnotes in his opinions. In a 1995 interview he elaborated:

> Sometimes it's awkward to use none at all, but if in fact you even use one, then you cannot make the point. And it is an important point to make if you believe, as I do, that the major function of an opinion is to explain to the audience of readers why it is that the Court has reached that decision.
>
> It's not to prove that you're right: you can't prove you're right, there is no such proof. And it's not to create an authoritative law review on the subject. Others are better doing that than I.

---

[34] Ronald Dworkin, "The Center Holds," *New York Review of Books,* August 13, 1992, pp. 29–33.

It is to explain as clearly as possible and as simply as possible what the reasons are for reaching this decision. Others can then say those are good reasons or those are bad reasons. If you see the opinion in this way, either a point is sufficiently significant to make, in which case it should be in the text, or it is not, in which case, don't make it.[35]

Breyer embraces what is sometimes called "intellectual honesty," a willingness to humbly acknowledge the limitations of one's own conclusions and so take seriously the views of others. Our culture is concerned with intellectual honesty in many different settings beyond the law. In science, Richard Feynman has written that the ideal is

a kind of scientific integrity, a principle of scientific thought that corresponds to a kind of utter honesty—a kind of leaning over backwards. For example, if you're doing an experiment, you should report everything that you think might make it invalid, not only what you think is right about it.[36]

We must next ask whether laypeople, those outside the legal system, also value these qualities. What evidence supports the position that trustworthy legal officials (as opposed to, say, officials who favor one's interests) cause people to support the legal system? In his book *Why People Obey the Law*, Professor Tom Tyler concludes that people obey the law primarily for noneconomic reasons. People do not comply because compliance costs them less. Rather, Tyler concludes they do so when they approve of the moral position the law takes and when they feel law is procedurally fair. The perception that the law is fair—and hence the willingness to comply—depends not on winning or losing but on such moral factors as whether people trust the system to hear their arguments.[37]

Similarly, Scott Barclay concludes in *An Appealing Act: Why People Appeal in Civil Cases* that litigants decide to appeal a trial court decision not so much based on their prospect of winning in the appeal court but rather because they felt they were treated unfairly and disrespectfully in the lower court. Even knowing they had a very small chance of having the trial court decision overturned, the appellants in Barclay's study still chose to go ahead. They thought the lower-court judges did not focus on the relevant issues, did not understand their claims, and in some cases had treated them rudely. They wanted their "day in court," a chance to tell the appellate judges how badly they had been treated in the lower court. The four losing litigants in the study who felt that the trial court was fair decided not to appeal.[38]

---

[35] "In Justice Breyer's Opinion, a Footnote Has No Place," *The New York Times,* July 28, 1995, p. B13. Compare this statement by legal scholar and Seventh Circuit Court of Appeals Judge Richard A. Posner, an appointee of Ronald Reagan:

Judges have a terrible anxiety about being thought to base their opinions on guesses, on their personal views. To allay that anxiety, they rely on the apparatus of precedent and history, much of it extremely phony. I do think judges can and should get away with a lot more candor. . . .

Linda Greenhouse, "In His Opinion," *The New York Times Book Review,* September 2, 1999, Section 7, p. 14.

[36] Quoted by Philip J. Hilts, "The Science Mob," *New Republic,* May 18, 1992, p. 24 at p. 31.

[37] Tom R. Tyler, *Why People Obey the Law* (New Haven: Yale University Press, 1990). In his most recent book, Tyler argues that judges and police officers can best improve compliance with the law by acting in ways that increase social trust in the legal system. See Tom R. Tyler and Yuen J. Huo, *Trust and the Rule of Law* (New Haven: Yale University Press, 2001). And see Peggy Noonan's *What I Saw at the Revolution* (New York: Random House, 1990), which links Ronald Reagan's political success to the public's trust in him.

[38] Scott Barclay, *An Appealing Act: Why People Appeal in Civil Cases* (Evanston: Northwestern University Press, American Bar Foundation, 1999).

Applying the Theory

Let us now apply our theory of legal reasoning to some of the cases this book has applauded and some it has criticized.

Consider first the *Prochnow* blood test case. We are tempted to condemn the judge's opinion for flying in the face of science: The court reached a result that we all know couldn't be true. If so, we would simply criticize the opinion for its failure to harmonize in its reasoning the social background facts in the case. But the difficulties with the *Prochnow* opinion go deeper. If the opinion means to tell us that juries should be free to speculate on whether God or nature or some hidden force temporarily suspended the laws of science, the opinion should have addressed that claim head on. Such a principle would revolutionize our entire notion of how law works, for if a jury verdict based on speculations about God's will can stand, a jury can find anything it wants, and no judge would or could ever overturn a jury verdict for being inconsistent with the weight of the evidence.

We have seen another less supernatural and more plausible explanation for the *Prochnow* result. Perhaps the legislature favored fatherhood so strongly that it authorized juries to disregard science for the sake of allowing children to grow up with fathers. It might have done this in part to protect children who would otherwise be labeled illegitimate—a real disadvantage at that time. But if that was the basis on which the court acted, it should have said so, partly to give the legislature a chance to react if the court had misread the statute, and partly to explain why, if the statutory purpose was to protect children, the legislature had authorized blood tests in the first place. The majority opinion read the statute legalistically, that is, without attention to the other three elements in legal reasoning. It said the words of the statute make the tests admissible but not conclusive; therefore, the law allows juries to disregard the tests.

Instead it could have harmonized all four elements by saying, "We know all about science, and we know the blood tests in this case are incompatible. We admit that no evidence in the trial contradicted the blood tests, but we read the purpose of this law to favor paternity and we believe this value is widely shared in the community." That reasoning would give us a coherent vision of the community that we can discuss and seek to sustain or change. Instead the majority implies that we live in a confusing and unknowable world in which anything can happen, one in which we can't trust either science or God or the conventional trial court methods of fact-finding.

The legal reasoning of *Repouille v. the United States* also fails. Here a clear precedent stated law that seemed to apply directly to the case. The *Francioso* opinion said that the naturalization decision should rest on judgments about the person seeking naturalization, a generalized inquiry into the person's life and the particularities of the moral decisions the applicant has made. Yet in *Repouille*, Learned Hand did quite the opposite, moving away from the facts of the applicant's life and resting his decision instead on the morality of euthanasia in the abstract. The reasoning in *Repouille* leads us to believe that law doesn't matter. It increases our mistrust.

We do not argue that *Prochnow* and *Repouille* "came out wrong." We argue that the results were not well reasoned or justified. A different opinion could have persuasively justified the result each case reached, but the opinions we read fail to do so. They are incoherent. They only confuse lawyers who must advise future clients with similar cases—confuse and thereby perhaps encourage litigation when law should instead encourage cooperation. Worse, they leave lay readers with the suspicion that those with power over them have lied to them.

You should, we hope, be able to see in each of the cases that this book has criticized one or more of the four elements that were not harmonized. The evidence introduced in trial about baseball in *Toolson* made a strong case that baseball was a business in interstate commerce that monopolized the sport. Why does the Court ignore that evidence? In *Lochner,* the bakers' hours case, the Court ignored the social background evidence that baking was unhealthy. *Repouille* ignores a legal rule created by precedent. The majority in *Fox v. Snow* ignored the ethical value of carrying out the hopes of those who write wills, and so on.

We should, of course, turn this analysis on the cases these pages have applauded. For example, *Hynes*, the diving board case, harmonizes (1) the fact in Harvey's case that the wire might have killed him had he been a swimmer lawfully using the river and the fact that the railroad had not maintained the wires and poles; (2) the social background fact that property boundaries become increasingly hard to learn of and remember as life becomes more complex, urban, and interconnected; (3) a plausible reading of the thrust of the *Hoffman* and *Beck* precedents; (4) the deeply ethical value that law should promote cooperation—that the law of tort ought to encourage the railroad, a powerful economic entity, to prevent the dangerous wires it owns and controls from injuring others.

Finally, let us apply the four elements of good legal reasoning so as to test Roy Moore's claim that he, not the federal courts, honors the rule of law. The case is so rich that discussion could go on for many pages. Here are just a few ways to question whether he has harmonized the four elements of legal reasoning.

1. The Legal Rules

In a sense, the legal issue in this case was very simple. Judge Moore was under a federal court order to remove the monument. While we might say that a private citizen has some kind of "right" to disobey a court order and accept punishment for contempt of court, it is legally difficult to argue that a sitting judge has a right to disobey a court order. But why does a *federal* trial judge's order, in this case Judge Thompson's order, bind the chief justice of a *state* court?

Before the Civil War, much of Moore's legal argument would have seemed to many people entirely valid. The First Amendment forbids the establishment of religion, by Congress, not the states ("*Congress* shall make no law . . ."). Indeed, though Americans in some sense fought the Civil War over slavery, the war might be more broadly understood as resolving the question of whether the federal government has the power to enforce its reading of law over and against the states. Union victory in the Civil War generated the Thirteenth, Fourteenth, and Fifteenth Amendments. These legal additions to "the supreme law of the land" enacted the triumph of federal over state legal authority and power. The Fourteenth Amendment, for example, commands: "nor shall any State deprive any person of life, liberty, or property without due process of law; nor deny to any person within its jurisdiction the equal protection of the laws."

Starting in the early twentieth century, the Supreme Court began using this language to protect persons against state violations of the rights guaranteed to them by the original Bill of Rights, including the First Amendment. Thus in the 1947 case *Everson v. Board of Education*, Justice Black for the Court wrote: "Neither a state nor the Federal Government can, openly or secretly, participate in the affairs of any religious organizations or groups and *vice versa*."[39] Since that time, the federal courts have interpreted the establishment clause so as to unambiguously to prohibit religious displays such as Moore's.[40] In 1993, the Eleventh Circuit reaffirmed

---

[39] 330 U.S. 1.

[40] Two years after Moore's suspension, the Supreme Court decided a pair of cases involving government buildings and the Ten Commandments. In *McCreary v. ACLU*, 545 U.S. 844 (2005), the Court declared unconstitutional a recently installed courthouse exhibit of documents illustrating "The Foundations of American Law and Government" that included the Ten Commandments. In *Van Orden v. Perry*, 545 U.S. 677 (2005), the court ruled that a monument inscribed with the Ten Commandments that had stood on the Texas State Capital grounds since the 1960s was constitutional; the monument was one of three dozen historical markers and displays on the grounds.

a trial judge's order to remove a display of the Ten Commandments, created with private funds, from the Cobb County, Georgia, superior court unless the display was part of a historical display of secular as well as sacred sources of American law.[41] Judge Moore invoked the Ninth and Tenth Amendments to support his case. From the texts of the Ninth and Tenth Amendments (footnote 2, above), you can judge whether the words of these amendments plausibly support Moore's case. But even if they did, do not the later amendments after the Civil War amend the Ninth and Tenth amendments along with the rest of the Constitution?

2. The Facts of the Case

Case law has regularly permitted publicly funded and maintained museums and cemeteries to contain religious imagery along with other nonreligious images. The Court, though sharply divided, has also upheld the display of Christmas nativity scenes on public property as long as they were part of a general holiday display of reindeer, plastic Santas, and other popular symbols of the season.[42] Indeed, it would make no sense for a museum to exclude works on religious themes as part of an art collection or a historically continuous depiction of the evolution of artistic themes and styles, precisely because religion and artistic expression are closely connected. And cases, including the Cobb County case, make it very clear that courts may display the Ten Commandments in such a historical context. This, of course, is what Roy Moore expressly refused to do.[43] In fact, the only way to explain his express refusal would be to take him at his word. He wants his court and his state to honor God, which is precisely what federal precedents, from *Everson* forward, consistently forbid. Moore also cites the Alabama constitution's invocation of the "favor and guidance of Almighty God." Thus the case facts on the record indicate that Moore's purpose was to promote the idea that God, and not the laws on the books, must guide the decisions of the Alabama courts.

3. Social Background Facts

One of the intriguing facts about the Ten Commandments as a biblical text is that there is no single agreed-upon translation of the Decalogue into English. Different faiths have different translations. Roy Moore used the King James translation, an Anglican work perceived, at least when King James promulgated it, as hostile to Roman Catholicism. Hence Roy Moore's message expresses not just the generic religious message of, say, the motto "In God We Trust," but a particular sect's translation of that message, one inconsistent with other translations, both Christian and Jewish.

Consider another social background fact, about the place of courts in society. Is not a courthouse *about* the business of following rules—legal "commandments"—in the way that a museum is not? To believers such as Roy Moore, the Ten Commandments are most certainly law. Does not a display of the Decalogue *in a courthouse* send a message to the effect

---

[41] *Harvey v. Cobb County*, 811 F.Supp. 669 (1993).

[42] *Lynch v. Donnelly*, 465 U.S. 668 (1984) is the "plastic Santa" case.

[43] "Roy's Rock" did have, inscribed on its sides, quotations from other political sources that supported, he claimed, his theocratic view of the state. These included the motto "In God We Trust" and the phrase "under God" from the Pledge of Allegiance. Several months after he installed the monument, he installed two plaques, about 75 feet removed from the monument and on the side wall behind columns. One plaque quoted the Bill of Rights. The other quoted from Martin Luther King, Jr.'s, "Letter from Birmingham Jail" and from the works of Frederick Douglass, both endorsing the importance of divine moral law. Judge Myron Thompson's opinion with appendices describing Moore's displays in Alabama's Judicial Building may be found at http://www.almd.uscourts.gov/Opinions/index_of_opinions.htm

that "The law we will follow in this building is not the law of the state but of some higher power"? If Alabama law and the Ten Commandments somehow did not conflict with each other, this problem might not seem so severe, but in fact, they do. Alabama law, for example, does not require businesses to "keep the Sabbath holy" by ceasing commerce on that day. Would not a claim to follow religious law as opposed to state law make it impossible to do law at all because law would no longer "resolve conflicts using rules made by the state as a starting point"?

Finally, having studied legal reasoning, are you willing to say that Blackstone is wrong as a matter of fact when he argues that judges only interpret but do not make law? Might we at least say that lawmaking and lawinterpreting are, in the actual behavior of judges, two sides of the same coin?

4. Widespread Social Values

Judging by the prayer gatherings outside the Alabama courthouse as this drama played out,[44] the social values of many Alabamians, and presumably of Christian fundamentalists around the country, supported Moore. Alabama voters elected him to the Alabama Supreme Court because he campaigned to bring the Ten Commandments back into Alabama public life. Does this support for the value of a theocratic government resurrect Moore's argument?

No. Good legal reasoning requires a judge to harmonize together all four elements. No matter how sincerely he held it, Judge Moore did not harmonize the fundamentalist value, widely shared though it was in Alabama, with the other three elements above, and it is not clear how anyone could do so. Other values, also deeply woven into American legal and political culture, seem far more relevant. These include tolerance for religious diversity and equality before the law, to name just two. Can we say that a display of one Christian sect's translation of the Decalogue displayed in a courthouse reassures members of, say, the Jewish, or Muslim, or Baha'i faiths—not to mention atheists—that they will receive equal treatment before the law?

Alert readers may well challenge this analysis. We seem to claim that Roy Moore was legally wrong. But how can we say Moore is wrong if legal reasoning does not generate "correct" answers in the first place? First of all, we do not argue that Moore is in some objective sense wrong. We only suggest that the legal argument he in fact made is atrociously bad. His argument boils down to the assertion that "the law is whatever I feel it ought to be," and so it does not square with any accepted meaning of "the rule of law." As we saw in the *Prochnow* case, the invocation of God as ultimate authority for a legal decision makes law itself impossible. Perhaps we can trust Moore's sincerity as a Christian, though it's possible that Moore was merely using this cause to advance his own political career. But his argument does not enable us to trust him as a sitting and impartial judge.

Could Moore have defended his position in a well-reasoned way and stayed within the rule of law? Of course. Such an argument might have two parts. First, Moore would have admitted that no body of existing precedents supports the placement of this monument, standing alone, in the courthouse. But he would then invoke the necessity, deeply valued in our political traditions, of peaceful civil disobedience. He might even have cited Martin

---

[44] The *New York Times* described the crowd as "wearing their beliefs on their backs, with T-shirts reading 'Jesus is the Standard' and 'Satan is a nerd'. . . . All day they blew ram's horns, shook Bibles, passed out cans of Coke, and knelt on the courthouse steps under a punishing sun." Jeffrey Gettleman, "Monument Is Out of Sight, but Not Out of Mind," *The New York Times*, August 28, 2003, p. A12.

Luther King, Jr.'s practice of that very value in Alabama. Second, he would argue that the Supreme Court's cases applying the establishment clause to the states are themselves badly reasoned. The establishment clause is part of the First Amendment, and because the First Amendment only forbids Congress, not Alabama, from establishing religion, Moore's opponents must rely on the due process clause of the Fourteenth Amendment, which has long been held by the Court to require states not to establish religion. But how, he might argue, does his monument "deprive any person of life, liberty, or property . . ." under the Fourteenth Amendment? He would defend his action in terms of the need to bring a test case to the Supreme Court in which the Court might revise a constitutional mistake, the extension of the Fourteenth Amendment to disputes about religious displays.

The Court's decisions in the religion cases, including its interpretation of the Fourteenth Amendment, are rooted in part in the belief that religion and the state both flourish when they are put at some distance from another. Strong historical evidence suggests that fanaticism in all its forms, including religious fanaticism, has too often fueled the fires of hatred that ignite human atrocities. The Founding Fathers well knew the horrors of the religious wars of Europe and of the Spanish Inquisition. The Holocaust only continued a pattern of Jewish persecution dating back more than a thousand years. As we write, Osama bin Laden has sworn enmity on the United States because we blaspheme, in his eyes, his one true religion. Israelis and Palestinians fight an endless war over what is to them holy space.[45] If the human race hopes to minimize such atrocities and maximize peaceful cooperation, it will embrace the liberal institutions that we described at this chapter's beginning.

But for all its social, political, and historical persuasiveness, this argument for strong separation of church and state is not a *legal* argument. It is a historical argument. Moore's hypothetical defense, couched in terms of the traditions of civil disobedience and of the possibility that the Supreme Court's establishment jurisprudence misinterprets the Constitution, would come much closer to honoring the rule of law than did the argument he actually made, though even this better-reasoned argument does not justify his deliberate refusal to obey the court order to remove the monument after he lost on appeal.[46]

---

[45] For a well-documented case arguing that a person's feelings of humiliation, frustration, and anger over the insult to his or her religion and homeland trigger terrorism and other human atrocities rather than a person's condition of poverty, see Alan B. Krueger and Jitka Maleckova, "Does Poverty Cause Terrorism?" *New Republic,* June 24, 2002, pp. 27–33.

[46] Nothing in our criticism of Roy Moore in any way suggests that sound legal analysis cannot incorporate widely shared Biblical principles and values. For example, University of Alabama Law School professor Susan Pace Hamill, who also earned a degree in divinity from a conservative evangelical seminary, specializes in taxation law and policy. In her book *As Certain as Death,* she argues that nearly every American state imposes taxes with such regressive consequences on poor people as to violate the many Biblical injunctions to help the poor. (Durham, N.C.: Carolina Academic Press, 2007) David Cay Johnson, commenting on the book, wrote, "The worst violator, in her view, is her own state of Alabama, which taxes its poor more than twice as heavily as its rich, while holding a tight rein on education spending." (Johnson, "Report Finds the Rich are Getting Richer Faster, *The New York Times,* December 25, 2007) Separation of church and state casts doubt on legal conclusions that rest *only* on religious principles and nothing else. Many secular arguments also oppose regressive taxation, not least the historical evidence of the social and political disruptions that follow when the spread between the wealth and incomes of the richest and poorest segments of society gets too large, as it did before the French Revolution.

Ultimately, then, it does not and should not matter whether judges' decisions are in some psychodynamic sense shaped and conditioned—even predetermined—by their political philosophies, ideological visions of the "good society," or what they ate for breakfast. What Roy Moore personally believes or feels should not matter to us in the slightest. We should care only that judges justify their results by using the elements of legal reasoning—facts, rules, and shared values—rather than bald assertions of personal belief and feeling. When Justice Scalia, during an interview with CBS's *60 Minutes,* defended the Supreme Court's decision in *Bush v. Gore* primarily by saying, ". . . get over it; it's so old by now," he gives his own opinion, but he gives us no reason to believe him or see why his opinion alone ought to matter. Scalia did not, on that occasion, talk legal talk.[47]

With the following illustrative case we end this chapter. Unlike the cases that end the preceding chapters, this one is hypothetical. However, in solving its problems, you will find yourself using many of the tools of good legal reasoning that apply to real-life cases. You will find as you delve deeper into it that focusing only on your own moral views about "right and wrong" will distract you from analyzing wisely how to resolve this legal reasoning challenge.

But must we conclude that, except for the role played by widely shared social values in good legal reasoning, law has no morality of its own? In one of the twentieth century's great works of legal theory, Harvard's Lon Fuller insisted that law does have its own morality. In his book *The Morality of Law,* he wrote:

> If I were asked . . . to discern one central indisputable principle of what may be called substantive natural law . . . I would find it in the injunction: Open up, maintain and preserve the integrity of the channels of communication.[48]

"Open up, maintain and preserve the integrity of the channels of communication." In a nutshell, this is precisely what reason, done intelligently and impartially in law, strives to achieve.

ILLUSTRATIVE CASE

Professor Sanford Levinson of the University of Texas School of Law presents his students with the following problem at the beginning of their study of constitutional law.[49] We urge you to use Levinson's "adulterer's hypothetical" to further explore the many facets of legal reasoning that we've discussed in this book. How would you answer the questions he poses?

---

[47] "Justice Scalia on the Record," *60 Minutes,* CBS News, April 27, 2008, transcript available at: http://www.cbsnews.com/stories/2008/04/24/60minutes/main4040290.shtml

[48] Lon Fuller, *The Morality of Law* (New Haven: Yale University Press, 1964), p. 186.

[49] "On Interpretation: The Adultery Clause of the Ten Commandments," 58 *Southern California Law Review* 719 (1985).

In 1970 a number of concerned citizens, worried about what they regarded as the corruption of American life, met to consider what could be done. During the course of the discussion, one of the speakers electrified the audience with the following comments:

> The cure for our ills is a return to old-time religion, and the best single guide remains the Ten Commandments. Whenever I am perplexed as to what I ought to do, I turn to the Commandments for the answer, and I am never disappointed. Sometimes I don't immediately like what I discover, but then I think more about the problem and realize how limited my perspective is compared to that of the framer of those great words. Indeed, all that is necessary is for everyone to obey the Ten Commandments, and our problems will all be solved.*

Within several hours the following plan was devised: As part of the effort to encourage a return to the "old-time religion" of the Ten Commandments, a number of young people would be asked to take an oath on their eighteenth birthday to "obey, protect, support, and defend the Ten Commandments" in all of their actions. If the person complied with the oath for seventeen years, he or she would receive an award of $10,000 on his or her thirty-fifth birthday.

The Foundation for the Ten Commandments was funded by the members of the 1970 convention, plus the proceeds of a national campaign for contributions. The speaker quoted above contributed $20 million, and an additional $30 million was collected—$15 million from the convention and $15 million from the national campaign. The interest generated by the $50 million is approximately $6 million per year. Each year since 1970, 500 persons have taken the oath. *You* are appointed sole trustee of the Foundation, and your most important duty is to determine whether the oath-takers have complied with their vows and are thus entitled to the $10,000.

It is now 1987, and the first set of claimants comes before you:

1. Claimant *A* is a married male. Although freely admitting that he has had sexual intercourse with a number of women other than his wife during their marriage, he brings to your attention the fact that "adultery," at the time of Biblical Israel, referred only to the voluntary intercourse of a married woman with a man other than her husband. He specifically notes the following passage from the article *Adultery*, I JEWISH ENCYCLOPEDIA 314:

    > The extramarital intercourse of a married man is not *per se* a crime in biblical or later Jewish law. This distinction stems from the economic aspect of Israelite marriage: The wife as the husband's possession . . ., and adultery constituted a violation of the husband's exclusive right to her; the wife, as the husband's possession, had no such right to him.

    A has taken great care to make sure that all his sexual partners were unmarried, and thus he claims to have been faithful to the original understanding of the Ten Commandments. However we might define "adultery" today, he argues, is irrelevant. His oath was to comply with the Ten Commandments;

---

* Cf. Statement of President Ronald Reagan, Press Conference, February 21, 1985, reprinted in the *New York Times*, February 22, 1985, § 1, at 10, col. 3: "I've found that the Bible contains an answer to just about everything and every problem that confronts us, and I wonder sometimes why we won't recognize that one Book could solve a lot of problems for us." [note in original]

he claims to have done so. (It is stipulated that A, like all the other claimants, has complied with all the other commandments; the only question involves compliance with the commandment against adultery.)

Upon further questioning, you discover that no line-by-line explication of the Ten Commandments was proffered in 1970 at the time that A took the oath. But, says A, whenever a question arose in his mind as to what the Ten Commandments required of him, he made conscientious attempts to research the particular issue. He initially shared your (presumed) surprise at the results of his research, but further study indicated that all authorities agreed with the scholars who wrote the *Jewish Encyclopedia* regarding the original understanding of the Commandment.

2. Claimant B is A's wife, who admits that she has had extramarital relationships with other men. She notes, though, that these affairs were entered into with the consent of her husband. In response to the fact that she undoubtedly violated the ancient understanding of "adultery," she states that that understanding is fatally outdated:

   a. It is unfair to distinguish between the sexual rights of males and females. That the Israelites were outrageously sexist is no warrant for your maintaining the discrimination.

   b. Moreover, the reason for the differentiation, as already noted, was the perception of the wife as property. That notion is a repugnant one that has been properly repudiated by all rational thinkers, including all major branches of the Judeo-Christian religious tradition historically linked to the Ten Commandments.

   c. She further argues that, insofar as the modern prohibition of adultery is defensible, it rests on the ideal of discouraging deceit and the betrayal of promises of sexual fidelity. But these admittedly negative factors are not present in her case because she had scrupulously informed her husband and received his consent, as required by their marriage contract outlining the terms of their "open marriage."

   (It turns out, incidentally, that A had failed to inform his wife of at least one of his sexual encounters. Though he freely admits that this constitutes a breach of the contract he had made with B, he nevertheless returns to his basic argument about original understanding, which makes consent irrelevant.)

3. C, a male (is this relevant?), is the participant in a bigamous marriage. C has had no sexual encounters beyond his two wives. (He also points out that bigamy was clearly tolerated in both pre- and post-Sinai Israel and indeed was accepted within the Yemenite community of Jews well into the twentieth century. It is also accepted in a variety of world cultures.)

4. D, a practicing Christian, admits that he has often lusted after women other than his wife. (Indeed, he confesses as well that it was only after much contemplation that he decided not to sexually consummate a relationship with a coworker whom he thinks he "may love" and with whom he has held hands.) You are familiar with Christ's words, *Matthew* 5:28: "Whosoever looketh on a woman to lust after, he hath committed adultery with her already in his heart." (Would it matter to you if D were the wife, who had lusted after other men?)

5. Finally, claimant *E* has never even lusted after another woman since his marriage on the same day he took his oath. He does admit, however, to occasional lustful fantasies about his wife, *G*, a Catholic, and is shocked when informed of Pope John Paul II's statement that "adultery in your heart is committed not only when you look with concupiscence at a woman who is not your wife, but also if you look in the same manner at your wife." The Pope's rationale apparently is that all lust, even that directed toward a spouse, dehumanizes and reduces the other person "to an erotic object."

Which, if any, of the claimants should get the $10,000? (Remember, *all* can receive the money if you determine that they have fulfilled their oaths.) What is your duty as Ttrustee in determining your answer to this question?

Introduction to Legal Procedure and Terminology

Here is a short but complete judicial opinion. This "case of the stolen airplane" makes a brief appearance in Chapter 1 and plays a more important analytical role in Chapter 4. At the end of the case, this appendix introduces you to most of the more common terms of judicial organization and procedure, using the case to illustrate each term as it arises.

THE CASE

McBoyle v. United States
Supreme Court of the United States
283 U.S. 25 (1931)

Mr. Justice HOLMES delivered the opinion of the Court.

The petitioner was convicted of transporting from Ottawa, Illinois, to Guymon, Oklahoma, an airplane that he knew to have been stolen, and was sentenced to serve three years' imprisonment and to pay a fine of $2,000. The judgment was affirmed by the Circuit Court of Appeals for the Tenth Circuit. 43 F.(2d) 273. A writ of *certiorari* was granted by this Court on the question whether the National Motor Vehicle Theft Act applies to aircraft. Act of October 29, 1919, c. 89, 41 Stat. 324, U.S. Code, title 18, § 408. That Act provides: "Sec. 2. That when used in this Act: (a) The term 'motor vehicle' shall include an automobile, automobile truck, automobile wagon, motor cycle, or any other self-propelled vehicle not designed for running on rails . . . Sec. 3. That whoever shall transport or cause to be transported in interstate or foreign commerce a motor vehicle, knowing the same to have been stolen, shall be punished by a fine of not more than $5,000, or by imprisonment of not more than five years, or both."

Section 2 defines the motor vehicles of which the transportation in interstate commerce is punished in Section 3. The question is the meaning of the word "vehicle" in the phrase "any other self-propelled vehicle not designed for running on rails." No doubt etymologically it is possible to use the word to signify a conveyance working on land, water, or air, and sometimes legislation extends the use in that direction, e.g., land and air, water being separately provided for, in the Tariff Act, September 21, 1922, c. 356, § 401 (b), 42 Stat. 858, 948. But in everyday speech "vehicle" calls up the picture of a thing moving on land. Thus in Rev. St. § 4, intended, the Government suggests, rather to enlarge than to restrict the definition, vehicle includes every contrivance capable of being used "as a means of transportation on land." And this is repeated, expressly excluding aircraft, in the Tariff Act, June 17, 1930, c. 497, § 401 (b), 46 Stat. 590, 708. So here, the phrase under discussion calls up the popular picture. For after including automobile truck, automobile wagon, and motor cycle, the words "any other self-propelled vehicle not designed for running on rails" still indicate that a vehicle in the popular sense, that is a vehicle running on land, is the theme. It is a vehicle that runs, not something, not commonly called a vehicle, that flies. Airplanes were well known in 1919 when this statute was passed, but it is admitted that they were not mentioned in the reports or in the debates in Congress. It is impossible to read words that so carefully enumerate the different forms of motor vehicles and have no reference of any kind to aircraft, as including airplanes under a term that usage more and more precisely confines to a different class. The counsel for the petitioner have shown that the phraseology of the statute as to motor vehicles follows that of earlier statutes of Connecticut, Delaware, Ohio, Michigan, and Missouri, not to mention the late Regulations of Traffic for the District of Columbia, title 6, c. 9, § 242, none of which can be supposed to leave the earth.

Although it is not likely that a criminal will carefully consider the text of the law before he murders or steals, it is reasonable that a fair warning should be given to the world in language that the common world will understand, of what the law intends to do if a certain line is passed. To make the warning fair, so far as possible the line should be clear. When a rule of conduct is laid down in words that evoke in the common mind only the picture of vehicles moving on land, the statute should not be extended to aircraft simply because it may seem to us that a similar policy applies, or upon the speculation that if the legislature had thought of it, very likely broader words would have been used. *United States v. Bhagat Singh Thind,* 261 U.S. 204, 209, 43 S.Ct. 338.

Judgment reversed.

LEGAL TERMS

When a person feels disappointed by the result a court reaches in a lawsuit in which he or she is a **party,** he or she may (unless a "court of last resort" has heard the case) **appeal** to a higher court. In an appeal the **appellant** (the party taking the appeal up) argues that the lower-court judge interpreted and applied the law of the case erroneously. Appeals do not reopen the facts of the case or consider new testimony or evidence. Appeals are limited to questions about whether the lower court reasoned well about the legal issues in the case. In *McBoyle,* the appellant (Mr. McBoyle) argued successfully that the lower courts wrongly interpreted the National Motor Vehicle Theft Act to include airplanes. Thus in this case the **appellee,** the U.S. government, lost in the U.S. Supreme Court, the "court of last resort" in the *McBoyle* case.

In this and all cases, the initial **plaintiff** (in this case the United States) must prove it has a **cause of action.** That is, the plaintiff must find some official legal text somewhere that says that what the initial **defendant** (McBoyle) did was wrong. A cause of action clearly exists in this case, since McBoyle obviously helped transport something stolen. But not all harms are legal causes of action. If, for example, a professor wears an offensively ugly necktie to class and a student sues him for the pain he suffers at having to stare at its rank ugliness for 50 minutes, the student will lose because no legal text makes such an offense **actionable.** Note, however, that the student can sue the professor. The interesting question in the legal system is never "Can I sue?" (The answer is always *yes.* All it takes to sue is to fill out the appropriate forms and pay the appropriate fees at a courthouse.) The question is whether the court will have some reason to throw the suit out without hearing its merits. If an official legal text made recovery actionable for the tort of having to look at ugly neckties, then the plaintiff might recover money **damages** from the professor or might win a court **injunction** in which a court would order him never to wear such a tie again.[1]

A cause of action existed in *McBoyle* because the plaintiff, in this case the U. S. government, could claim that the defendant, Mr. McBoyle, violated a legal rule enacted by Congress: the National Motor Vehicle Theft Act. No statutes, common-law cases, or bureaucratic regulations protect against the pain caused by seeing an ugly necktie, so viewers of ugly neckties have no legal cause of action. There are, however, common-law rules of negligence. If a professor wears a combination of pants, jacket, and necktie that causes a student to have a severe seizure, and if that student then explains to the professor the problem and asks him not to wear that combination again, and if the professor then forgets and causes a second seizure requiring medical attention, the rules of negligence would give the student a cause of action.

The legal system normally classifies legal actions as either **civil** or **criminal**. As long as we don't think about it too much, we think we know the difference: In a criminal case like McBoyle's a governmental official—a **prosecutor**—has the responsibility for filing complaints for violations of laws that authorize the judge to impose a punishment—usually a fine, imprisonment, or both—on behalf of the polity. *McBoyle* is a criminal case, prosecuted by a U.S. attorney working for the U.S. Department of Justice, because the National Motor Vehicle Theft Act prescribes a punishment for those convicted under it.

In a civil case, on the other hand, the plaintiff seeks a judicial decision that will satisfy him personally. Civil remedies usually consist of a court award of money damages to compensate for harm already done or of a court order commanding the defendant to stop doing (or threatening to do) something injurious.

In practice, these distinctions between civil and criminal actions blur at the edges. Units of government, acting as civil plaintiffs, may file lawsuits to enforce policies that benefit the entire country. The United States government does so when it files civil antitrust actions. A private citizen may file and win a lawsuit in which the judge imposes "punitive damages" on defendants, which like criminal penalties are aimed at punishing bad conduct. Punitive damages can far exceed the harm the plaintiff actually experienced.

Occasionally in public debate there is talk about "decriminalizing" some form of behavior. To decriminalize something does not automatically legalize it. Jurisdictions that decriminalize marijuana use merely reduce the penalty to the equivalent of a parking ticket. This prevents prosecutors from seeking criminal penalties for possession of small amounts of pot. And, if marijuana were legal, lawsuits over marijuana use would remain possible. For example, a person injured in an accident could still bring a personal injury claim against a "stoned" and therefore allegedly negligent driver. When a legal issue is civil rather than criminal, the rules of evidence change significantly. For example, in the civil trial brought against O. J. Simpson for wrongful death by the heirs of Ron Goldman and Nicole Brown, Mr. Simpson could not refuse to testify. Double jeopardy protections apply only to defendants in criminal cases, and Simpson no longer faced criminal prosecution for these deaths.

The kind of rule on which a lawsuit is based very much shapes the **evidence** that the parties introduce in trial. We can, for example, imagine that when the owner of the airplane McBoyle transported got it back, he found that it needed $1,000 of repairs. The owner of the

---

[1] For a thorough (and dramatic) description of the details of litigation at the trial level, see Jonathan Harr, *A Civil Action* (New York: Random House, 1995).

plane might file a civil suit against McBoyle seeking to recover damages from McBoyle to pay for the repairs plus the damage the owner suffered by not having use of his vehicle. At this imaginary trial, McBoyle's lawyers might try to introduce evidence that the airplane needed the repairs before McBoyle transported it. In the actual criminal case, however, the facts at issue and the evidence presented are completely different. The evidentiary questions at this trial might wrestle with whether McBoyle knew the plane was stolen. In the actual criminal trial, McBoyle denied any involvement, but the trial court found that he had hired a Mr. Lacey to steal the airplane directly from the manufacturer and fly it to Oklahoma. The jury found that McBoyle paid Lacey over $300 to do so. See *McBoyle v. United States,* 43 F. (2d) 273 (1930).

The four elements of legal reasoning introduced in Chapter 1 include two kinds of facts about which lawyers and judges may reason. One set of facts we may call the facts of the dispute at issue between the parties. These are events and observations that the people in the lawsuit must either prove or disprove through their evidence to prevail at trial. Thus the United States government had to prove that McBoyle knew the plane he transported was indeed stolen. These facts are settled one way or the other by the **trier of fact:** a jury or a judge sitting without a jury. (Jury trials are longer and more costly than "bench trials." The large majority of lawsuits filed are in fact settled by negotiation without any trial, and most trial court proceedings take place without juries.)

A second kind of fact, which we have labeled a "social background fact," also influences legal reasoning. In *McBoyle,* the court, including the trial judge, must interpret the word *vehicle* in this statute so as to decide whether it covers airplanes. Social background facts help decide that question: How common were airplanes when Congress passed the statute in 1919? Did congressional debates discuss and reject the idea of including the word *airplanes* in the statute? What social problem prompted busy Congress members to pass the National Motor Vehicle Theft Act? Every state had laws prohibiting theft. Why, historically, was a national law about stealing and transporting motor vehicles necessary in 1919?

Notice that, unlike the facts at issue between the parties, these social background issues have no direct connection with the parties at all. They do not have to be proved at trial. Sometimes lawyers at trial will address them, but just as often these factual issues will arise only on appeal, where the lawyers can argue them orally and in their written briefs. Furthermore, judges are free to research such issues on their own or through their clerks with no help from the parties before them, and base their legal conclusions on them. Often the social background facts appear only implicitly in the opinion. They are the judge's hunches about the way the world works that we can only infer from what the judge does say. Every appellate opinion reviewed in these pages rests on such explicit or implicit hunches.

In addition to the requirement of a cause of action, litigants must meet a number of other procedural requirements before courts will decide their case "on the merits." For our purposes we may divide these procedures into requirements for **jurisdiction** and **justiciability.**

"Jurisdiction" prescribes the legal authority of a court to decide the case at all. More specifically, a court must have (a) **jurisdiction over the subject matter** and (b) **jurisdiction over the person** before it can decide. Neither of these requirements is terribly mysterious. Subject matter jurisdiction refers to the fact that all courts are set up by constitutions and statutes that authorize the court to decide some kinds of legal issues but not others. A local "traffic court" has jurisdiction to hear only a small subset of cases: criminal traffic violations. State probate courts hear issues about the wills and estates of the deceased. The federal court system has a variety of specialized courts, such as the United States Tax Court and the United States Court of International Trade. In both federal and state judicial systems, some courts have statutory authority to hear a broad scope of cases. These are called courts of "general jurisdiction."[2] The U.S. District Court and (in most states) state "superior courts" serve as the trial courts in which most serious lawsuits begin. The U.S. District Court for the Western District of Oklahoma is such a court, and it therefore had subject matter jurisdiction to try the criminal case against McBoyle.

Jurisdiction over the person refers to the fact that agents of a court must catch the defendant and serve him with the papers notifying him that a suit has been filed against him before the court can enter a judgment against him. The agents who "serve process" on defendants—sheriffs in the states and U.S. marshalls in the federal system—have authority to find people and serve notice on them only within the geographic territory the court governs.[3] A sheriff working for a Superior Court in Georgia cannot serve someone who lives in Alabama unless the sheriff can catch the person (or attach land of his) in Georgia. This jurisdiction over the person is sometimes called **territorial jurisdiction**.

McBoyle's case raises an interesting problem of jurisdiction over the person. Federal law requires that defendants be tried in the district where the crime was committed. McBoyle claimed that because he never flew the airplane, or left Illinois for that matter, he could not have committed a crime in the Western District of Oklahoma, Mr. Lacey's destination. The U.S. Court of Appeals for the Tenth Circuit rejected that argument, saying that the crime ran with the airplane, and that the crime was committed in Oklahoma, even if McBoyle wasn't in Oklahoma at the time. See 43 F. (2d) 273 at 275 (1930).

Most courts in the United States possess authority to decide what the U.S. Constitution (in Article III) calls "cases" and "controversies." Over the years this phrase has become synonymous with a genuinely adversarial contest in which plaintiff and defendant desire truly different outcomes. While judges can issue contempt citations against those who refuse to play by the court's rules, judges cannot start lawsuits from scratch. They respond to the initiatives taken by the litigants.

---

[2] The U.S. Supreme Court has subject matter jurisdiction, according to Article III of the Constitution, to sit as a trial court when one state sues another state, for example, over a boundary dispute. Thus, in 2008, the legislature of Georgia, which had suffered a severe drought in 2007, claimed that, due to a surveyor's error over 200 years earlier, Georgia's northern boundary with Tennessee actually reached just enough further into Tennessee as to locate a part of the Tennessee River near Chattanooga in thirsty Georgia. Were Georgia to get serious about pursuing its claim, it would presumably file its lawsuit in the U.S. Supreme Court. Shaila Dewan, "Georgia Claims a Sliver Of the Tennessee River," *The New York Times*, February 22, 2008, A14. As we write, two such original jurisdiction border dispute cases are pending at the Supreme Court, *South Carolina v. North Carolina* and *Montana v. Wyoming*. Some recent original jurisdiction cases decided by the Supreme Court include *New Jersey v. Delaware* 552 U.S. _____ (2008), *Virginia v. Maryland* 540 U.S. 56 (2003), *Arizona v. California*, 530 U.S. 392 (2000), and *New Jersey v. New York*, 523 U.S. 767 (1998).

[3] In November of 2006, a collection of civil rights groups filed a lawsuit in Karlsruhe, Germany, against former Secretary of Defense Donald Rumsfeld and eleven other members of the Bush administration charging them with war crimes committed against detainees in military prisons in Guantanamo and elsewhere. German law gives its courts "universal jurisdiction," empowering them to prosecute anyone for crimes committed anywhere in the world, hence the German courts had subject matter jurisdiction. They did not, however, have jurisdiction over the persons of these named defendants unless they were physically served in Germany itself. The lawsuit was thus primarily a political statement. Mark Landler, "12 Detained Sue Rumsfeld in Germany, Citing Abuse," *The New York Times*, Wednesday, November 15, 2006, p. A17. The Bush administration claimed that American courts lacked jurisdiction over the person to hear challenges to treatment of detainees in Guantanamo, since Guantanamo is legally part of Cuba, but the Supreme Court in 2004 rejected the argument on the basis that the United States had "complete jurisdiction and control" over the Guantanamo base. *Rasul v. Bush*, 542 U.S. 466 (2004).

Rules of **justiciability** ensure that judges decide true adversary contests. These rules serve three functions: (a) To avoid wasting judicial time and resources on minor matters; (b) to improve the quality of information that reaches them by hearing opposing points of view; (c) to justify refusing to decide politically delicate cases that might damage the courts' political support.

Thus courts generally refuse to hear **moot** cases, cases in which the harm the plaintiff tried to prevent never happened or, for whatever reasons, cannot happen in the future. Plaintiffs must have **standing**, which means that the plaintiff must be among those directly injured (or directly threatened) by the defendant's actions. To illustrate, in 1996 federal courts held that the city seal of Edmond, Oklahoma, violated the "establishment clause" of the Constitution because it contained a Christian cross. The plaintiffs in that case, Unitarian and Jewish residents of Edmond, argued successfully that their very membership in a community with a religious symbol directly injured them enough to have standing to sue. By contrast, a federal court in 2004 denied claims for damages filed by descendants of African American slaves against corporations. The plaintiffs claimed that the corporations had been unjustly enriched by slave labor over 150 years earlier, but the court dismissed the case on standing grounds because the descendants themselves were not directly enough injured by the practice of slavery.[4] In February of 2008 the U.S. Supreme Court let stand a lower court holding that plaintiffs challenging the legality of domestic wiretapping lacked standing to sue because they could not prove their own communications had ever been wiretapped. Providing proof was not possible because national security statutes required the government to keep secret the names of Americans whose phone and e-mail conversations were being wiretapped.[5] **Exhaustion** requires that plaintiffs exploit their primary opportunities for settling a case, especially through bureaucratic channels, before going to court, and **ripeness** requires that the defendant actually threaten what the plaintiff fears. Thus, partly to avoid getting itself in hot political water, the U.S. Supreme Court at first refused to consider the constitutionality of Connecticut's laws against distribution and use of birth control devices. It insisted that Connecticut wasn't bothering to enforce these laws and that therefore the case wasn't ripe. No justiciability problems arose in *McBoyle*.

McBoyle's case reached the U.S. Supreme Court in this fashion: The trial court found McBoyle guilty. (In criminal cases the trial court expresses its **disposition** in terms of guilt and innocence. Civil dispositions find defendant "liable" or "not liable.") McBoyle appealed, and the Court of Appeals, ruling on both the jurisdictional claim and the statutory interpretation claim, **affirmed** (upheld) the trial court's decisions on these two matters of law. McBoyle appealed again, and the U.S. Supreme Court **reversed**.

---

[4] The court's decision is critiqued in Anthony J. Sebok, "The Lawsuit Brought by African-Americans Seeking Compensation from Corporations for the Wrongs of Slavery: Why the Opinion Dismissing the Suit is Unpersuasive," *Findlaw's Writ,* August 8, 2005, available at: http://writ.lp.findlaw.com/sebok/20050808.html

[5] *ACLU v. National Security Agency,* 493 F.3d 644 (6th Circuit, 2007). In *Massachusetts v. EPA,* 549 U.S. 497 (2007), twelve states and several cities of the United States brought suit against the United States Environmental Protection Agency (EPA) to force that federal agency to regulate carbon dioxide and other greenhouse gases as pollutants. Many observers predicted the U.S. Supreme Court would dodge this politically hot potato by holding that the future potential harm of global warming was speculative and not specific to these plaintiffs and therefore would deny their standing to proceed with the lawsuit. However, the Court accepted the plaintiffs' standing and decided the issue on the merits.

The Rule of Law and the Presidency of George W. Bush

"When I use a word," Humpty Dumpty said, in a rather scornful tone, "it means just what I choose it to mean— neither more nor less."

"The question is," said Alice, "whether you can make words mean so many different things"

"The question is," said Humpty Dumpty, "which is to be master—that's all."

—LEWIS CARROLL: *ALICE'S ADVENTURES IN WONDERLAND AND THROUGH THE LOOKING GLASS*

In the framework of our Constitution, the President's power to see that the laws be faithfully executed refutes the idea that he is to be a lawmaker.

—JUSTICE HUGO BLACK FOR THE MAJORITY IN *YOUNGSTOWN SHEET AND TUBE V. SAWYER,* 343 U.S. 579 (1952)[1]

This book began by describing the dramatic legal confrontation in Attorney General John Ashcroft's hospital room. Two of President Bush's advisors, Andrew Card and Alberto Gonzales, attempted to take advantage of Ashcroft's illness to get him to authorize electronic surveillance—wiretapping, as it used to be called—that he considered illegal. This story is one of many that sparked widespread accusations that the Bush administration acted in ways that dishonored the rule of law. These accusations came from legal professionals like Jack

---

[1] On related grounds, a federal trial judge in 2006 held that the Bush warrantless surveillance program violated the Constitution, saying at one point, "There are no hereditary Kings in America and no power not created by the Constitution. So all 'inherent power' must derive from that Constitution." *American Civil Liberties Union v. National Security Agency,* 438 F. Supp. 2d 782 (2006). This decision was reversed by the Sixth Circuit Court of Appeals on the grounds that the ACLU and other plaintiffs lacked standing. 493 F.3d 644 (2007); see Appendix A.

Goldsmith, a Bush appointee, and from voices in the popular media such as *Frontline's* PBS programs *Cheney's Law* and *Bush's War* to Jon Stewart's *Daily Show,* and from Republicans and Democrats alike. Thus Republican Bruce Fein, an associate deputy attorney general under President Ronald Reagan, told Jane Mayer that Bush

> made claims that are really quite alarming. He's said that there are no restraints on his ability, as he sees it, to collect intelligence, to open mail, to commit torture, and use electronic surveillance. . . . All the world's a battlefield—according to this view, he could kill someone in Lafayette Park [located across from the White House] if he wants! It's got the sense of Louis XIV: "I am the State."[2]

This appendix explores more thoroughly what it might mean to accuse someone of dishonoring the rule of law. We are learning more about actions the Bush administration took, and the legal reasoning it used to justify its actions, but many details remain unclear.[3] We do not know what future investigations of the Bush administration, if they happen, will turn up. In this appendix, then, we will use what has been revealed publicly, mostly through the efforts of journalists and congressional investigators, as the basis for an analysis of the Bush administration's approach to the rule of law.

Our goal in this appendix, as in the rest of this book, is to equip nonlawyer readers with the tools they need to judge the plausibility of the legal claims that powerful people make throughout political life. Just as knowing the basic rules of sports allows fans to tell if the referees and umpires corrupt the game by favoring one team over another, so knowing the basics of legal reasoning allows nonlawyers to judge whether the "fix is in" and our public lives corrupted. As in previous editions of this book, we examine a major political and legal controversy to analyze critically the quality of the legal reasoning used to resolve it.[4]

The legal history of the Bush administration presents two issues. The first is whether the justifications it offered for its positions satisfactorily harmonized the four elements of legal reasoning. The second issue poses deeper challenges: If the Bush administration did act unlawfully, does that necessarily count as dishonoring the rule of law? The answer is not at all clear, because as you will see below, law itself cannot answer the critically important question: Why does law matter?

Legal Reasoning in the Bush Administration

We limit this appendix to five Bush administration legal positions and practices that have triggered charges of lawlessness—its surveillance of electronic communications, its detention of "enemy combatants," its use of torture on and inhumane treatment of suspected terrorists, its claim of an executive privilege against testifying before Congress, and its argument that

---

[2] Jane Mayer, *The Dark Side* (New York: Doubleday, 2008), p. 71.

[3] The Obama administration on April 15, 2009 released four previously classified Bush administration memos authorizing the CIA to use a range of harsh interrogation techniques. Mark Mazzetti and Scott Shane, "Interrogation Memos Detail Harsh Tactics by the C.I.A.," *The New York Times,* April 16, 2009, p. A1.

[4] The sixth edition's Appendix B reviewed the failed reasoning behind the Supreme Court's decision in *Bush v. Gore.* Analyzing the reasoning in that case makes it difficult if not impossible to conclude that the Supreme Court harmonized the four elements of legal reasoning so that Americans could trust in the Court's impartiality. The seventh edition's Appendix B explained why, in the public debate over whether to remove the feeding tube from the already brain-dead Terri Schiavo, lawyers who took the "pro-life" position of the Bush administration and nearly all Republican officials (including Bush's brother Jeb, then the Governor of Florida) found it hard to square their position with the rules of law and facts in the case. You can read both of these previous appendices at: http://www.pearsonhighered.com/carter8e.

under the Constitution, in matters of national security the president cannot be restricted by Congress. The last of these issues looms largest: If the president has "unitary executive" powers, he can make his own law, even if it contradicts legal precedents or statutory commands passed by Congress. The scope of statutes that seek to constrain executive power would then be irrelevant because the statutes are unconstitutional.[5]

The following cases put the burden of persuasion on those who claim the Bush administration acted unlawfully. To determine whether the Bush administration's positions were badly reasoned, we examined how they tried to "harmonize," that is, bring together, the four elements that we claim make up legal reasoning—case facts, rules of law, social background facts, and shared values. In judging the legal reasoning of the Bush administration we must use the same standards that we apply to judical opinions.

1. Eavesdropping on telephone, e-mail, and Internet communications among American citizens

We begin by returning to the drama in the hospital room. Just what were the legal reasoning elements in that case? First the legal rules. The Fourth Amendment of the Bill of Rights states:

> The right of the people to be secure in their persons, houses, papers, and effects, against unreasonable searches and seizures, shall not be violated, and no Warrants shall issue, but upon probable cause, supported by Oath or affirmation, and particularly describing the place to be searched, and the persons or things to be seized.

Katz v. United States, 389 U.S. 347 (1967) reversed the case we feature in Chapter 5, *Olmstead v. United States,* by holding that this text applied to the intercepting of private telephonic conversations. In old fashion and high-tech contexts alike, the key question is whether searchers need a warrant in the first place. But if it is not "reasonable" to expect an officer to go to court to get a warrant, the Fourth Amendment does not require one. If, for example, a credible person reports to a patrol officer that "a bomb in that car over there in front of the bank is set to go off in thirty minutes," the officer can reasonably search the car without getting a warrant.

Is it "unreasonable" for the federal government to listen in on phone conversations and e-mails between the United States and other nations to stop terrorist plots? Don't considerations of national security preclude the government from the normal process of getting a warrant, since the government might have to reveal secret information in order to convince a judge that a warrant is appropriate? These are big questions, but Congress wrestled with them more than 30 years ago, when it enacted the Foreign Intelligence Surveillance Act (FISA) in 1978. This law created a special "FISA" Court, which meets secretly to approve or deny requests for warrants to engage in electronic and physical searches for "foreign intelligence information" between or among "foreign powers." If the search involves a U.S. citizen,

---

[5] We do not address here the instances in which Bush officials admitted that they violated the law, for example the violations of Civil Service hiring laws, designed since the nineteenth century to insure a nonpartisan public service, by screening employees, particularly in the Department of Justice, to insure that they were Republicans, "loyal Bushies," Christian, and sexually straight. See the case of Monica Goodling, a graduate of Televangelist Reverend Pat Robertson's Regent University Law School, who took the Fifth Amendment when asked to testify about her role in screening Justice Department employees. Granted partial immunity from prosecution, she admitted that she "may have taken inappropriate political considerations into account." David Johnston and Eric Lipton, "Ex-Justice Aide Admits Politics Affected Hiring," *The New York Times,* May 24, 2007, p. A1. See also Eric Lichtblau, "Report Faults Aides in Hiring at Justice Department," *The New York Times,* July 29, 2008, p. A1, and Charlie Savage, "White House Pushed List of 'Loyalists' for Hire," *The New York Times,* July 31, 2008, p. A17.

a lawfully admitted permanent resident alien, or a U.S. corporation, FISA requires that the secret court approve the search within 72 hours after the search was initiated. If the court refuses to warrant the search, the operation must end. Violation of this provision subjects its violators to both criminal and civil penalties and liabilities.

The framework for determining statutory purpose in Chapter 4 would seem to suggest, given that the words of the statute explicitly cover the gathering of "foreign intelligence," that the statute covers gathering electronic information about Al Qaeda.[6] In fact the FISA law includes a provision stating that the FISA procedure is to be "the exclusive means by which the electronic surveillance . . . may be conducted."[7] Nonetheless, the Bush administration refused to follow the FISA procedure. The administration acknowledged that it electronically intercepted communications involving U.S. citizens without complying with the warrant requirements of FISA, but, in effect, it claimed that social background facts and widespread values validated its legal position. The administration pointed out, for example, that nonstate terrorist organizations such as Al Qaeda have no physical headquarters. They coordinate their hostile operation electronically via technologies invented after the FISA law was enacted, through the Internet, encrypted e-mails, and disposable cell phones. "It seemed crazy," wrote Bush appointee Jack Goldsmith, "to require the Commander in Chief and his subordinates to get a judge's permission to listen to each communication under a legal regime that was designed before technological revolutions brought us high-speed fiber-optic networks, the public Internet, email, and ten-dollar cell phones."[8] Modern technology minimizes the cost of intercepting, storing, and analyzing these messages. It also minimizes intrusion into personal privacy. Indeed, the very point of surveillance requires that the subject not know the government has invaded his or her privacy. If the subject has done nothing wrong, the argument goes, no harm is done. And finally, the most effective way to uncover terrorist messages is to screen *all* traffic through word- and content-analysis filters, and it is impossible to name in advance whose communications will be intercepted in such a search. As for values, protecting the lives of people against lethal attacks by criminals and terrorists, or more generally, keeping the peace and protecting human life, is one of the paramount functions of government.[9]

Critics of the Bush administration, however, pointed out that the FISA law was written to be extraordinarily flexible, anticipating the difficulties of detecting terrorist activity over electronic media, and that it had been updated several times, most notably by the Patriot Act in 2001.[10] From 1978 to 2005, the special FISA court issued 18,748 warrants while refusing only five.[11] To the extent that some provisions in FISA continued to create obstacles to effective

---

[6] Pub.L. 95-511, 92 Stat. 1783, enacted 1978-10-25, 50 U.S.C. Ch. 36.

[7] Quoted in James P. Pfiffner, *Power Play: The Bush Presidency and the Constitution* (Washington, D.C.: The Brookings Institution, 2008), p. 177.

[8] Goldsmith, *The Terror Presidency* (New York: Norton, 2007), p. 181.

[9] For a more complete analysis of these political, legal, and technological issues, see Jack Goldsmith, *The Terror Presidency,* and his article, "Secrecy and Safety," *The New Republic,* August 13, 2008, pp. 31–36. Goldsmith begins by observing that in 1940 President Franklin Roosevelt ordered secret wiretap searches for information on Nazi espionage within the United States in violation of the Communications Act of 1934.

[10] John Yoo, the Bush appointee who wrote several memos for the administration justifying Bush administration policies regarding the detention and interrogation of "enemy combatants," and who strongly supported the Bush's surveillance program, nonetheless notes that the Patriot Act "adapted FISA for terrorism." Yoo, *War by Other Means* (New York: Atlantic Press, 2006), p. 79.

[11] Pfiffner, *Power Play,* p. 175.

antiterrorism measures, these critics noted that the Bush administration could have asked Congress to amend the law to remove those particular barriers. Indeed in 2008, after years of controversy over the Bush administration's surveillance program, Congress enacted several amendments requested by the Bush administration.[12]

2. Detaining American citizens and noncitizens indefinitely without affording detainees habeas corpus proceedings or any other legal opportunity to show that their detention was factually, and therefore legally, erroneous

After the World Trade Center attacks on September 11, 2001, the Bush administration designated virtually anyone arrested on charges associated with Al Qaeda as an "illegal enemy combatant" and imprisoned them in military prisons. Most commonly we think in this context of foreign nationals arrested overseas, principally in Afghanistan, and held, in due course, in the military prison at the Guantanamo U.S. naval base.[13] However, the Bush administration handled U.S. citizen-suspects the same way. José Padilla, for example, was born in Brooklyn, N.Y., and arrested in Chicago in May of 2002 on claims that he was part of a conspiracy to plant "dirty bombs" in the United States. He was held in solitary confinement in a military prison until early 2006, when he was transferred to the regular court system. He was eventually convicted for conspiracy to help raise money for allegedly radical Islamic groups, and therefore indirectly to conspire to kill others. He was never charged with any of the crimes for which the government imprisoned him as an illegal enemy combatant. Yaser Hamdi, also a U.S. citizen, had been taken by The Northern Alliance and turned over to U.S. forces in 2001 near the beginning of the U.S. invasion of Afghanistan. The Bush administration claimed he was fighting for the Taliban; Hamdi claimed he was in Afghanistan doing relief work. The administration contended that his enemy combatant status allowed it to hold him in a military brig without benefit of a lawyer or any other legal avenue to claim his innocence. However, a key rule of law in this case, the Sixth Amendment to the Bill of Rights, states:

> In all criminal prosecutions, the accused shall enjoy the right to a speedy and public trial, by an impartial jury of the State and district wherein the crime shall have been committed, which district shall have been previously ascertained by law, and to be informed of the nature and cause of the accusation; to be confronted with the witnesses against him; to have compulsory process for obtaining witnesses in his favor, and to have the assistance of counsel for his defence.

More importantly, the Constitution's Article I, Section 9, states: "The Privilege of the Writ of Habeas Corpus shall not be suspended, unless when in Cases of Rebellion or Invasion the public Safety may require it." The Fifth Amendment, which governs the national

---

[12] See Georgetown law professor Marty Lederman's analysis of FISA issues in the blog "Balkinization" at http://balkin.blogspot.com/2008/06/what-fisa-debate-is-not-about.html. Lederman, who has been highly critical of the Bush administration's legal reasoning, has since been appointed assistant attorney general in President Obama's Office of Legal Counsel (OLC), taking a position that had been previously held by John Yoo, the Bush appointee whose legal memos are at the center of several Bush administration controversies.

[13] One legal justification for holding prisoners in Guantanamo, Cuba, was the Bush administration's belief that courts would have no territorial jurisdiction to review its denial of legal rights to these prisoners. See Appendix A, fn. 3. The Supreme Court rejected this claim in *Rasul v. Bush,* 542 U.S. 466 (2004).

government, states that "No person shall be . . . deprived of life, liberty, or property without due process of law."[14]

The Bush administration, however, refused to grant these legal protections to its citizen and noncitizen prisoners. The administration claimed that Congress' Authorization for Use of Military Force (AUMF) Against Terrorists, passed on September 18, 2001, authorized the president to refuse all legal rights and protections to prisoners because the AUMF authorized the president to use all "necessary and appropriate force" against those whom he determined "planned, authorized, committed or aided" the September 11 attacks, or who harbored said persons or groups. These prisoners thus had no opportunity to show that they were factually not enemy combatants—to show, for example, that someone had turned them over to U.S. authorities merely to collect the cash payments offered by the United States, or that a rival turned over a suspect merely to settle a grudge or get the suspect "out of the way."[15]

The writ of habeas ("we command to have") corpus ("the body") is the primary guarantee against the age-old and tyrannical political practice of eliminating the enemies of the king, or of the state, by killing them or otherwise shutting them up. That is, no one can be imprisoned without showing in open court a factual and legal basis for the imprisonment. From the time of Magna Carta, the writ has been the critical "firewall" for safeguarding individual freedom against arbitrary state action. The Bush administration's denial of habeas corpus to those it chose to imprison thus, among other things, prevented prisoners from demonstrating, as in Padilla's case, that whatever they might have done, it was in no way related to the attacks on 9/11 and therefore not covered by the AUMF of 2001. Studies suggest that a large percentage of enemy combatants held in Guantanamo and at Iraq prisons such as Abu Ghraib were there by mistake; in one study only 8 percent of Guantanamo detaineees were found to be Al Qaeda fighters.[16] The military commission systems that the Bush administration designed were weighted heavily against the detainees. Those who staffed the commissions were under strong pressure to find, no matter how fragmentary and inconsequential the evidence, that the detainees were "enemy combatants." In 2007, the chief prosecutor for the military commissions resigned from his post, citing this pressure.[17]

The Bush administration claimed that trying "enemy combatants" through the criminal justice system was inappropriate because the detainees were not ordinary criminals but

---

[14] Testifying before the Senate Judiciary Committee on January 18, 2007, then Attorney General Alberto Gonzales said, "There is no expressed grant of habeas in the Constitution; there's a prohibition against taking it away." Gonzales attempted to show that this wording permitted the Bush administration not to grant habeas corpus review to detainees in the "war on terror" if it so chose. He did not explain how the Constitution could prohibit taking away a right that doesn't exist in the first place, or why the Fifth Amendment guarantee of due process of law would not include a right of habeas corpus. Bob Egelko, "Gonzales says the Constitution doesn't guarantee habeas corpus," *San Francisco Chronicle*, January 24, 2007, p. A1.

[15] Jane Mayer reports that an unidentified CIA agent fluent in Arabic visited Guantánamo and reported to the White House in late 2002 that at least a third of the detainees were there by mistake. She reports later studies concluding that the vast majority of detainees were not captured by military forces but turned in by bounty hunters. Mayer, *The Dark Side*, pp. 182–185. When John Bellinger, the top national security lawyer for Condoleezza Rice, and General John Gordon tried together to communicate these facts to White House Counsel Alberto Gonzales, they were confronted by vice presidential aide David Addington, who told them, "No, there will be no review. The President has determined that they are ALL enemy combatants. We are not going to revisit it!" (186).

[16] James Pfiffner reviews some of the studies in *Power Play*, pp. 114–115.

[17] Ibid., p. 111.

participants in a war, and thus like prisoners in other wars, subject to detention without the legal protections given to criminal suspects. Giving enemy combatants the rights of criminal suspects, they argued, would endanger national security, because the government could not prove in open court their guilt beyond a reasonable doubt and because any effort to do so might reveal national secrets. Yet the administration also argued that "enemy combatants" were ineligible for the legal protections provided to prisoners of war because they were not uniformed soldiers but instead agents of Al Qaeda, which is not a signatory to international agreements about the conduct of war.[18]

Students who wish to explore the full range of legal issues in these cases will have no trouble finding on the Web the judicial opinions in *Hamdi v. Rumsfeld*, 542 U.S. 507 (2004), *Rasul v. Bush*, 542 U.S. 466 (2004), *Hamdan v. Rumsfeld*, 548 U.S. 557 (2006), and *Boumediene v. Bush*, 553 U.S, _____ (2008). These searches will also produce a trove of wiki entries and other essays on these cases.

The case of Mr. Hamdan, a Yemeni citizen with a fourth-grade education, is particularly instructive. Held since the invasion of Afghanistan and eventually accused of war crimes and conspiracy to commit terrorism, Hamdan insisted that he, desperate for work, merely applied for and got a job as Osama bin Laden's driver.[19] After the Supreme Court rejected the Bush administration's military commission system for handling enemy combatants as unconstitutional, Hamdan was finally tried before a properly constituted military tribunal in the summer of 2008. The prosecution asked that he be sentenced to a term of 30 years to life. The jury of six military officers found him not guilty of conspiracy to commit terrorism or of any war crime. It convicted him for giving aid to terrorists and sentenced him to 5½ years, with 5 years credit for time served. Hamdan was moved to a prison in his native country, Yemen, and released from jail in January 2009.[20]

3. Harsh interrogation of suspected terrorists—"torture"

In the wake of 9/11, fears of a continuing terrorist assault on the United States fueled an intense effort to uncover the plans of Al Qaeda. The Bush administration believed that through harsh interrogation of suspected terrorists it could prevent another attack on American soil and also protect American troops in Iraq and Afghanistan from ambushes and bombings.

---

[18] Yoo, *War by Other Means*, pp. 128–164.

[19] Hitler's driver, Erich Kempka, was never prosecuted in the war crimes trials at Nuremberg after World War II. Indeed, the legal definition of a war crime deserves careful consideration. Obviously it cannot be a "war crime" to kill or help others kill the enemy in warfare. That, sadly, is the purpose of war itself. See Aryeh Neier, *War Crimes: Brutality, Genocide, Terror and the Search for Justice* (New York: Times Books & Random House, 1998).

[20] William Glaberson, "Panel Convicts Bin Laden Driver in Split Verdict," *The New York Times*, August 7, 2008, p. A1; "Panel Sentences Bin Laden Driver To a Short Term," *The New York Times*, August 8, 2008, p. A1; and "Yemen Releases Former bin Laden Driver From Jail," *The New York Times*, January 11, 2009. During his confinement, Hamdan had been completely cooperative with his captors. He said that the taking of innocent lives in the World Trade Center appalled him and that he had been betrayed by bin Laden and Al Qaeda. Nevertheless, at the time of the trial, the government continued to assert that Hamdan was an enemy combatant and that therefore the government could legally continue to hold him until the official end of the "war on terror" in spite of the jury's verdict. One of the six officers who sat on Hamdan's jury and described the jury's reasoning in an interview on National Public Radio objected vigorously to that position. See "Juror: Hamdan Didn't Seem Like Al-Qaida Warrior," *Morning Edition*, August 11, 2008, http://www.npr.org/templates/story/story.php?storyId=93490163

We cannot adequately convey in a couple of pages all the complexities of the debate over techniques of interrogation that followed, some of which continue to preoccupy the Obama administration. The Bush administration's interrogation policies evolved throughout 2002–2008 in response to court decisions, public criticism, and a federal law enacted in 2005, the Detainee Treatment Act. Those interested in the Bush record on interrogations can consult a profusion of books and movies on the topic.[21] That said, the Bush administration's legal reasoning regarding interrogations can be outlined briefly.

Several international treaties and national laws forbid torture and other kinds of degrading treatment of detainees. Among the most significant of the international treaty agreements is Common Article Three of the Geneva Conventions:

> In the case of armed conflict not of an international character occurring in the territory of one of the High Contracting Parties, each Party to the conflict shall be bound to apply, as a minimum, the following provisions:
>
> (1) Persons taking no active part in the hostilities, including members of armed forces who have laid down their arms and those placed hors de combat by sickness, wounds, detention, or any other cause, shall in all circumstances be treated humanely . . . To this end the following acts are and shall remain prohibited at any time and in any place whatsoever with respect to the above-mentioned persons:
>
> a. violence to life and person, in particular murder of all kinds, mutilation, cruel treatment and torture;
> b. taking of hostages;
> c. outrages upon personal dignity, in particular, humiliating and degrading treatment;
> d. the passing of sentences and the carrying out of executions without previous judgment pronounced by a regularly constituted court affording all the judicial guarantees which are recognized as indispensable by civilized peoples.

The prohibitions in sections a–d seem to apply literally only to conflicts "occurring in the territory of one of the High Contracting Parties" and only to "armed conflict not of an international character." President Bush concluded that because Al Qaeda was not a signer of the Geneva Conventions, Common Article 3 did not apply to suspected Al Qaeda terrorists. Further, Bush claimed that because the conflicts with Al Qaeda and with the Taliban in Afghanistan were international in scope, Article 3 did not cover them. Bush's determination followed the "plain meaning" of Article 3, but ignored a large body of case law, commentary, and practice establishing the principles of Article 3 as minimum standards of conduct in *all* conflicts. The interpretation of Article 3 followed in this body of law is *even more literal* than the Bush administration's. According to the dominant interpretation, "international" means "between nations," so the conflict with Al Qaeda falls under Article 3; it is "not of an international character" because it is not "between nations."[22] The Bush administration's

---

[21] See, for example, the movie *Taxi to the Dark Side* (2007), the television documentary by PBS's *Frontline, The Torture Question* (2005) (available at http://www.pbs.org/wgbh/pages/frontline/torture/view/), and two collections of books and documents, Sanford Levinson, ed., *Torture: A Collection* (New York: Oxford University Press) and Karen J. Greenberg, ed., *The Torture Debate in America* (New York: Cambridge University Press, 2006). For a defense of the administration's position, see John Yoo, *War by Other Means*, pp. 18–47 and 165–203.

[22] This was the interpretation of Article 3 adopted by the Supreme Court in *Hamdan v. Rumsfeld*, 548 U.S. 557 (2006), which rejected the Bush administration's position.

contrary position was rooted in the belief that terrorists who did not agree to follow the rules of war should not be protected by those rules, including the rule against "humiliating and degrading treatment" of detainees.[23]

Several federal laws also prohibit forms of interrogation amounting to torture. Among the most significant is the Anti-Torture Act, which defines torture as:

> An act committed by a person acting under the color of law specifically intended to inflict severe physical or mental pain or suffering (other than pain or suffering incidental to lawful sanctions) upon another person within his custody or physical control . . .[24]

The Bush administration's initial attempt to interpret this statute came in a memo mostly written by John Yoo, an assistant attorney general, in 2002 and signed by Yoo's boss, Jay Bybee. Yoo interpreted the statute to cover only the kind of physical suffering associated with "death, organ failure or permanent damage resulting in a loss of significant body function." To reach this conclusion, Yoo took his definition of severe physical suffering not from international or national law regarding torture but from an unrelated statute governing health benefits. He concluded that mental suffering, to be counted as torture, would require suffering "not just at the moment of infliction" but "lasting psychological harm, such as seen in mental disorders like posttraumatic stress disorder." Yoo also interpreted the words "specifically intended" in the statute to mean that the "precise objective" of the torturer must be to inflict severe pain; if an interrogator had the objective of eliciting information but knew that his techniques would create severe pain, he was not guilty of torture. In practice, because of the difficulty of proving intent, this would make it extraordinarily difficult to convict anyone of torture.[25]

Based on Yoo's memo and several others, the Bush administration authorized techniques such as sleep deprivation, food and water deprivation, a variety of psychological humiliations, forced standing, confinement in "stress positions," hooding, exposure to extreme noise, forced feeding, forced enemas, forced nudity, exposure to cold and heat, exposure to attack dogs, and waterboarding, in which the detainee is bound and smothered with a wet towel to make him think he will die of drowning. The cumulative effect of these techniques on some detainees was profound. One Guantanamo detainee, Mohamed al-Qahtani, became incoherent, crying for days and begging his captors to allow him to

---

[23] See Philippe Sands, *Torture Team: Rumsfeld's Memo and the Betrayal of American Values*, (New York: Palgrave, 2008), pp. 31–36; and George W. Bush, "Humane Treatment of al Qaeda and Taliban Detainees," February 7, 2002, available at: http://www.gwu.edu/∼nsarchiv/NSAEBB/NSAEBB127/02.02.07.pdf

[24] 18 U.S.C. 2340, available at: http://www4.law.cornell.edu/uscode/18/usc_sec_18_00002340—000-.html

[25] Office of the Assistant Attorney General, "Memorandum for Alberto R. Gonzales, Counsel to the President, Standards of Conduct for Interrogation Under 18 U.S.C. 2340–2340A," August 1, 2002, Washington, D.C. Available at news.findlaw.com/nytimes/docs/doj/bybee80102mem.pdf. The Bush administration in 2004 replaced the memo with another legal opinion that renounced some aspects of Yoo's reasoning, though not its conclusions. Office of the Assistant Attorney General, "Memorandum for James B. Comey, Deputy Attorney General, Legal Standards Applicable Under 18 U.S.C. 18 2340–2340A," December 30, 2004, Washington, D.C., see especially fn. 8, available at http://www.usdoj.gov/olc/18usc23402340a2.htm. See the analysis of the Yoo memo in Pfiffner, *Power Play*, pp. 154–157.

commit suicide.[26] Abuses of detainees in Iraq and Afghanistan prisons were widespread. At least 43 detainees died as the result of homicide by U.S. personnel, and though some of these have been ruled justifiable (for example, to stop escape attempts), many involved beatings, strangulation, and injuries sustained because of interrogation techniques such as stress positions.[27] When photos of abuses at Abu Ghraib prison were leaked to the press they created an international scandal. The Bush administration, however, argued that such abuses resulted from the actions of rogue officers, not its own policies.

Among the social background facts that are disputed in this controversy is whether torture "works," that is, provides useful information that can save lives. The Bush administration asserted that its harsh interrogation techniques had led to the arrests of Al Qaeda leaders such as Khalid Sheikh Mohammed, and so prevented terrorist attacks, saving American lives. Critics, however, argue that the administration got the information that led to these arrests from other sources and failed to document a credible connection between the arrests and interrogations. They argue that "softer" methods of interrogation are far more effective in eliciting accurate information.[28] Some researchers contend that torture rarely provides truthful information, especially when the interrogation takes place weeks after capture. Indeed, some of the techniques the Bush administration used were adapted from communist regimes that intentionally used torture to produce *false* confessions from dissidents. And there is at least one documented example in which the administration relied on false information provided by a detainee through harsh interrogation.[29]

In defending its actions, the Bush administration pointed to the paramount value of national security—protecting Americans from harm—and argued that terrorists did not deserve the civil liberties afforded to domestic criminal defendants. Critics, however, argued that harsh techniques such as waterboarding violated American traditions and ideals, diminishing the United States in world opinion, and encouraging other nations to use torture, even against American troops. In a concurring opinion in *Hamdan v. Rumsfeld*, which found that detention of "enemy combatants" is covered by the Geneva Conventions, Justice Kennedy argued that "The Constitution is best preserved by reliance on standards tested over time and insulated from the pressures of the moment." Kennedy concluded that violations of Article 3 are war crimes punishable under federal law, thus raising the possibility of criminal investigations of Bush administration officials.[30]

As we write, the Obama administration continues to wrestle both with calls to investigate the Bush administration's handling of enemy combatants and with the legal status and

---

[26] Mayer, *The Dark Side*, p. 208. On waterboarding, see Christopher Hitchens, "Believe Me, It's Torture," *Vanity Fair*, August, 2008, and watch the author's experience with waterboarding at http://www.youtube.com/watch?v=4LPubUCJv58. A conservative radio talk show host, Erich "Mancow" Muller, immediately changed his mind about waterboarding after suffering it, declaring it "absolutely torture." See this video at http://www.nbcchicago.com/news/local/Mancow-Takes-on-Waterboarding-and-Loses.html

[27] Pfiffner, *Power Play*, p. 133.

[28] See Yoo, *War by Other Means*, pp. 165–168 and Mayer, *The Dark Side*, pp. 171–181.

[29] The administration made much of a purported connection between Al Qaeda and Iraq, arguing that this connection justified the invasion of Iraq and removal from power of Saddam Hussein. The evidence of a connection between Al Qaeda and Iraq was based in part on statements made by detainee Ibn al-Shaykh al-Libi, but al-Libi later recanted his statements. See Pfiffner, *Power Play*, pp. 137–139. The U.S. Army Field Memo rejects torture and any form of inhuman treatment in part because it yields unreliable results; see Sands, *Torture Team*, pp. 7–9 and 144–148.

[30] *Hamdan v. Rumsfeld*, 548 U.S. 557 (2006).

disposition of those imprisoned at the Guantanamo military base. President Obama, in his inaugural address, broadly rejected the Bush administration's approach to the war on terrorism:

> As for our common defense, we reject as false the choice between our safety and our ideals. Our founding fathers faced with perils that we can scarcely imagine, drafted a charter to assure the rule of law and the rights of man, a charter expanded by the blood of generations. Those ideals still light the world, and we will not give them up for expedience's sake.[31]

In line with this statement, Obama issued an order banning the use of "enhanced interrogation techniques" against detainees, arguing that these techniques "undermine the rule of law" and so "did not advance our war and counterterrorism efforts." Obama has also ordered the closing of the prison at Guantanamo yet has advocated the indefinite detention without trial of some enemy combatants, a position that has put him at odds with both conservative and liberal critics. Controversy over how to square the handling of enemy combatants with federal, constitutional, and international law appears destined to continue for years to come.[32]

4. Refusing to honor congressional subpoenas commanding administration officials to testify regarding alleged violations of law

While the Constitution does not specifically give Congress the power to subpoena witnesses and thus compel people to testify truthfully or face prosecution for perjury and/or for contempt of Congress, it is settled law that Congress does have such power incidental to the lawmaking powers that Article I explicitly grants it. Thus on June 13, 2007, the Senate and House Judiciary Committees issued subpoenas to command testimony from Harriet Miers, former White House General Counsel, and Sara M. Taylor, former deputy assistant to President Bush and the White House director of political affairs, to testify about the firing of eight U.S. Attorneys. It was suspected that members of the Bush administration might have fired these attorneys, who served as heads of various regional offices of the Justice Department, in order, among other things, to prevent them from investigating and bringing charges of corruption against certain Republicans. Such firings, if so motivated, could count as a criminal conspiracy to obstruct justice. These subpoenas also ordered Miers and Taylor to produce all unprivileged documents, that is, those not classified for national security reasons, for committee inspection. Former Bush White House aides Karl Rove and Joshua Bolten were, separately, called to testify for similar reasons. All these parties refused to comply or, for that matter, even appear in Congress on the dates specified in the subpoenas. The

---

[31] Barack Obama, Inaugural Address, January 21, 2009, available at http://www.whitehouse.gov/blog/inaugural-address/

[32] Obama outlined and defended his approach to enemy combatants in a May 21, 2009, speech. See "Text: Obama's Speech on National Security," *The New York Times*, May 21, 2009, available at: http://www.nytimes.com/2009/05/21/us/politics/21obama.text.html?pagewanted=1&ref=politics. That same day, former Vice President Dick Cheney made a speech defending the Bush administration's approach and attacking the Obama administration's policies as dangerous for the United States. "Remarks at the American Enterprise Institute," May 21, 2009, available at: http://www.aei.org/docLib/Vice%20President%20Cheney%20Remarks%205%2021%2009.pdf. Jack Goldsmith concludes that Obama's policies represent only a modest shift from those of the Bush administration, but that Obama is a much more persuasive defender of his approach, and thus a more effective leader in the struggle against terrorism. See Goldsmith, "The Cheney Fallacy," *The New Republic*, May 18, 2009, available at: http://www.tnr.com/politics/story.html?id=1e733cac-c273-48e5-9140-80443ed1f5e2&p=1

Bush administration insisted that a "blanket executive privilege" absolutely immunized it from any need to comply. The administration contended that, to be effective, a president must have "candid and unfettered advice" from his aides, and that the executive branch could only function with "free and open discussions" among its officers. Presidential advisors, the administration argued, would not be candid if they had reason to fear that their comments could be revealed publicly, and the need for candor outweighed the interest Congress had in the advisors' testimony and memos.[33]

A major problem for the Bush administration was that the Supreme Court, in *U.S. v. Nixon*, rejected similar arguments made by President Richard Nixon during the Watergate scandal.[34] Nixon had argued that, as a matter of constitutional law, the only legal control on either the president or his executive assistants is impeachment in the House of Representatives and removal from office by the Senate.[35] President Nixon had refused to comply with a subpoena to turn over tapes of recorded conversations in the White House that allegedly would establish that Nixon and his aides had committed the crime of "obstruction of justice" after Republican operatives had burglarized Democratic Party offices in the Watergate building. Nixon's lawyers held that a U.S. president had absolute immunity from judicial process and was indeed limited only by his own judgment. The Supreme Court, by an 8-0 vote (Justice Rehnquist, having been plucked from Nixon's Justice Department to serve on the Court, did not participate), rejected Nixon's claim and held that, when allegations of specific legal violations (as opposed to "fishing expeditions") were plausibly supported by specific evidentiary requests that could prove a violation, not even a president was above the law.

After suffering setbacks in court, the former members of the Bush administration who had asserted executive privilege eventually gave up their claims. In March 2009, both Karl Rove and Harriet Miers made a deal in which they agreed to testify before Congress, though without television cameras and without disclosing the contents of any conversations with President Bush.[36]

---

[33] Fred Fielding, Counsel to the President, Letter to Senate Judiciary Committee Chairman Patrick Leahy and House Judiciary Committee Chairman John Conyers, June 27, 2007; and Paul Clement, Acting Attorney General, Letter to the President, June 27, 2007, available at: http://www.talkingpointsmemo.com/docs/fielding-exec-priv/?resultpage=1&

[34] *U.S. v. Nixon*, 418 U.S. 683 (1974).

[35] President Jefferson made the same argument early in his presidency, but the Supreme Court rejected it in dictum in the classic case of *Marbury v. Madison* (1803).

[36] David Johnston, "Top Bush Aides to Testify in U.S. Attorney's Firings," *The New York Times*, March 5, 2009, p. A1. On July 31, 2008, Federal District Court Judge John D. Bates concluded that "The executive's current claim of absolute immunity from compelled Congressional process for senior presidential aides is without any support in the case law." *Committee on the Judiciary v. Miers, et al.*, D.C. District Court, 08-0409.

Vice President Cheney made a kind of "non-executive branch privilege" claim when he refused to comply with laws ordering members of the executive branch to provide various documents to the National Archives by insisting that "the vice presidency is a unique office that is neither a part of the executive branch nor part of the legislative branch, but is attached by the Constitution to the latter." (Quoted in Josh Meyer, "Cheney's executive decision," *Los Angeles Times*, June 22, 2007, p. A1.) The Bush administration eventually abandoned the claim that the vice-presidency is not a part of the executive branch. Jim Rutenberg, "White House Drops Vice President's Dual-Role Argument as Moot," *The New York Times*, June 28, 2007, p. A15.

5. Ignoring the case law defining constitutional limits on presidential power

For the sake of argument, let us assume that the Bush administration's legal positions in our first four cases so far fail to meet the harmonization test. Assume, for example, that the warrantless wiretaps cannot be harmonized with the language of FISA. Assume that the constitutional clause about suspending habeas corpus combined with its venerable history cannot be squared with denying the writ, plus other protections declared in the Bill of Rights, to U.S. citizens, who clearly qualify as "persons," because factually there has been no rebellion in or invasion of the United States. (Immediately after the 9/11 attacks, the President, belying the notion of an invasion, urged the nation to continue shopping in order to keep the economy going.) Assume that some of the interrogation techniques approved by the Bush administration constitute "humiliating and degrading treatment" under Common Article 3 of the Geneva Conventions, or torture under the Anti-Torture Act. Assume that the Bush administration's claim of blanket immunity cannot be squared with the *Nixon* precedent. We must still ask whether the Constitution's text and the case law interpreting those texts gives a president some alternative but trustworthy legal basis for arguing that he can disregard the law. John Yoo, the assistant attorney general who, with David Addington, legal counsel to Vice President Cheney, was a primary architect of many of the administration's legal arguments outlined above, has contended that the president has broad, unilateral power as commander and chief to make war as he sees fit, subject only to Congress's powers over the raising of armies and the funding of hostilities. Congressional limits on war making, such as restrictions on surveillance or interrogation, are unconstitutional incursions into executive power.[37]

How credible are arguments like Yoo's that presidents can ignore statutes enacted by Congress? For starters, recall that the U.S. Constitution is the law that governs the government and declares itself to be "the supreme law of the land." With respect to the power to make law, this document's first sentence states: "All legislative powers herein granted shall be vested in a Congress of the United States." The categorical word "all" reappears at the end of Article I, Section 8, which spells out the powers specifically "herein granted" to Congress:

> The Congress shall have Power . . . To make all Laws which shall be necessary and proper for carrying into Execution the foregoing Powers, and all other Powers vested by this Constitution in the Government of the United States, or in any Department or Officer thereof.

Note that the last clause grants the Congress power to make laws governing any "department or officer" of the U.S. government, which would seem to include FISA.

What, then, does the Constitution say about presidential powers and responsibilities? Section 1 of Article II, the article that describes presidential powers and responsibilities, concludes this way:

> Before he enter on the Execution of his Office, he shall take the following Oath or Affirmation:—"I do solemnly swear (or affirm) that I will faithfully execute the Office of President of the United States, and will to the best of my Ability, preserve, protect and defend the Constitution of the United States."

Section 3 of Article II includes the command that the president "shall take Care that the Laws be faithfully executed."

---

[37] See Yoo, *War by Other Means*, and *The Powers of War and Peace: The Constitution and Foreign Affairs After 9/11* (Chicago: University of Chicago Press, 2005).

Analyzed in isolation, the logic of these words compels the conclusion that presidents do not have the constitutional power to make law in violation of either the Constitution or of specific statutory commands like FISA. (What parts of "all" and "faithfully execute," we might ask, did the Bush administration not understand?) No clause in the Constitution grants the president the power to declare martial law or otherwise ignore the Constitution's legal commands in times of emergency.

But, as we saw in *Home Building and Loan* in Chapter 5, the logic of constitutional words in isolation does not end the matter. A president could, for example, argue that his power as commander in chief confers on him, in times of war, powers in foreign policy that he does not have in domestic policy, or even the power to ignore legal commands made by Congress for the sake of national security. Presidents might also argue that the paramount duty to "preserve, protect and defend the Constitution" does not mean honoring its legal commands but protecting the country that the Constitution creates. Lincoln, after all, insisted that his first duty in the Civil War was to preserve the Union, not obey the law. The destruction of the Union would necessarily destroy, not protect, the Constitution.

Ours being a common-law based system, the rubber of our legal rules only meets the road as the judicial system declares in individual cases what the law means. What, then, have the umpires and referees of our political game said about the president's power to ignore the Constitution and the acts of Congress, at least in times of emergencies? On this question the precedents from the earliest days are surprisingly clear. *The Federalist* #s 23 and 28 particularly articulate that the Constitution is designed to cover all emergencies. In 1866 the Court overturned the conviction of a U.S. citizen in a military tribunal, declaring that "The Constitution of the United States is a law for rulers and people, equally in war and in peace. . . . [T]he government, within the Constitution, has all the powers granted to it which are necessary to preserve its existence."[38] In *Duncan v. Kahanamoku*, 327 U.S. 304 (1946) the Court struck down as unconstitutional the imposition of martial law in Hawaii after Pearl Harbor. Indeed, in *Home Building and Loan* itself, Chief Justice Hughes said for the majority of the Court: "The Constitution was adopted in a period of grave emergency. Its grants of power to the federal government . . . were determined in the light of emergency and they are not altered by emergency."[39]

Thus constitutional cases do not carve out a general exception, in times of emergency, for presidents to make their own law, and it is a stretch to equate "faithfully executing the laws" with "whatever I say goes." But we must look at case law more carefully. If the case law carves out specific instances in which the president may disregard the law of "normal times," the Bush team might then be on sound legal ground in some if not all of the four cases above.

In fact, however, in a surprisingly consistent line going back to the early nineteenth century, case law on presidential power has said quite the opposite. In a nutshell, these cases hold that congressional silence on a matter, and of course even the most indirect hint of congressional approval, leaves the president with very wide latitude to make his own law, or interpret what Congress has written in his favor, but that when Congress enacts restrictions, even on the war power, the president is subject to them.[40] Thus the Supreme Court upheld Lincoln's blockade of the Confederacy after the fall of Fort Sumter, imposed before Congress

---

[38] *Ex Parte Milligan*, 71 U.S. 2 (1866).

[39] *Home Building and Loan Assn. v. Blaisdell*, 290 U.S. 398 (1934) at 425.

[40] In fact, our epigraphic quote from Justice Black at the beginning of this appendix expresses a view that, though never directly rejected by the Court, is hard to square with the long line of cases giving the president ample freedom to act without authorization from Congress. The case law only holds that the president may not violate a specific command of Congress.

reconvened and hence without Congress' explicit authorization, *because* statutes from 1795 and 1807 authorized the president to call out the military, including the U.S. navy, in times of insurrection against the United States. This decision, known as *The Prize Cases,* was decided 5-4. The dissenters argued that the Constitution's words grant only Congress the power to declare war, and that Congress had not declared war against the Confederacy.[41]

In the definitive Steel Seizure Case, *Youngstown Sheet and Tube v. Sawyer,*[42] the Court held that the president could not, even during the Korean War, disobey an act of Congress. The Court struck down President Truman's assumption of the power to run the steel mills so as to avoid a strike and keep steel rolling for the war effort in Korea. A constitution designed to apply in times of emergencies does not permit a president legally to suspend its provisions guaranteeing habeas corpus. A president has no basis for claiming blanket immunity after the *Nixon* decision. If a president can, like Humpty Dumpty, twist the words of constitutions, statutes, and judicial precedents to mean whatever he chooses them to mean, then he can, like Humpty Dumpty, become "master" and throw the founders' ideal of a government limited by checks and balances out the window.

Did the Bush Administration Dishonor the Rule of Law?

This appendix thus far has only set the stage for analyzing the questions that really matter. If we had found a legal basis by which to harmonize the fifth claim, namely that the president has the constitutional authority to act in express violation of the Constitution in times of emergency, the actions in the first four instances would, in turn, have a legal basis. But we did not, and the question then arises: So what? Recall that our basic question calls on us to decide if the Bush administration has dishonored the rule of law. Since there are no right answers in law, "dishonoring the rule of law" must be different from unpersuasive legal reasoning in specific cases. We have concluded that the Bush administration's positions on several issues relating to executive power were not well reasoned, and in several instances federal courts, including the Supreme Court, have also come to this conclusion. But does a president have an obligation to obey a law with which he disagrees?

These questions inevitably take us back to the intersection between law and politics. Martin Luther King, Jr.'s most effective tactic of opposing segregation laws was to violate deliberately criminal trespass laws. We believe that King's civil disobedience served valid purposes. But at the same time we know that if, on a called strike three, a batter insisted that the pitch was a ball four and trotted to first base, and then refused to budge when the umpire ejected him, the batter would destroy the integrity of the game. The tools of legal reasoning may lead us to conclude that the Bush administration did not comply with the law, but we must probe deeper before deciding whether his acts resemble the heroically illegal acts of those who opposed racial segregation, on one hand, or of someone who, in refusing to play by the rules, destroys the very system in which he operates.

The best defense of the Bush administration, we think, would insist that the president, like every other politician who is not a judge (or a member of the bar and thus an "officer of the court") is a partisan player in the game of politics.[43] Like any other player in the games

---

[41] 67 U.S. 635 (1863).

[42] 343 U.S. 579 (1952).

[43] For the full argument that American law and politics function at their best when they take on the structural elements of good games (one of which is always respecting the decisions of referees and umpires), see Lief H. Carter, "Law and Politics as Play," 83 *Chicago-Kent Law Review* 1333–1384 (2008). Carter argues that treating politicians as players striving to win competitive political games is a useful way to understand the limits of their ethical responsibilities.

we all play—of speeder versus cop on the highways, of organized sports, and of politics—Bush's only obligation is to accept and pay the consequences if caught violating the rules. At no point did the Bush administration refuse to comply with a direct judicial ruling ordering it to correct some violation of law. The Supreme Court ruled that the detainees in Guantanamo and elsewhere deserved the basic protections of habeas corpus and due process, and Hamdan eventually got his military trial. The Bush administration may have acted like the batter who insists that the call strike three was ball four, but it has not refused to leave first base when ejected from the game.

An equally strong argument supports President Bush personally. He is not a lawyer or an officer of the court. As many descriptions of the legal battles within the Bush administration make clear, extended legal analyses developed by attorneys John Yoo, Jay Bybee, David Addington, and others gave the President unambiguous counsel that his administration's actions were legal. On June 10, 2004, President Bush was asked to comment on whether torture was legally justified. He responded, "We're a nation of laws. We adhere to laws. We have laws on the books. You might look at these laws, and that might provide comfort for you."[44] Uninformed as his comment may sound to us, there is still no reason, and certainly no legal basis, for condemning a client, in this case President Bush, for accepting the confidently given advice of his attorneys. We have said throughout this book that the question can never be, "Did decision X get the law right or wrong?" Law is too indeterminate to let us make such judgments. Instead we have insisted that lawfulness requires public justifications for legal decisions that cohere well enough that we can trust their impartiality. President Bush, like any president, merely took a legal position that his lawyers recommended and stuck to it until the courts told him he must change.

A "yes" answer to the question of whether the Bush administration dishonored the rule of law, though, might take the following form: Those who hold positions of political power have an obligation to do more than merely accept the consequences when they are caught not playing by the rules. Some make that case by referring to the president's constitutionally prescribed oath of office quoted above. The argument holds that being under oath is somehow different, as if someone who took an oath never to drive faster than the speed limit would somehow violate the law "more" by speeding than someone who did not take the oath. But this argument is both circular and indeterminate. If one need not obey the Constitution, why then obey the oath it prescribes? How much "more" bad is it to disobey an oath than some other law? Was Lincoln somehow "more bad" for ignoring the Constitution, because he was under oath, than King was for engaging in criminal trespass?

We think the case against the Bush administration must rest on different grounds. First, the administration did not make a good faith attempt to publicly justify its decisions in legal terms. Second, doing law in good faith is, we argue, a prerequisite for social stability and cooperation. Throughout this book we have emphasized the importance of individual trust in legal and political systems. Specifically we know that dispute resolution by impartial third parties keeps the peace, because both sides trust it. For these reasons, Chapter 6 urged readers to criticize our methods of selecting judges, methods that encourage selecting judges because, unlike professional sports umpires and referees, they have already taken partisan political stands and prejudged important legal and political issues. But of course judges, like all humans, have political views that affect their decisionmaking. Judges, like all actors in a rule of law system, must nonetheless reassure us that they are thinking beyond their own particular desires in interpreting the law. The commitment to law, then, is ultimately a

---

[44] Mayer, *The Dark Side*, p. 182.

commitment to the discipline of giving reasons for decisions publicly and defending and justifying those reasons in terms that appear to come from something shared, not merely from what a politician or judge personally feels is right.

And this is exactly where the Bush administration fell down. It tried to avoid the task of justifying its decisions publicly, and where it could not avoid this task, it justified itself in lazy and unconvincing ways that did not reassure those who disagreed with the administration that it was acting in good faith.

First, on many issues, the Bush administration made its legal reasoning secret and thus immune from scrutiny. For example, the memo in which John Yoo interpreted laws governing torture was classified and not revealed until two years after it was drafted. Similarly, the administration hid the existence of the surveillance program and many aspects of its system for detaining and interrogating enemy combatants. The administration claimed that revealing its policies would give the advantage to terrorists, and so it had to keep all these matters from the public. It certainly would be prudent to keep all the operational details of the surveillance program, or perhaps its interrogation practices, away from the public, but does the administration's defense explain why it kept its legal reasoning secret? The Yoo torture memo, when revealed, included nothing that affected national security. Some administration defenders argued that just acknowledging the existence of the surveillance program, or of interrogation procedures, would benefit the terrorists, but is it likely the members of Al Qaeda did not suspect they were being surveilled, or that they might be interrogated if captured? (Is it likely the members of Al Qaeda cared whether the Bush administration did or did not use the FISA procedure? Why was the president's bypassing of FISA kept not only from the public but also from all but a few members of Congress?) The administration acted not only against the predominant interpretation of several federal laws but also kept secret its refusal and the justifications for it.

The administration tried to keep its legal reasoning secret even from legal experts within the executive branch. For example, in weighing the legality of the surveillance program, the administration failed to consult with lawyers in the security agencies, the group most expert on surveillance law, refusing even to let them review the memos the administration wrote justifying the legality of the program.[45] When the Bush administration received answers from legal officials it did not like, it tried to bypass or punish them. For example, a Justice Department lawyer who questioned the legality of the FBI's handling of John Walker Lindh, the "American Taliban," was told to find a new job, and her memos on the case were suppressed.[46] And when, as we have seen, Bush's advisors could not convince Attorney General Ashcroft or his top aides that the surveillance program could be squared with federal law and the Constitution, they shamefully tried to take advantage of Ashcroft's illness to get him to sign an order authorizing the program.

Finally, the administration's legal reasoning justifying its decisions was often deficient. Take for example Yoo's torture memo. A section of the memo is devoted to arguing that

---

[45] Mayer, *The Dark Side*, pp. 79–80. The administration's policy on what techniques the military could use in interrogating detainees was made without consultation with the top lawyers in the military. The president's order creating the military commission system for detaining suspected "enemy combatants" was signed without consultation with any lawyer or official from the National Security Council or the State Department, and without the review of a special task of experts on international law and military justice *specifically convened to advise the Administration on handling terrorism suspects.* See Charlie Savage, *Takeover: The Return of the Imperial Presidency and the Subversion of American Democracy* (New York: Little, Brown, 2007), pp. 181, 136–138.

[46] Mayer, *The Dark Side*, p. 96.

Congress cannot constitutionally limit the power of the president to torture. As discussed above, the leading case on Congress's power to limit the president is the "Steel Seizure case," *Youngstown Sheet and Tube v. Sawyer*, the beginning of almost any legal discussion of legislative limitations on "emergency" executive power. But Yoo's memo fails even to mention *Youngstown*, an omission that Yoo's successor, Jack Goldsmith, found deeply troubling.[47] Yoo later argued that the reference was omitted because *Youngstown* took place on American soil and thus did not involve the conduct of war. As we have argued, the use of precedent involves "fact freedom," and Yoo was certainly entitled to distinguish *Youngstown*, though his approach would have been unusual.[48] But Yoo failed even to explain in his memo his reasoning in distinguishing the case because he failed to acknowledge its existence. Thus he failed to "harmonize" a key precedent. Dawn Johnsen, whom President Obama has appointed to head the legal advising agency in which Yoo worked during the Bush administration, has written that the Yoo torture memo is "an extreme example of poor lawyering" and that "A strong case can be made that the Opinion does not meet the professional standards that define any transactional attorney's ethical obligations in advising a client."[49]

The administration gave every indication that it did not care much about the persuasiveness of its legal opinions. It did not consult those within the executive branch who best understood the legal issues involved, nor experts outside the government, but instead employed a small coterie of lawyers that could be predicted to support whatever the administration wanted to do. When the Bush administration found policies that it felt were outdated or needed amending, it failed to work with members of Congress to revise them, opting instead to reinterpret the law as it liked, or to declare the law unconstitutional. The Bush administration's lawyers often ignored or dismissed inconvenient rules of law, social background facts, or values that went against the administration's position.

But, one might ask, why did the administration produce the opinions in the first place? Didn't the fact that it at least attempted to justify its conduct, however secretly, and in such haphazard ways, demonstrate a concern for acting according to law? Doesn't the profusion of legal memos in the Bush administration in itself indicate a sign of respect for the rule of law? It's true that Bush officials, unlike their predecessors in, say the Lincoln administration during the Civil War, encountered a welter of legal restrictions on their conduct in confronting security threats, and it is also true that the administration formally responded to these restrictions by writing memos and orders full of legal reasoning.[50] There is reason to suspect, however, that this profusion of legal argument was aimed not only at justification but also insulation—Bush administration officials wanted to protect themselves from criminal prosecution. By finding lawyers willing to conclude that their actions were legal, and having them make a record of that determination, members of the administration may have thought they were immunizing themselves against future prosecution on national or international war crimes charges, a "golden shield." So, for instance, Defense Secretary Rumsfeld and others who issued orders to use torture techniques that resulted in the deaths of prisoners[51] could defend themselves against war crimes charges by saying they were relying on legal advice.

---

[47] Goldsmith, *The Terror Presidency*, p. 149.

[48] Yoo, *War by Other Means*, p. 184.

[49] Dawn E. Johnsen, "Faithfully Executing the Laws: Internal Legal Constraints on Executive Power," 54 *UCLA Law Review* 1559 (2007): 1578–1579.

[50] Jack Goldsmith describes the many restrictions on the Bush administration's conduct in *The Terror Presidency*, pp. 64–70.

[51] Brian Ross & Richard Esposito, ABC News, "CIA's Harsh Interrogation Techniques Described," cited in Dawn E. Johnsen, "Faithfully Executing the Laws: Internal Legal Constraints on Executive Power," fn. 45, 1571. See more generally Philippe Sands, *Torture Team*.

Whatever its motivation, much of what the Bush administration did reflected a belief that it had no obligation to submit its legal arguments, transparently and openly, to the judgment of others. When those in power say, "I believe that this is what the law says, therefore this is the law," the rule of law has broken down, for what "I believe" may be the product of magical thinking or baseless hopes. The rule of law requires those in authority to look beyond their own standards and convince others they are acting according to law. Thus when the Bush administration tried to justify the detention of a Muslim Chinese citizen (a Uyghur, whose group opposes the Chinese government on a variety of issues) who had no connection to 9/11 or any other anti-American activity of any kind, the court that reviewed the detention found the administration's argument to be little more than an assertion that it should be trusted to do the right thing:

> First, the government suggests that several of the assertions in the intelligence documents are reliable because they are made in at least three different documents. We are not persuaded. Lewis Carroll notwithstanding, the fact that the government has "said it thrice" does not make an allegation true. See LEWIS CARROLL, THE HUNTING OF THE SNARK 3 (1876) ("I have said it thrice: What I tell you three times is true."). In fact, we have no basis for concluding that there are independent sources for the documents' thrice-made assertions. To the contrary, . . . many of those assertions are made in identical language, suggesting that later documents may merely be citing earlier ones, and hence that all may ultimately derive from a single source.
>
> Second, the government insists that the statements made in the documents are reliable because the State and Defense Departments would not have put them in intelligence documents were that not the case. This comes perilously close to suggesting that whatever the government says must be treated as true, thus rendering superfluous both the role of the Tribunal and the role that Congress assigned to this court. We do not in fact know that the departments regard the statements in those documents as reliable; the repeated insertion of qualifiers indicating that events are "reported" or "said" or "suspected" to have occurred suggests at least some skepticism. . . . [52]

Too often, the Bush administration's argument amounted to little more than a demand to "trust us" despite legitimate questions about its interpretations of rules of law and case facts.

The question for readers to decide about the Bush administration boils down to the same questions we asked about Judge Roy Moore in Chapter 6. There we saw that we might have trusted Moore if he, like Martin Luther King, Jr., had publicly claimed that the law on the books was wrong, had given reasons for why it was wrong, and had explained how his preferred legal position would better harmonize the four elements that good legal reasoning always takes into account. The Bush administration might have done the same, defending its need to change the law in light of the changing technological realities of modern terrorism. Instead the administration largely ignored the discipline of law, and the rule of law itself, making no coherent public attempt to justify its legal conclusions on commonly accepted principles. In so doing, the Bush administration damaged the community's sense that law can be a basis for trusting one another.

And so we come to our fundamental premise, a belief based not in law but in political philosophy: The main difference between democratic and totalitarian leaders is that democratic leaders assume responsibility for maintaining social trust, and this in turn requires them to do law in good faith. Without law, communities fall apart. Lacking a legal system to settle disputes peacefully, people have no alternative but to fight those with whom they disagree.

---

[52] *Parhat v. Gates*, 532 F.3d 834 (D.C Cir., June 20, 2008).

This fact of life is perhaps most eloquently described in literature. Here, for example, is an excerpt from William Butler Yeats's perhaps most well-known poem, *The Second Coming*:

> Turning and turning in the widening gyre
> The falcon cannot hear the falconer;
> Things fall apart; the center cannot hold;
> Mere anarchy is loosed upon the world,
> The blood-dimmed tide is loosed, and everywhere
> The ceremony of innocence is drowned;
> The best lack all conviction, while the worst
> Are full of passionate intensity.[53]

In Robert Bolt's epic play *A Man for All Seasons*, a fanatical friend of Thomas More's named Roper insists that illegal acts should be taken if necessary to defeat the Devil. More responds to Roper:

> And when the last law was down, and the Devil turned round on you—where would you hide, Roper, the laws all being flat? . . . This country's planted thick with laws from coast to coast—man's laws, not God's—and if you cut them down—and you're just the man to do it—d'you really think you could stand upright in the winds that would blow then?[54]

A CONCLUDING THOUGHT

We condemn terrorism precisely because its lawlessness brings both tyranny and chaos. It destroys individuals, deforms communities, and ruins the lives of many of those who survive its horrors. But does this lawlessness achieve the ends of those who practice it? Our concluding thought, an entirely pragmatic one, is this: Honoring the rule of law is smart politics. It is especially smart for political leaders who are tempted, perhaps out of fear, to think short-sightedly and selfishly, especially when they need not justify their actions in public. George Washington knew this. During the Revolutionary War the British forces treated the American soldiers they captured as traitors, as "illegal combatants." They tortured and murdered American captives brutally. Washington, on the other hand, issued orders to his forces to treat its prisoners:

> . . . with humanity, and let them have no reason to complain of us copying the brutal manner of the British Army. . . . While we are contending for our own liberty we should be very cautions of violating the rights of conscience in others, ever considering that God alone is the judge of the hearts of men, and to Him only in this case are they answerable."[55]

We seem to have strayed far from the topic of legal reasoning, and yet the comparison of two presidents, Bush and Washington, reminds us that legal reasoning and political leadership, even leadership in war, are intertwined. And so we ask of these two leaders, not who was the better legal reasoner, but who was the better commander in chief?

---

[53] "The Second Coming," first printed in *The Dial* (November 1920) and afterwards included in his 1921 verse collection *Michael Robartes and the Dancer* (New York: Kessinger, 2003).

[54] Act One, Scene 7.

[55] Mayer, *The Dark Side*, p. 84.

Credits

Thomas S. Currier, "Time and Change in Judge-Made Law: Prospective Overruling," 51 *Virginia Law Review* 201 (1965), 235–238. Reprinted by permission.

"In Justice Breyer's Opinion, A Footnote Has No Place," *The New York Times,* July 28, 1995, B13. Reprinted by permission of the *New York Times.*

Sanford Levinson, "On Interpretation: The Adultery Clause of the Ten Commandments," 58 *Southern California Law Review* 719 (1985), 719–723. Reprinted by permission.

Index

Index of Cases

Boldface page numbers indicate pages that contain a significant excerpt from an opinion in the case. All other page numbers denote in-text case references. This index excludes cases of minor significance—cases, for example, cited only within other quoted cases and secondary citations, particularly in footnotes.

CPSIA information can be obtained
at www.ICGtesting.com
Printed in the USA
FSOW02n0229280915
11602FS